DARK MAJESTY

DARK MAJESTY

The Secret Brotherhood and the Magic of A Thousand Points of Light

TEXE MARRS

LTP Living Truth Publishers
8104 Caisson Circle • Austin, Texas 78745

ACKNOWLEDGEMENTS

The author would like to acknowledge the very special contributions of the following individuals to the successful completion of this book: to my wife, Wanda Marrs, for her love and her faith; to Sandra Schappert, our business administrator, for her loyalty, gifted talents, and dedication; to our secretary, Cathy Earles, whose typing and editing skills were superb; and Beckie King, whose outstanding service is so essential to Living Truth Publishers. I am grateful, too, for the many persons who care and who have been so kind and thoughtful in sending me research materials and also warm letters of support and encouragement. May God richly bless you all!

Dark Majesty: The Secret Brotherhood and the Magic of A Thousand Points of Light

 Published by Living Truth Publishers, a division of Living Truth Ministries, 8104 Caisson Circle, Austin, Texas 78745.

Scripture quotations are from the King James Version of The Holy Bible.

Cover design: Texe Marrs, Wanda Marrs and Sandra Schappert

Printed in the United States of America

Library of Congress Catalog Card Number 91-62296
Categories: 1. Current Events and Issues 2. Politics
3. Religion 4. Bible Prophecy

ISBN 0-9620086-7-2

Don't believe the human eye
In sunlight or in shade
The puppet show of sight and sense
Is the Devil's Masquerade.

Robert Anton Wilson
Masks of the Illuminati

OTHER BOOKS BY TEXE MARRS

Millennium: Peace, Promises, and the Day They Take Our Money Away

America Shattered: Unmasking the Plot to Destroy Our Families and Our Country

New Age Cults and Religions

Ravaged by the New Age

Mystery Mark of the New Age

Dark Secrets of the New Age

Mega Forces

TABLE OF

Contents

PREFACE

Is there behind the scenes an *Illuminati*, a secret clique of wealthy men masterminding a massive conspiracy to rule the world? Are these powerful and influential men behind the frenzied campaign for World Government and a New International Economic Order? If such a hidden group of elitists and occultists does exist, will their carefully contrived plot succeed?

As unlikely as it may seem, the astonishing answer is *yes*, there is a secret organization of illuminized men that exists. It is the Money Power of America, Europe, and Asia. I call the men who lead it the *Secret Brotherhood*. The members of this clandestine group believe themselves to be men of a superior race and bloodline. They are convinced that their destiny is to be served. *We are to become their economic slaves.*

Over the centuries, these diabolical men, agents of a magical underworld known to only a few, have banded together in secret societies, amassing untold wealth and material treasures. But because greed is never satiated, their hungry appetite for more and more money—and for more and more absolute, unchallenged power—grows daily.

Frankly, during the first 42 years or so of my life, I did not believe that such a group of men existed. I found the conspiracy "theory" of history somewhat amusing, if not absurd. When I encountered otherwise highly intelligent people who seemed to be consumed by notions of a hidden conspiracy of international bankers bent on ruling the world, I typically put them in the category of being either bizarre eccentrics or, quite possibly, nuts and overly bright wackos. "Surely," I thought, "their research and findings must be marred and their conclusions defective. The world simply can't be organized that way!"

A Startling Discovery

Then, six years ago, I made a startling discovery. While investigating a weird but sometimes fascinating worldwide spiritual and social movement called the "New Age," I stumbled onto something strange. Something gigantic. Yes, even something scary.

At first I could not believe it. I did not *want* to believe it. But there it was: the evidence. An undeniable body of evidence. Eventually, my defense mechanisms collapsed. I knew the *truth*.

The day that I discovered the terrible truth about the *Secret Brotherhood* was a day I shall never forget. It changed me in some kind of unfathomable, mysterious way. And I will never again be the same person, now that I know.

Winston Churchill once made the keen observation that, "Most people, sometime in their lives, stumble across the *truth*. Most jump up, brush themselves off, and hurry on about their business as if nothing had happened."

That is exactly what happened to me that fateful, unforgettable day when I stumbled onto the truth. At first, I, too, was staggered, almost to the point of being incoherent. But I could not simply get up off the floor, dust myself off, and go about my business, pretending I didn't know. *I did know*.

In the Bible, in *Proverbs 25:2*, is found this intriguing passage:

> "It is the glory of God to conceal a thing: but the honor of kings is to search out a matter."

A man or woman of honor, the scriptures tell us, is a majestic, *kingly* person. Such a person searches out a matter to see if it be so. Though it may be elaborately concealed, the honest and dedicated inquirer will eventually be rewarded with the truth. The shackles of deceit will fall off his eyes and the rays of truth will shine through with sparkling clarity.

Are you a kingly person? Can you endure the Truth? Do you have the courage to tear off the masks of deceit worn by the men of the Secret Brotherhood? Are you prepared to pay the price of being scornfully called a kook, a troublemaker . . . or worse?

If your answer is "yes," then *Dark Majesty* will be of benefit to you. It will enable you to discern and discover the truth and to reject the lie. I am, of course, referring to the truth that so many—indeed, the vast majority—find too painful, too horrible, even to contemplate: that there is indeed a World Conspiracy. Moreover, this World Conspiracy is led by men of immense influence who have taken a solemn oath to ever favor their own kind, and to willingly and without hesitation deceive all those outside their fold.

The calculatingly shrewd men of the Secret Brotherhood have convinced themselves that *they* know what is best for mankind. They believe also that their natural superiority over the rest of us gives them the right to conceal and cloak their true intentions.

The Truth Can be Disturbing . . . and Frightening

Why would so many prefer to listen to men who have repeatedly *sworn* to deceive them rather than to investigate the facts and discover the truth for themselves? The answer, regrettably, is that the very real idea of a monstrous worldwide conspiracy at work intensely disturbs the average man or woman. It shatters their comfort zone. It's outside the realm of usual thinking and what's socially "correct."

Their secure feeling about the current system is threatened. Their emotional well-being is left exposed and raw.

They don't want to learn the truth because it would be too discomforting—too alarming. If they were to accept the fact that much of what they think they know about their government and its leaders, the economy, and where society is heading are simply elaborate myths, concealing and insulating a hidden elite from opposition and exposure, they would then be faced with a horrible dilemma: What can they do about it?

Even more scary, it would also become mandatory that they ponder the question of *what will happen to them* if they *try* to do something about it.

Self-deception, the tendency to *want* to believe in a lie, to *want* to remain convinced that "all is well" regardless of overwhelming evidence to the contrary, is the greatest weapon in the Secret Brotherhood's vast armory of weapons. Truth that rattles one's nerves and unsettles one's inner security is truth that must be rejected. It simply must, or many believe they might go insane—or suffer an emotional breakdown.

Once you read this book, you will know for a certainty—if you don't already know it—that there *is* a World Conspiracy by a hidden elite. You will just know it. Period. All the evidence is there—mountains of evidence. No other conclusion is possible. A World Conspiracy that deeply and severely affects you and me exists. *It is for real.*

And that's a shattering—and frightening—thought. Moreover, it is a dangerous thought that, at first, we desperately want to suppress, to dismiss. But we can't. That numbing, unsettling reality sinks in. It's there, and it won't go away. It gnaws at our stomach, and gradually assaults our mind. Eventually we must either reject it outright and refuse to listen to the truth, or finally, reluctantly, we are compelled to accept it, along with all the horrible complications and ramifications that come with that acceptance.

You are Invited

I invite you, then, to read this book with an open mind and to discover the truth for yourself—the same truth that I eventually discovered after my own struggle to seek out this knowledge. I began my investigations with an objective and discerning spirit, honestly desiring to ferret out the facts, whatever they may be. I trust that you will do the same.

What I uncovered in my research and my earnest inquiry first startled, then scared, then angered me. I finally realized just what a sucker I had been, how I had been deceived all my life. And that hurt. It hurt deeply. But thankfully, I'm fast getting over my hurt and my frustration. What's left now is the anger and indignation. Righteous indignation.

The men of the Secret Brotherhood have no right to do what they are doing. *No right.* And I'm not going to look the other way, not since I found out the truth. Not since I realized that *it is possible* to set things right, to fight back, to win.

I admit, it *may* be too late for us to stop the men of the Secret Brotherhood. But I'm not yet ready to concede defeat. I know this: It's *not* too late to warn as many men and women as we can about the miserable fate that the hidden elite have in store for them. It's *not* too late to protect as many innocent people as we can from the savage destiny that otherwise awaits them.

The ruthless and unfeeling men of the Secret Brotherhood can only get their way if they are allowed, without opposition, to hide, cover up, and elude the light of discovery. Well, let's not allow them that freedom of maneuver. *Dark Majesty* is designed to broadcast light deep into dark crevices and concealed cracks. Believe me, having light shined on their repugnant activities causes these otherwise confident, even arrogant and despicable men to desperately scurry about seeking cover. And that is exactly what should happen to them.

As it now stands, they believe themselves to be invincible, oblivious to detection, and too strong to be successfully confronted. I believe they're wrong. I believe that the tens of thousands of good, honest people who, by the grace of God, obtain this book and read it, are going to prove them wrong.

"One Word of Truth Outweighs the World"

Alexander Solzhenitsyn, the courageous Russian dissident writer exiled by communist tyrants for standing up to their cowardly atrocities, once wrote:

> The simple step of a courageous individual is not to take part in the lie. One word of truth outweighs the world.[1]

What a thought-provoking declaration for free men to ponder! Yes, it's okay to be surprised and alarmed when you first discover the terrible truth about the monstrous men who intend to be our masters. It's okay to have unsettling feelings and experience moments of depression and even chilling fright.

But then, after the initial shock wears off, we must—*we must*—take that bold yet simple step. We must decide that, no, we won't—*we will not take part in the lie.*

Having finally made that momentous decision, our lives will never, ever be the same. But always, we can rest calm in this assurance, that just as Solzhenitsyn said, *one word of truth does, indeed, outweigh the whole world.*

Texe Marrs
Austin, Texas

ONE

The Illuminati—Secret Brotherhood of Destiny

It was the third Thursday in May, 1947. The crescent quarter moon was all but obscured by the hazy fog and mysterious, drifting clouds that seemed to fill the dark sky. A tall, thin, and gaunt figure moved briskly across the landscape of the old campus of ancient and prestigious Yale University. The lithe young man was accompanied on each side by escorts sent to fetch him.

As the chapel bell struck eight, the lanky figure and his two "aides" stepped off the curb of High Street. Fast as lightning, they traversed the short distance to the Tomb, their destination.

Greeted at the front door of the massive and imposing structure and giving the necessary password, the two aides ushered their new initiate down a musty corridor into a darkened side room. Instructed to "strip completely," the young man obeyed, not uttering a word. A sense of excitement—and dread—filled every atom, sinew, and corpuscle of his being. His heart raced with anxiety and anticipation. Vague, unnamed fears began to infiltrate his mind.

Silently, in the dark he waited. Minutes passed. A sense of quiet desperation soon enveloped his brain. He felt trapped, yet hopeful and expectant. No way could he back out now, he thought. No way.

Then suddenly, the room began to bristle with activity. The door flung open and a band of "ruffians" rushed in. Grabbing him roughly but firmly by the shoulders they placed a blindfold over his eyes and led him out—in and out of corridors and up a long series of stairs and landings.

Along the way, he heard noises—terrible noises—moans, screams and wails, some muffled, some hollered out in total terror. Fear would have overtaken him but for the fact that it was all happening so very, very fast. He had little time to think, let alone evaluate these unexplainable events.

Then, entering a large, red velvet room, he felt hands and arms shoving, mauling, pressing his body into what seemed to be a box or container. (Later, the initiate was to discover that this container was, in fact, a crude coffin.)

The new man heard a brusque voice announce his arrival, and the rite of passage commenced. Members in black-hooded robes carrying flickering candles crowded around the candidate, some chanting, others muttering strange and bizarre incantations, and still others—perhaps more inebriated—huskily mouthing epithets and curse words. The smell of liquor combined with a dank, unidentifiable odor wafted about the room.

> "Tonight," the leader's voice intoned, "he will die to the world and be born again into the Order as he will thenceforth refer to it. The Order is a world unto itself in which he will have a new name and fourteen new blood brothers, also with new names."

Then, abruptly, on command, all in the room ceased their voices. It was time for the connubial bliss portion of the ritual. The candidate was ordered to begin his confession. As he lay in the coffin and poured out his heart about his sexual experiences and fantasies, as he began to reveal to the utmost depths his hidden desires and passions, a clamor began around him. He was being accused of "covering up," of lying, of stretching the truth, of omitting pertinent facts.

He was warned that unless he truthfully and completely told all, until he shared every bit of intimacy with his future "brothers," he would be deemed to be unfit for service as an honorable, esteemed Knight of the Order.

It did no good to protest of his veracity. The howls, threats, and verbal abuse simply escalated. The initiate felt rotten. He was overcome with an overpowering and consuming need to comply, to please, to conform. Pliantly and with intense concentration he searched the deepest recesses of his mind and soon was able to recall additional bits of data.

His performance obviously pleasing to the assembled members, there was a brief pause. The new man was lifted out of the coffin and his blindfold removed. As he blinked his eyes and gazed about the room, he was shocked at the scene: he saw before him members in skeleton suits, in red suits, in bloody, torn, scroungy garb, and in ghostly costume. Some wore campus attire but their heads were covered with black hoods. And he noticed that some wore sparsely cut, grayish robes with strange symbols inscribed or sewn thereon.

Stage one was over and the candidate had passed with flying colors. But more trials were to come. There would be the naked wrestling as he and the other 14 candidates plunged into and wallowed in a mud pile, to the taunts, cries, cheers, and roars of the spectators. Busily, up and down the stairs he went, from sanctum to inner sanctum, sometimes threatened and prodded, at other times encouraged.

Once, in a tower room, he was brought before a mysterious hooded and crowned figure who sat regally on a throne. "Bow to the Master," the order came from attendants. Feeling uneasy at so bold a request to demonstrate his servility, yet desperately not wishing to offend and anger, the initiate meekly—and promptly—complied.

Finally came the climactic ceremony of the "bones," the moment when he and the other candidates were "awarded" and assigned their new, esoteric names.

"This is our new brother "Poppy," the leader reported." He is a Knight. May he *ever remember* that he is a bonesman and a member of the Order, and may he *never forget* that all those creatures outside the Order are barbarians, vandals, and gentiles."

That's the way it was that night, over four decades ago, when George Herbert Walker Bush—"Poppy" to his blood brothers—was initiated into the privileged, much revered ranks of the notorious, yet powerful, Skull & Bones Society.[1]

The Grand World Conspiracy

The Skull & Bones is only one of several key groups and secret societies we will be examining in this book. The men whom we shall unmask are central to a grand, world conspiracy. They operate behind a number of shadowy covers and fronts. Among these are the Vatican's Sovereign Military Order of Malta (SMOM), the Priory of Sion, the Grand Orient Lodge, the Knights Templar, the Royal Order of the Garter, and the Rosicrucians.

They have also established some very special and highly influential organizations, many of which have clandestine aims and goals. Included in this category are the Bilderbergers, the Club of Rome, the Aspen Institute, the Trilateral Commission, the Council on Foreign Relations, the Bohemian Grove, the Lucis Trust, and World Goodwill.

All of these groups—and many more which we will expose—are part of one gigantic, unified, global network known collectively as the *Secret Brotherhood*. In the past they have also been identified as the *Illuminati*. And at the top, at the very pinnacle of this network, is a hidden combine: a small clique, or committee, of plotters. Currently, there are nine illuminized men who sit on this exclusive committee. Eventually, a tenth will join them, but for now his seat remains vacant.

These nine men possess more power and authority than any other group in all of human history. They meet regularly at various locations around the globe and plot out the future of the world and humanity.

Once they make a decision or set a policy, the entire apparatus of the Secret Brotherhood snaps together to implement it, like some piece of complex, intricate, well-oiled machinery.

The Three Objectives of the New World Order

The nine men who now rule the world from behind closed doors do not, at present, wish to have their existence made known to the public at large. The reason for their secrecy and reluctance becomes most clear when we consider their three major objectives, which are, in priority sequence, the establishment of a New World Order comprising:

(1) A World Economy
(2) A World Government
(3) A World Religion

These three objectives are startlingly close to fulfillment. It has taken the Secret Brotherhood hundreds of years of labor and dedication to arrive at this crucial juncture point. Today, almost all of the obstacles which once prevented the establishment of a unified world economy, a world government, and a cooperative world religious system have been successfully overcome.

The fantastic conspiracy revealed in the pages of this exposé will soon explode with such force and impact that every man, woman, and child on this planet is going to personally feel the shocks and repercussions. Most will be staggered and overwhelmed. But those who read *Dark Majesty* will have been forewarned in advance. Their knowledge and understanding gained may very well be the keys to their survival during the massive period of devastation and betrayal that lies just ahead.

The Conspiracy is For Real

I do not believe that my description of the present danger that now confronts us because of the hidden work of the Secret Brotherhood is overly dramatic. To the contrary, mine is a realistic assessment based on careful analysis and evaluation, and on meticulous research and documentation. The world conspiracy is *real.* Just as the secret society known as the Order of Skull & Bones is *real*; and the fact that George Bush, President of the United States of America, is a member of this sordid group is also *real.*

Furthermore, as incredible as all this appears to be, I believe that the scene I've painted here is remarkably close to exactly what occurred that eventful night in 1947 when candidate George Bush was initiated into Yale's Skull & Bones Society. The details I've described harmonize to an astonishing extent what actually goes on behind the closed doors of The Tomb, the Skull & Bones mausoleum, on initiation night.

True, I have no hard facts about George Bush's sex life before Yale, and cannot, therefore, speak to this part of the Skull & Bones initiation process, nor do I wish to inquire into this area of a man's life. That is not my purpose in this book. Instead, I am concerned about how a sordid and notorious *secret society* has not only molded and shaped the entire adult life of a president of the United States, but has been able to gain a deadly stranglehold on the political, economic, and spiritual realms of the whole world.

However, the required *connubial bliss* ritual *is* most definitely a standard for new bonesmen, and on that night in May of 1947, George Bush no doubt revealed himself to his fellows in living technicolor, and with any and all lurid or unseemly details stitched into his personalized account. Obviously, such dramatic, gut-wrenching, and detailed disclosures of one's most intimate personal life to other men—especially men who are to become one's "blood brothers" for life—is a soul tie and emotional bond of incredible strength and endurance.

Occultic and Gruesome: A Harrowing Ritual

Coffins, black-hooded men with lit candles, skeletons and bones—these are all grotesque images and reveal to us the occultic nature of the Skull & Bones initiation. But is my account of what goes on behind the closed doors of the Tomb accurate? The definitive answer is *yes*. Other investigators report similar gruesome events remarkably parallel to my own descriptions.

For example, Ron Rosenbaum, in his exposé article, "The Last Secrets of the Skull & Bones" (*Esquire* magazine, Sept. 1977) wrote extensively of the "harrowing" and grueling ordeal and test to which the newly tapped members voluntarily submit. According to Rosenbaum, accompanied by "strange cries and moans coming from the bowels of the tomb," the initiate must undergo *as a minimum* the following:

- Lying completely nude in a coffin, he confides to bystanding members, or Knights, the most intimate "secrets" of his sex life.

- A naked wrestling match with other candidates in a sloppy and messy mud pile.

Roger A. Javens, a friend of mine and a dedicated Christian who just happens to be a Yale graduate—though not a bonesman—investigated and researched the Order of Skull & Bones while still a student on campus. In his extensively documented report, Javens states that:

> Each member is required to give his autobiography . . . Fellow members are assembled in black-hooded robes with candles as a member shares his life story from a coffin.[2]

Javens adds that this ritual can be traumatic: "This is known to be a powerful and emotional experience as a member shares his childhood, his experiences (including his sexual experiences), and his ambitions and goals in life."[3]

A Mind-Jarring Ritual

"Moreover," says Javens, "the bizarre initiation rituals of the Skull & Bones Society are not simply juvenile, fun and games sessions. Their purpose is a serious one. They are, in fact, calculated to produce enduring, lasting behavior and thorough changes. They serve as an intense, ritualistic form of "psychological conditioning."

> The initiation process, undoubtedly, as the evidence suggests, is a humiliating and traumatic psychological experience. Like other initiations . . . theirs is also a form of peer pressure, encounter group therapy. All inhibitions and defense mechanisms are broken down.
>
> The individual is then built back up after he has been sufficiently demoralized.[4]

The Ritual Making of A "New Man"

I myself am keenly aware of the psychological conditioning process—of the sometimes startling changes that are induced in men who undergo initiatory programs such as George Bush experienced at Yale that fateful night some four decades ago. In the U.S. Air Force (I am a retired career U.S. Air Force officer), I served for four years at Lackland Air Force Base, Texas, near San Antonio, a major basic training ("boot camp") installation. There, I frequently witnessed the dramatic transformation in the minds and lives of young men who underwent rigorous ordeals and tests. Military boot camp is designed to be a unique form of mental conditioning, as any former serviceman can attest.

Later, as an instructor in the R.O.T.C. program, I put hundreds of young and bright new officer candidates through their paces. Again, I often observed remarkable changes in behavior and thought. In some cases, after the training programs (initiation) were successfully completed, the new officer seemed to literally be a "new person." As if by magic, he was endowed with all the traits and characteristics desired by the programmers—those who designed the training program curricula.

More important, the successful military initiate had incorporated into his own personality a team perspective, a specific set of attitudes which made him a cooperative and cohesive member of the group. His individuality being assaulted and then submerged, he had become a valued "Team Player."

Once the individual is voluntarily sheared of his distinctiveness and unique persona and fully accepts the principle that his own fate is inseparably linked with the fate of his peers, he is ready to undertake the most arduous, demanding, and dangerous of missions. Often, he will submit to the harshest circumstances, even deprive himself of basic sustenance, for his fellows—his brothers in arms. If called upon, he may even give the ultimate sacrifice—his very life.

In a military environment, such "new paradigm" men, endowed with a sharply focused group perspective, are needed. I am no critic of the military initiation system. It has served our nation well.

For Sinister Purposes

But the same type of intense psychological conditioning process, induced in a far different environment—that of the secret society—can be cunningly calculated to serve a more devious and sinister purpose. It can produce, for example, a blood thirsty terrorist, a mafia hit man, a deluded but fanatical member of an Eastern New Age cult—or a loyal and obedient servant of a conspiratorial and dangerous occult secret society.

The George Bushes, Potter Stewarts, and David Borens of the Skull & Bones no doubt experienced a similar, dramatic life "turning point" as a result of their initiation. They, too, have integrated and fused their once separate minds in the interest of becoming a valued member of a *group collective.*

As Roger Javens writes in his investigative report, "Skull & Bones and The Secret Society System at Yale:"

> This (initiation) process serves to increase dependence and reliance on the group, but ultimately places an individual in a position of compromise.
>
> The individual's independence in a sense is sacrificed on the "altar of collective dependency." He then becomes involved in something larger than himself.[5]

Following that extraordinary night, when the candidates of the Order experienced the most unusual and arcane rites of passage, an event involving bones and mud piles, coffins, and hazing, did George Bush become a *dependent* and docile servant of a dangerously occultic secret society? Did he allow himself to become an initiated and cooperatively functioning *cog* in a heavily oiled, precision-made machine—an international collective whose leadership is bent on world domination? Did he give up his independence as a unique person to join something larger than himself?

Was it a part of the bargain that he compromise himself as an acceptable sacrifice for the sumptuously seductive benefits offered initiates who are slated to become the globe's top elite—the cream of Earth's bankers, financiers, politicians, and corporate board chairmen?

Significantly, Malachi Martin, author of the bestselling book, *Keys of This Blood*, which examines Pope John Paul II's grand plan for the Vatican to become *the* leading global authority in the New World Order, has described President Bush as a "servant of the Council of Wise Men." The Council of Wise Men is one of the synonyms for the Illuminati, otherwise known as the Secret Brotherhood. The symbol of the Illuminati is the unfinished Egyptian pyramid crowned by the all-seeing eye of Horus the Sun God.[6]

33° Mason Ties Bush's New World Order to All-Seeing Eye

James G. Martin, a 33° Mason who is Governor of North Carolina and a leading Republican party big-wig, has warmly praised President Bush's plans for a "New World Order." Writing in Raleigh's daily newspaper, *The News and Observer* (Mar. 24, 1991), Martin stated, "President George Bush . . . has revitalized an old but timely idea: the realization of a New World Order."

Martin noted that this was the same visionary idea as depicted on our U.S. one dollar bill--the all-seeing eye above the pyramid with the Latin inscription below of *Novus Ordo Seclorum*. This, Martin explained, is interpreted as either "A New Order of the Age," "a New Secular (or Worldly) Order," or simply a "New World Order."

Unfortunately, in his article Governor Martin failed to tell readers these significant facts: that the pyramid and its all-seeing eye was first printed on the U.S. dollar bill in the 1930s at the insistence of President Franklin D. Roosevelt, a Mason, and his vice president, Henry Wallace. Wallace, a fellow Mason as well as an ardent communist sympathizer, later ran for president as a Socialist.

Reprinted from Texe Marrs' newsletter, Flashpoint (April, 1991).
For a free subscription to this monthly publication, simply write to:
8104 Caisson Circle, Austin, Texas 78745 or phone toll free 1-800-234-WORD.

A Price to Pay . . . But Enormous Rewards

Obviously, there is a price one must pay to enter the exalted ranks of the world's most exclusive men's club. Psychological conditioning takes its toll. But the greatest sacrifice made, quite possibly, is the new initiate's independence. Now an active member of a *group collective*, he is expected to comply with the group's demands and support its goals. His own destiny and future is tied to the fortunes of the greater group collective. He has become the servant of the group and it is his acknowledged and unquestionable master.

The servant aspect, bonesmen realize, is the price they must willingly and eagerly pay for all the enormous rewards to be accrued through membership in the world's most elite Brotherhood. In light of the substantial rewards offered the initiate, the price probably does not seem to be onerous. It is, in fact, a bargain. The new bonesman finds that he is immediately tied into the "old boys" network of the Skull & Bones in innumerable ways. He quickly discovers, too, that it is a network that operates throughout the planet and holds the levers of power in almost every nation on earth. From the moment he is initiated and given a *new name*, an ancient recognized symbol of unity among those in cultic groups, a young man of the Order finds that his life is guided by a powerful, often invisible silver cord. He himself is but one of the interlinking and braided threads in a closely woven, rigid, and inelastic network of power and influence.

In a fascinating recent article on President Bush in the *Guardian Weekly*, an insert tabloid of *The Washington Post*, the authors allude to the guiding, yet unseen, power network that influences the policies and political life of the President. Referring to the book, *The Wise Men*, in which the authors *favorably* look at the secret societies and their works, the article stated:

> What he (George Bush) may be guided by is a *thread* that runs deep through his own life and times. Like the

> "wise men" chronicled by authors Walter Isaacson and Evan Thomas in their 1986 study of six influential men who shaped American policy, Bush can trace his own roots back to bastions of the establishment such as . . . Yale. His father, Prescott Bush was a friend and business associate of these men, including . . . W. Averell Harriman.
>
> They were an elite group . . . who helped shape a New World Order . . . They steered the United States . . . toward a new and difficult international role . . .[7]

President Bush's Unchanging Allegiance to the Brotherhood

As President, George Bush has surrounded himself with fellow brothers of the Skull & Bones and interlinking, related groups, such as the Council on Foreign Relations and the Trilateral Commission. Indeed, on the very day he kicked off his presidency, Bush signaled his unchanging allegiance to the Brotherhood.

At his inauguration ceremony, his Oath of Office was sworn as George Bush's hand rested on the Masonic bible furnished him by his brothers at St. John's Masonic Lodge, 71 West 23rd Street, New York City. It was the same bible, printed in London in 1767, that was used at the inauguration of Warren G. Harding, Dwight D. Eisenhower, and Jimmy Carter. These three Presidents were all Masons, as is George Bush.[8] (Ronald Reagan was not a Mason at the time of his inauguration. However, in 1987, only a few months before his second term of office was completed, President Reagan was inducted into the secret world of Freemasonry—as an honorary 33rd degree Mason, courtesy of the House of the Temple in Washington D.C., the 33rd degree Mother Council of Accepted Scottish Rite Freemasonry.)[9]

The Rockefeller Connection

For his National Security Advisor and right-hand man, Bush chose Brent Scowcroft. Scowcroft, an intelligence buff with international banker connections, had previously been President of Kissinger & Associates.[10] This is the world's most prestigious and influential lobbyist firm, ruled and headed by Henry Kissinger former Secretary of State. In turn, Kissinger's mentor and benefactor has long been billionaire banker David Rockefeller.

David Rockefeller, indisputably one of the world's richest men—and also one of its chief power brokers—has the highest regard for the members of the Skull & Bones. Indeed, Rockefeller Financial Services, Inc., the main corporate entity in the Rockefeller family's extensive business empire, is personally managed by a bonesman, the aggressively brilliant J. Richardson Dilworth (Skull & Bones, class of '38).

In 1973, Rockefeller, with the help of disciples Zbigniew Brzezinski and Averell Harriman (bonesman, Skull & Bones class of 1917—the same as Prescott S. Bush, George Bush's father), founded the *Trilateral Commission*. The Trilateral Commission is a group with the goal of hastening the era of World Government and promoting an international economy controlled behind the scenes by the Secret Brotherhood. Brzezinski was President Jimmy Carter's National Security Advisor and intelligence coordinator, the same position held by Henry Kissinger in the Nixon and Ford administrations and now by Brent Scowcroft in the George Bush era.

Notably, George Bush has served in the past as a director of the globalist Trilateral Commission, while both Jimmy Carter and Henry Kissinger have long been active members of this same group. Moreover, as we shall discover in our detailed examination of the unusual and rapid rise to political stardom of George Bush, it was Richard Nixon who, as president, played a key role in catapulting the young

The Rockefeller clan (above) in a 1967 photo. Shown, from left to right: David, Nelson, Winthrop, Laurance, and John D. III.

At left is the current czar of the family, David Rockefeller.

bonesman to the top of the political heap. In turn, Richard Nixon's chief mentor and backer was David Rockefeller.

In other words, David A. Rockefeller, billionaire, chairman of multinational Chase Manhattan Bank, Council on Foreign Relations czar, Bilderberger overseer (see Chapter 5), and founder of the Trilateral Commission, has, through his minions and insiders in the Oval Office of the White House, successfully manipulated the foreign and economic policies of the United States for a quarter of a century—or more.

Events have proven that George Bush, though ever wary of his public image and vulnerability to the electorate, nevertheless has systematically carried out the blueprint and agenda of his benefactors in the Secret Brotherhood since his first days in public office as a young and aspiring U.S. congressman from Houston, Texas.

Indeed, George Bush has always been keenly aware that his power base depends not on his standings in the polls, but on the degree to which he is able to please and mollify his superiors and peers in the Skull & Bones and the even more powerful elite of the Secret Brotherhood, the group that oversees and directs the activities of all the secret societies. As Guy Molyneau recently noted in his political newsletter, *The Commonwealth Report*, this is "Bush's only existential belief: that politics is based on the personal relationships of leaders, that "doing politics" means hammering things out with a handful of major figures."[11]

That "handful of major figures" most certainly includes his bosses in the Brotherhood. My research and investigation reveals that George Bush, as president of the world's greatest military nation, the U.S.A., is the *ultimate insider*. While the people of the United States and the other 226 countries of the world view the President as *the* central figure in world affairs, the real truth is that George Bush is only one of the directors. He is not chairman of the board, though his personal influence is considerable and should not be discounted.

The Real Power

The Rockefellers, Rothschilds, and a few others—numbering less than a dozen leaders of international finance—are the real power behind the visible thrones of world government. No major policy is formulated without their input, no major plan of action is implemented without their specific "go" signal. To act independently and thus incur the wrath of the fearsome and marvelous Council of Nine is political and financial suicide.

Rebellion by a maverick president, prime minister, legislator, bureaucrat, corporate head, or banker may result in the most stringent of penalties, sanctions and punishments, up to and including death.

The embryonic New World Order is ruled over by men whom George Bush has long served in a subordinate capacity. Yet, his association and service to the upper echelons of the Brotherhood has been a *mutually rewarding* experience for the President.

In Part II of *Dark Majesty*, I will further examine the meteoric career of George Bush and demonstrate how his path to the presidency was conveniently paved by influential friends in the upper echelons of the Secret Brotherhood. We will also take an in-depth look at the mysterious, yet unknown power that this one secret society, the Order of Skull & Bones, has been able to exert over the years on American institutions and global politics.

But the fantastic story of the men whom I call the *Secret Brotherhood* involves much more than revelations about just one secret society.

It also entails more than the drama of just one man's story, no matter how intriguing that may be. Instead, in this book I will provide a documented account of a colossal group of men who now control a vast, pyramidal empire of unparalleled influence and authority. The men at the top of the empire are billionaires many times over. Yet, they still want *more* money. Their power, too, is awesome, and with the nod of their heads, nations have fallen, governments have collapsed, and opponents have been assassinated. Yet they continue to seek and amass even *more* power.

These corrupt men are of no particular political persuasion or party—they are neither republican nor democrat, nor can they be neatly categorized as liberal or conservative. But what they all have in common is this: every initiate of the Secret Brotherhood is an *internationalist* and an avid proponent of the *New World Order*. Moreover, every initiate has committed his or her life to the attainment of an enduring dream: the unity of all things on planet Earth under the leadership and control of an enlightened few, the illuminized men who make up the hierarchy of the Secret Brotherhood.

The men of the Secret Brotherhood therefore view the New World Order as a clever vehicle for the attainment of their most cherished and ancient objectives and goals.

The sometimes strange, secretly coded illuminist speeches of President George Bush in which he repeats the term, the "New World Order," over and over must, therefore, be considered in light of the fact that he is a Skull & Bones alumni and a dedicated and loyal servant of the Secret Brotherhood. The secret societies, including the "invisible college" behind the highest levels of Freemasonry, fervently believe that their current campaign for a New World Order will culminate in the fulfillment of all the dreams of their *Illuminati* forefathers.

The ages-long conspiracy and cult of the all-seeing eye is now thought to be unstoppable. Victory appears to be imminent, certainly by the year 2000. The New Millennium, the conspirators believe, will be crowned with success.

Global governance, in the form of World Government, an international commercial economic system, and the unity of all religions and cults into a sublime fraternity—that is the unwavering, unquenchable goal of the Secret Brotherhood. It is also the all-consuming objective of every secret society founded on illuminist principles.

Three Directives of the Secret Brotherhood

To attain its objectives, the men who lead the Secret Brotherhood have promulgated three key directives. The *prime directive* of the Secret Brotherhood is this: that the *Glory of the One* shall be paramount. *Unity out of diversity* must be achieved in every arena of life, in every avenue of human endeavor. As the inscription on the U.S. one-dollar bill signifies in Latin: *E Pluribus Unum*—"*out of many, one.*"

The second, related directive of the Secret Brotherhood and its affiliated secret societies and organizations is that the hierarchy of the Secret Brotherhood shall control the One. The few, the elite, the Illuminati, shall reign over the many.

And we also have this third, important directive: that the many must never, ever realize that they themselves are not in control of their own destiny. Whether by manipulation, mind control, mass hypnosis, magic, or deceit and persuasion, every man and woman on planet Earth must be convinced of his or her own autonomy and power.

Men cannot be allowed to discover the horrible truth: that the *democracy* which they all so vitally crave, clamor for, and demand is, like some fantastic global shell game, only a mental concoction dreamed up by a tiny but ruthless band of hidden persuaders and master illusionists.

The Shrinking Competition

The conspirators of the Secret Brotherhood, the Illuminati, today have few rivals to preclude their achieving their goals of global conquest by the year 2000. They have systematically either *destroyed* their competitors . . . or *merged* with them. At one time, both the Catholic Church and the Protestant Christian establishment opposed the Brotherhood. But no longer.

In addition, in decades past the secret societies themselves warred against one another, each vying for control and absolute power. Today, however, the leaders of the secret societies have all come together as one. They have found that greater rewards are possible only if *unity* is practiced, in purpose and organization.

Astonishingly, my investigation has revealed that almost all the world's secret societies, banking and financial organizations, crime syndicates, intelligence agencies, and occult groups have merged. All now come under the direct command and authority of the elite, executive council of the Secret Brotherhood. *Never before in the annals of human history has so much power been reposited in the hands of so few.*

Still, as I will explain, the men of the Secret Brotherhood are not invincible. There is still hope that these evil and selfish men can be stopped. Those of us who truly care about truth and about freedom, liberty, and the future of our country can do something to stem the tidal wave of occultism and propaganda sponsored by these men and their associates. If it be God's will, *we can* restore the world to sanity and goodness.

But the first thing to be done is to unmask the plot of the Secret Brotherhood and shed some much needed light on their dangerous, often disguised activities. A perfect way to start is to focus our eyes and minds in the direction of a very wealthy man who currently wields tremendous power within the highest ranks of those who intend to rule the world. Let me, then, in the next chapter, introduce you to Mr. Maurice Strong, fervent New Ager, wealthy aristocrat, dedicated environmentalist, and a man with access to the inner circles of the Secret Brotherhood.

TWO

World Conspiracy: A "Novel" Idea

He lives in the beautiful Baca Grande area of the San Luis Valley in Colorado. He's one of the most wealthy and most staggeringly powerful men on the face of the earth. He counts among his closest friends such billionaires as David Rockefeller and Lord Rothschild, as well as Pope John Paul II. In 1992, as chairman of the United Nation's Earth Summit in Rio de Janeiro, he visited with President George Bush in the White House and gave the president a personal invitation to the gala affair, said to be *the* premier environmental event of the 21st century.[1]

If there is any one man who sits at the top echelon of authority in formulating the Plan for the New World Order, it is Maurice Strong, the Canadian financier and investor.

In 1990, Maurice Strong gave a fascinating series of interviews to Daniel Wood, a writer for Canada's *West* magazine.[2] Wood spent considerable time with Strong and evidently was able to gain his confidence. Indeed, on one particularly stunning occasion, Maurice Strong loosened up and let his guard down for a few, very revealing moments.

Here is how writer Daniel Wood describes a ride and conversation with Maurice Strong when visiting the ruggedly attractive Baca Grande ranch:

> I leave the Baca with Strong, retracing our route of a week earlier. We pass the Lazy U Ranch and turn South on Highway 17. Strong tells me he has often wished he could write. He has a novel he'd like to do. It's something he has been thinking about for a decade. It would be a cautionary tale about the future.
>
> "Each year," he explains as background to the telling of the novel's plot, "the World Economic Forum convenes in Davos, Switzerland. Over a thousand CEO's, prime ministers, finance ministers, and leading academics gather in February to attend meetings and set economic agendas for the year ahead."
>
> With this as a setting, he then says, "What if a small group of these world leaders were to . . . form a *secret society* to bring about an economic collapse? It's February. They're all at Davos. These aren't terrorists. They're *world leaders*."
>
> "They have positioned themselves in the world's commodity and stock markets. They've engineered a *panic*, using their access to stock exchanges and computers and gold supplies. They jam the gears. They hire mercenaries who hold the rest of the world leaders at Davos as hostages. The markets *can't close*. The rich countries . . ." and Strong makes a slight motion with his fingers as if he were flicking a cigarette butt out the window.
>
> I sat there spellbound. This is not *any* storyteller talking. This is Maurice Strong. He knows these world leaders. He is, in fact, co-chairman of the Council of the World Economic Forum. He sits at the fulcrum of power. He is in a position to *do it*.
>
> "I probably shouldn't be saying things like this," he says.[3]

Will the planned culmination of the New World Order conspiracy come about much the way the plot in Maurice Strong's "novel" develops? Do the super-rich money men intend to someday soon abruptly seize control of the world's banking and financial machinery, bringing the planet to a grinding halt—until their demands are met?

Though a possibility, my research indicates that Strong's dramatic plot is not the future scenario planned for mankind by the Secret Brotherhood. Actually, I see Maurice Strong's fascinating comments as more indicative of his own impetuous personality. Unlike most of his peers in the Illuminati fraternity, who rarely display their anger or emotion in public, Strong is well-known for openly expressing his dreams and frustrations. Obviously, this man is a *true believer*: he wants World Government and centralized authority *now*—and he's ready to do whatever it takes to hasten the process.

The Brotherhood has long been content to subvert and conquer its opposition bit-by-bit and piece-by-piece. It has shrewdly stayed behind the scenes in the calculated hope that by its stealth and by the covert nature of its operations, potential opposition would not become suspicious nor would enemies to its sinister goals be provoked and aroused. The

Maurice Strong, shown at left, has a "novel" idea about how a conspiratorial society of the super-rich can take over the world.

Secret Brotherhood's long range strategy has proven itself again and again.

Still, while Maurice Strong's threat of a global *coup d'etat* is not entirely unrealistic. The scenario he paints so vividly of a group of powerful, super-rich conspirators who meet each year to plan the world's economic and political future deciding to go for the jugular could just happen!

This conspiratorial group does exist, and its eventual aims are, indeed, exactly as Strong depicts. Their goal is to accumulate most all of this planet's wealth and power under their wings. *They intend to become our masters, our benefactors, and our gods.*

They Meet in Secret

It is not improbable, then, that at one or another of their meetings and conclaves, the super-rich clique who now have our financial destiny in their hands could decide to pull the plug on the world economy. Perhaps Strong's idea for a future "novel" is more than just the imaginative plot of a dreamer.

That the men of the Secret Brotherhood frequently meet at different locations throughout the world to plot out their plans and schemes is unquestionable. Comprising themselves in the form of the *Bilderberger Group*, they have met at least annually since 1954. The most recent conclave of this conspiratorial plan was held in the French resort city of Evian in June, 1992. The previous year, the secretive Bilderbergers conferred together in the secluded town of Baden Baden, a resort haven off the beaten path deep in the Black Forest region of Germany.[4]

There is also evidence that sets 1952 as a key date for the conspirators. On June 12th of that year, a group of representatives of the Brotherhood, organizing themselves under the name of the Order of the Temple, met in France, in the Castle of Arginy, near Charentay, Beaujolais.[5]

The significance of this location was unmistakable. The men who now oversee the global operations of the secret societies believe themselves to be the direct spiritual descendants of the original *Order of the Knights Templar*, the group from which today's Freemasonry, Knights of Malta, and Rosicrucianism sprang. And it was at the Castle of Arginy where the founder and first Grand Master of the medieval Templars, Hugues de Payns, and his comrades first took their vows in the year 1118.

The Revenge of the Knights Templar

Almost two centuries, later, on March 18, 1314, Jacques de Molay, the twenty-second and last Grand Master of the Order, was burned at the stake in Paris, having been first censured by Pope Clement V then condemned to death by France's King Philip the Fair. The Templars and their leader had been accused of numerous crimes, including a conspiracy to overthrow established authorities, acts of sodomy, and worship of the devil under the guise of Baphomet, the androgynous (male *and* female combined) goat god.

The last cry of Jacques de Molay, as he stood writhing in torment in the flames, reportedly was this ominous curse and threat: "Woe will come ere long, to those who condemn us without a cause. God will avenge our death."[6]

Today, the Masonic Lodge pays honor to martyr Jacques de Molay by naming their young boys' groups, the "Order of DeMolay." But how many of today's Freemasons know that their hero was reputed to be a traitor to his country, a blasphemer, a homosexual, and a devil worshipper?

With de Molay's death, the lodges of the Knights Templar were ordered shut down in France and the Order persecuted elsewhere in Europe. Then in 1717, the movement, which had gone underground, once again resurfaced in Great Britain and later in other countries in the guise of Freemasonry. About six decades later, in 1776, Adam Weishaupt founded the *Order of the Illuminati* which almost succeeded at the time in its incredible goal of totally conquering the world.

The Resurgence of the Brotherhood

Over the intervening centuries the Order has continued to be bold and defiant. But it has only been in the 20th century that the resurgence of the World Conspiracy has occurred with such awesome force and might.

My investigation has convinced me that the Secret Brotherhood and the reestablished Order of the Temple are one and the same group. Therefore, the meeting held in 1952 in the Castle of Arginy was a most auspicious event in the annals of the secret societies. This meeting marked the preparation for the final stages of the World Revolution which, by the year 2000, is expected to be completed and crowned with success.

Yet another important event for the Secret Brotherhood was a conclave that took place on March 21, 1981. Known only to a few outsiders and convened with the strictest of security, the meeting was held in Switzerland at an old but elegant manor once owned by the Order of the Knights of Malta.

According to one authoritative source, at that meeting in Switzerland were *nine* senior members of the Brotherhood, the executive council, each of whom had been initiated in the esoteric oral tradition of the ancient Order of the Knights Templar.[7] *This initiation ritual is virtually the same that is given new members of the Order of Skull & Bones.*

Why Occultists Favor the Number Nine

The Secret Brotherhood is therefore led by nine men who sit on its executive council. Why exactly nine? The number 9 has very important hidden, esoteric significance. The men of the Secret Brotherhood believe firmly in the power of ceremonial ritual, magical words, and occult numerology. In the science of occult numerology we discover that the number 9 is the ultimate number of power and authority.

A case in point is the *enneagram*, an occultic symbol that has several triangles and lines arranged so that *nine points* simultaneously touch an outer circle. Currently, the enneagram is popular in a number of Catholic and liberal Protestant churches. Recently, we found that it was even taught to Southern Baptists at a spiritual retreat in Texas.

There are a number of arcane reasons why occultists favor the number nine and promote the nine-point enneagram. First, Christ breathed His last breath on the cross at the *ninth* hour, an event perversely celebrated by the Adversary and his agents. Occultists teach that there are *nine* orders of devils in Hell. Satanists also take delight in noting that the number 9 upside down becomes 6, the number of the beast.

In pagan Greece it was taught that there were *nine* muses (or divine "spirits—e.g. demons") who guided mankind's efforts on planet earth.

The Etruscans, from whom the Romans took many of their religious mythologies, believed in *nine* gods whom they swore by. In Imperial Rome the Romans honored the goddess Nundina by holding a purification ceremony for

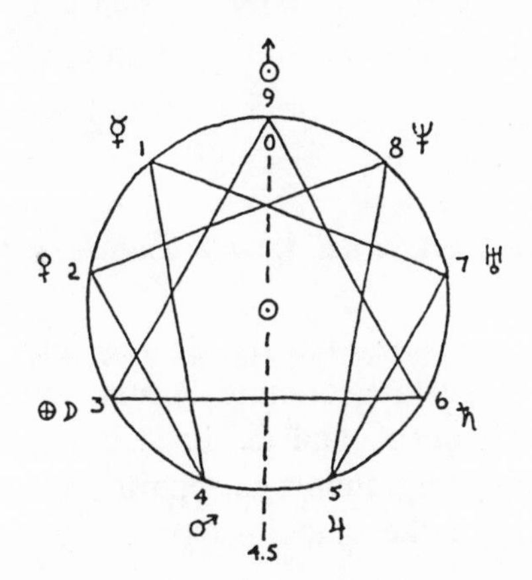

The enneagram is a triangle system of 9 points.

male infants on their *ninth* day of life. In addition, every *ninth* year the Romans held a feast in memory of the dead.

Moreover, according to the Rosicrucian magus W. W. Westcott, in his book *Numbers: Their Occult Power and Mystic Virtues*, the number *nine* also holds great significance among the Masonic orders and secret societies. "There is a Masonic order of Nine Elected Knights," wrote Westcott, "in which *nine* roses, *nine* lights, and *nine* knocks are used." Westcott also reported that in occult numerology *nine* is the number of "the earth under evil influences."

In my own book *Mystery Mark of the New Age*, I picture and discuss the enneagram symbol on pages 86 and 87. In the book I demonstrate its use by New Age authorities and Hindus alike, including Alice Bailey and Djwhal Khul of the Lucis Trust. I also explain how some confused Christian teachers are today claiming that the enneagram can be profitably used to provide people the key to unlocking their personality traits and curing their psychological compulsions.

Then, in my book *New Age Cults and Religions*, I discuss the use of the enneagram by a strange Hindu goddess sect which also believes the number 666 is holy. *Sri Aurobindo*, the late Hindu guru who founded this New Age-styled sect, claimed that whoever unravels the secrets of the enneagram "will enjoy riches and wealth and be sexually fertile."

In occult numerology, the digits 666 are added to produce a mystical sum; thus 6+6+6 equals 18; and 1+8 equals 9. So again, we have that most magical and profound of numbers: 9.

The Link Between Hindu Cults and World Leaders

Now consider this astonishing fact: Maurice Strong, the co-chairman of the powerful World Economic Forum, the chairman of the Earth Summit event, and the head of the United Nations Environmental Programme, is reportedly a devoteé and a stout believer in the teachings of the Sri Aurobindo cult![8]

Strong, a fabulously rich man, has also built a great and sacred temple to the sun god at his ranch in the Baca Grande of Colorado. Both he and his wife, Hannah, are fervent New Agers. Reportedly, Mrs. Strong believes that her 10-year-old grandson is the reincarnation of an 11th century Tibetan Buddhist monk named Rechung Dorje Drakpa.

Russian leader Mikhail Gorbachev also has his own Hindu guru, Sri Chinmoy, who mentors and guides him in the new spiritual ways. And Gorbachev, too, has demonstrated his own New Age beliefs and learnings.[9] So quite obviously, if Strong and Gorbachev are any indication—and they are!—the mystical foundations of the elitist membership of the Secret Brotherhood are deeply rooted in Hindu and New Age mythologies and religious dogma. And as we shall see, these mythologies and dogma are based on a belief in a "god of forces," pictured to be the great, central Sun. The religion of the Illuminati is of the ancient Solar Tradition of Mystery Babylon!

Solar Men, Solar Tradition and the New Rome

In 1984, this same group of nine influential leaders of the Illuminati met once again in France. Renewing their vows, they dedicated themselves to their goal of a New World Order to encompass the entire globe. These nine individuals, who believe themselves to be a sacred nobility and the forebearers of a new type of man, also gave their Order a new name. In French, that name is *L'Ordre International Chevaleresque, Tradition Solaire*, which, translated in English, is the *International Order of Chivalry, Solar Tradition.*[10]

It is interesting that Thomas Ehrenzeller, a director of the World Federalists Association, an influential group founded by the late Norman Cousins that has as its chief goal the setting up of World Government, wrote a book in 1976 entitled *Solar Man*. In that book, Ehrenzeller put forth a startling blueprint for exactly how the Secret Brotherhood intended to achieve the unity of all nations under one central authority.[11]

The plan calls first, for organizing the earth into regions (beginning with the European Community, with the Americas and others to follow), the breakdown and dissolution of the old Soviet communist empire, and finally, a strengthened United Nations with global military capability.[12]

All of these planks of the Brotherhood's plan have enjoying shockingly accurate fulfillment. The surprising, recent developments in the formation of the Europe Economic Community, President George Bush's proposal of a North American Free Trade Zone, and the resounding fall of communism and breakup of the Soviet Union, were exactly what Ehrenzeller had prescribed in *Solar Man.*

In fact, the term "Solar" is an illuminist code-word. George Bush's "Thousand Points of Light" phrase is also a byproduct of the "Solar Tradition" and the plan of the Illuminati to exalt "Solar Man." Bush's phrase literally means the sparks of divinity *within* illuminized, perfected man. Such men constitute the nobility who are to rule and manage our planet.

The ascendance to the pinnacle of global power of the Secret Brotherhood will, its members believe, mean that the Holy Roman Empire of the caesars is once again restored to its former heights of glory. The building of the *New Rome* has long been the dream of the Illuminati.

In the book *The Household of the Grail*, Robin Waterfield proposes that this yearning for the return of the imperial tradition is the key to what motivates the secret societies. For the secret societies, Waterfield writes:

> The Holy roman Empire was *restauratio* and *continuatio* (to be *restored* and *continued*) . . . which in its ultimate meaning implies a restoration of the Roman movement toward a world-wide "solar" synthesis, a restoration which logically, implies transcending Christianity.[13]

"Transcending Christianity" means to go beyond it, to leave it behind, to recognize it as lacking in value and no longer useful to humanity. The Illuminati despise true, traditional Christianity. This is why Maurice Strong has stated: "It must be clear . . . that if the world is to change, Christianity must change."[14]

No More Smoke-Filled Rooms

Investigative reporter Danny Casolero, who gave his life in an attempt to uncover the workings of this huge, conspiratorial financial behemoth which Casolero unaffectionately named *The Octopus*, told anyone who would listen that the tentacles of this beast extended in every direction across the face of the globe.[15] Given the astonishing advances and communications today, a conspiracy is much more likely to occur in our era than any other era in history.

Today, it is remarkably easy for conspirators to meet at any spot on the globe by jet within a few hours of a decision being made that a meeting is necessary. Moreover, personal, face-to-face meetings can be augmented or substituted with teleconferences, a method in which each participant can sit comfortably in a walnut-paneled board room and observe joint proceedings on a giant television screen.

Moreover, rapid communication, coordination, and command and control can be effected through lightning-fast and cryptologically coded and protected computer networks. Fax machines can be utilized to send documents in moments to hundreds of locations around the world.

My point is simply this: No longer do conspirators have to travel by slow boats, railroad, and other snail's pace forms of transportation to smoke-filled rooms, where they meet and plot the most devious and sinister of schemes to take over and control humanity. Instead, there are more than ample ways, many high tech in nature, which are being employed to coordinate and supervise the gigantic global empire put together by the Secret Brotherhood.

Conspiracy is a Natural Event

Actually, it is a natural thing for men to conspire and collude together to make more money and to promote common goals. I am always amused and perplexed over anyone who would deny that men's natural tendency is to organize themselves into a conspiracy. Certainly, the history of the world has given us many examples. In the 20th century alone, we have seen a conspiracy by Mao Tse-tung and a few Communists who instigated a rebellion that began in the snow-capped mountains of Manchuria and eventually became so immense that a nation of 600 million (now exceeding 1 billion!) was conquered.

The Communist successors of the dictator Mao still sit in hallowed halls, reigning over their far-flung oriental empire and subjecting almost 20 percent of the world's population to the basest and most vile forms of persecution, terror and control.

In our generation we also watched as a small conspiratorial group led by a man named Ho Chi Minh first took on the Japanese invaders, then conquered the French, and finally went head to head with about half a million American combat troops in a decade-long struggle for supremacy in Vietnam. Incidentally, though American troops were not directly defeated on the battlefield, the conspirators gained the victory when U.S. President Richard Nixon decided to cut and run.

Also in our generation we have witnessed the most criminal savagery and butchery that has ever been perpetrated on innocent men, women, and children. I am referring not only to Adolf Hitler's massacre of millions in concentration camps and his ruthless suppression of the peoples and the nations that he conquered in Europe, but also to Pol Pot, the Khmer Rouge monster. It was Pol Pot who led over one million of his countrymen to the killing fields in Cambodia where they were shot in the back of the head and bludgeoned with baseball bats, among other acts of unspeakable atrocities.

Need I refresh the reader's memory that Hitler took office in Germany with the strength of a small band of conspirators known as the Nazi Brown Shirts? And of Pol Pot, the hideous gangster of Cambodia—we must remember that he, too, came to power after founding a small, conspiratorial movement and insurrection that eventually succeeded in capturing the capitol city of Pnom Penh and extending its vise-like grip to all the provinces of that sad Southeast Asian nation.

We also should not forget the emergence of a communist dictatorship, Lenin's vanguard, in Moscow in 1917. Lenin, and subsequently Joseph Stalin, were co-partners in a conspiratorial scheme that at first consisted of only a handful of determined and ruthless Marxists. They were funded behind the scenes by secret societies and others in Germany and America. Their repugnant campaign to purify and cleanse Mother Russia and to seek world domination resulted in possibly as many as 100 million human beings wiped out and brutally purged and eliminated in a brief space of some 76 years.

So we cannot deny that conspiracies have been hatched even in our generation that have resulted in monumental transformations of human society and governments. Nor can we deny that these transformations have resulted in millions of deaths and untold counts of human suffering.

How amazing, then, that some today deny that a conspiracy could possibly exist!

Does the Bible Prophesy a World Conspiracy?

It is an astonishing fact that the Bible contains prophecies directly relating to the great world conspiracy now confronting mankind. If anything could make a man or woman perk up and pay attention to the Word of God, *this should*! Here are just a few of the incredibly accurate predictions found in the Bible regarding a conspiracy in the last days just before Jesus' return:

1. **Global Conspiracy**: The conspiracy will be *worldwide* and gigantic, involving many peoples, languages, ethnic groups, and nations. It will "devour the whole earth." *(Revelation 13:8; 17:15; Daniel 7:23)*
2. **The Illuminist Religion**: The conspirators will worship a strange "god of forces" rather than a personal God. Theirs will be a universalist, mystery religion. *(Daniel 11:36-39; II Thessalonians 2)*
3. **Mass Hypnosis**: The people of the world will be given a "strong delusion" so that they will believe "the Lie." *(II Thessalonians 2; Isaiah 28, 29; Revelation 13:14)*
4. **A Ruling Elite**: A small group will control the whole world. Ten world leaders will be "of one mind," and they will eventually give "all of their power and strength" in allegiance to one supreme leader. *(Daniel 11:23; Revelation 13:8; 17:12-17)*
5. **An International Economic Order**: The super rich will prosper through finance, international trade and commerce. *(Revelation 13:16-17; 18; Ezekiel 28:16)*
6. **Money Conspiracy**: The conspirators will gain their wealth and riches by defrauding working people. They'll also control the precious metals (gold and silver) markets. *(James 5; Daniel 11:37-38)*
7. **Occultism**: "Craft" (witchcraft) and magic will be employed by the conspiracy to seduce the masses. *(Isaiah 44; Daniel 8:23-25; 11:37-38; I Timothy 4:1-3)*
8. **Deception**: Because they are deceived, the masses will go along with the plot by an elitist clique to usher in a New World Order. *(Daniel 11:23-32; Isaiah 28:15-18; Revelation 13)*
9. **Crises and Chaos**: The conspirators will cause bloody and devastating wars, plagues, hunger, oil shortages, pollution of the environment, and nuclear catastrophes *(Revelation 6: Matthew 24:21; Zechariah 14:12; Isaiah 1:7; 12; 24:6; 25:5)*
10. **Ultimate Defeat**: In the end, the conspirators will be totally vanquished because God has been and always will be in control. He allows the conspiracy to exist only to fulfill His will. *(Philippians 2:9-11; Daniel 7:27; 28:18; Revelation 19; I John 5:4)*

The Revelations of A. K. Chesterton

In his book, *The New Unhappy Lords: An Exposure of Power Politics*, Britain's A. K. Chesterton, who fully investigated the reality of a world conspiracy a quarter of a century ago, made this emphatic declaration:

> I claim, with submission, that what has been written in these pages proves the existence of a conspiracy for the destruction of the traditional Western world as the prelude to shepherding mankind into a sheep's-pen run as a One World tyranny . . .
>
> If the idea of so large a conspiracy seems preposterous, it is not nearly so preposterous as the assumption that the post-war shaping of the world is innocent of design.[16]

A. K. Chesterton's study of the conspirators demonstrated that their's was a "frenzied assault on patriotism."[17] He further revealed that the plan of the conspirators was that "all remaining nations had to be softened up with a view to their absorption in federal bodies—such as the European Economic Community—and ultimately in a One World Federation."[18]

Isn't it an interesting fact that since the publication of Chesterton's book about 25 years ago, what he declared as the hidden objectives of the Secret Brotherhood is exactly what we have since seen accomplished? Moreover, the frenzied assault on patriotism and the absorption of individual nations into groupings such as the European Economic Community and a North American Free Trade Zone, and the establishment of the Trilateral Commission, which also divides the world up into three regions, has escalated. All these things have occurred since Chesterton's book came out. It is quite obvious, then, that Chesterton was fully on target with his analysis.

As I mentioned earlier, today, given the ample opportunities offered to conspirators to collude together through high tech communications and ultra-fast transportation, the concept of a conspiracy is made much more feasible and reasonable. But even 25 years ago, Chesterton noted that the Money Power of the globe was being concentrated into fewer and fewer hands. As Chesterton stated: "The money and credit monopoly is controlled by a very few men."[19]

In the natural state of human affairs, considering men's tendency to want more and more money and their natural desire to exercise greater and greater power, it makes sense that men of like mind would work together to enrich themselves as a team. As Chesterton observes:

> In brief, *if there is no conspiracy, why is there no conspiracy*? Why should nature abhor all power vacuums except this particular vacuum? If the means of controlling the lives and destinies of mankind exists, as undoubtedly they do exist, why should use of them go by default? It is not as though there was any shortage of unscrupulous manipulators.[20]

In other words, it makes no sense at all that sinister men, involving themselves in sordid secret societies, would not conspire together to achieve common ends, particularly when money is involved. And as Chesterton so astutely reflected, certainly today there is no shortage of unscrupulous manipulators. If anything, in the decades since Chesterton's book was first published, the number of unscrupulous manipulators, corrupt politicians, and greedy banking and financial con men has multiplied beyond our wildest imaginations.

Chesterton concluded his study of the secret elite with this final word: "A conspiracy of worldwide dimensions does exist and . . . unless we manage to defeat the conspirators, no matter how great the odds against us, we shall have nothing to pass on to our successors except the certainty of enslavement."[21]

THREE

What International Evil Lurks in Vaults of Banks?

Few would debate the proposition that if there is a great world conspiracy that surrounds us, *money* and its acquisition is at the heart of it. A famous novelist once said that bestselling novels must contain at least one of four essential ingredients: money, sex, power, and blood. But with enough money, the other three can be bought!

Increasingly, intelligent and thoughtful men and women are discovering the alarming truth: that a conspiracy of grotesquely evil dimensions does exist. Moreover, they are coming to this shocking conclusion based on what they see occurring today in the realm of money.

For example, take Steve Daley, a highly respected Washington, D.C. correspondent for the *Chicago Tribune*. Daley recently penned an article about a money conspiracy, specifically related to the BCCI banking scandal. When the internationalist Bank of Credit and Commerce International (BCCI) folded in 1991, ripples were felt around the globe.

How can it be, it was asked, that a fantastic, double-dealing but super-rich bank such as this could even exist!

The Bank of Crooks and Criminals International (BCCI)

Bill Gates, soon to become director of the CIA, once scathingly called BCCI the "Bank of Crooks and Criminals International." But if so, then—surprise of surprises—consider the rogues' gallery of famous names attached to this scandal. As it turns out, many of the very men who have in the past been suspected of being at the forefront in an international Illuminati conspiracy just happen to be the same ones implicated in the BCCI scam.

And so Steve Daley wisely entitled his article for the *Chicago Tribune*, "What International Evil Lurks in Vaults of Banks?" Here's a fascinating portion of that intriguing article:

> WASHINGTON - Like millions of my skeptical countrymen and women, I long have snickered at the conspiracy theorists among us.
>
> Wild talk of evil-doing by the shadowy Trilateral Commission, letter-writing Scientologists, followers of Sun Myung Moon, collegiate fun-seekers in Skull and Bones or Soviet moles burrowed inside the American intelligence community kept me changing the channel.
>
> By my lights, Skull and Bones, the subterranean society that President Bush joined while at Yale, was the province of dull rich guys. And those who got lathered up by the secret-handshake crowd were as easily dismissed as folks who call talk-radio programs three nights a week to discuss Elvis Presley's whereabouts.
>
> The headlines indicate that I've been wrong. Years after critics of the Warren Commission and yahoos who

trumpeted papal conspiracies have passed in review, along comes the Bank of Credit and Commerce International.

Time magazine calls the controversy swirling around the bank "the first global scandal . . ."

Begun in 1972 by a Pakistani financier with an eye toward Third World development, BCCI soon became an automatic-teller machine for bribery, fraud money-laundering, drug deals, arms shipments and terrorism.

The preferred bank of Philippines despot Ferdinand Marcos, Iraq's Saddam Hussein, Panama's Manual Noriega and Colombia's murderous Medellin drug cartel, BCCI also serviced the Central Intelligence Agency and sponsored the largest bank holding company in Washington, First American Bankshares, hiring long-time Democratic insider Clark Clifford as a front man.

Clifford, the subject of a New York grand jury investigation, has denied all wrongdoing and he's not alone.

But how can a conspiracy theorist resist a scandal that links British Prime Minister John Major and former President Jimmy Carter, Clifford and arms dealer Adnan Khashoggi, Attorney General Dick Thornburgh and former Peruvian President Alan Garcia?

None of these worthies has been found guilty of anything so far, and most of them are probably responsible for little more than bad judgment and low companions.

But the exploding scandal appears likely to damage reputations on four continents and enhance the belief there are international forces at work operating independent of accountability and control.

What was the bank up to? It will take years to sort out.

A British newspaper, citing French sources, says that four years ago the Kuwaitis deposited $60 million in a BCCI account to bankroll the Fatah Revolutionary Council, a terrorist front for the notorious Abu Nidal.

Closer to home, there are charges the bank was used by the CIA as a link to Nicaraguan Contras, Afghan rebels and a host of cloak-and-dagger operatives overseas.

In Florida there are continuing investigations into BCCI involvement with the savings and loan fiasco, and there is also a growing body of evidence to suggest the U.S. government was less than zealous in following up rumors and reports about the bank.

In testimony before Senator John Kerry's Senate subcommittee last Thursday, William von Raab, former commissioner of the U.S. Customs Service, said the Justice Department had "cut out" his investigation of BCCI.

Talking about the ability of the U.S. government to overlook this vast illegality despite warnings going back nearly a decade, Von Raab offered a remarkable civics lesson.

"There wasn't a single influence peddler who wasn't being used to work this case," he said.

"The result is that senior U.S. policy-level officials were constantly under the impression that BCCI was probably not that bad, because all these good guys they play golf with all the time were representing them."

Von Raab suggested that Kerry's subcommittee look into a special Treasury Department outfit unit called SinCen, which took over international coordination of the BCCI investigation after von Raab resigned two years ago.

We don't yet know what SinCen is, but it's fair to assume it's not a new cable channel.[1]

A Skull & Bones Cover-up?

It's a sure bet that the U.S. Senate won't *ever* get to the bottom of the BCCI scandal. How clever of the Senate leadership that the subcommittee chaired by Senator John Kerry (D.-Massachusetts), a Yale grad and a Skull & Bones Society man, was assigned the task of straightening out the sleazy mess. That's a little like throwing a rotting side of ham into a deep freeze, then tossing the deep freeze into the bottom of the Pacific Ocean!

If the common, everyday people of the United States *were* to discover the true facts about BCCI, the whole scam of the world conspiracy would begin to unravel. This is because the conspiracy is fueled *by* money and is engaged in by the Illuminati so that they can acquire *more* money.

International banking is at the very core of this present evil force. Indeed, wherever we turn today in the field of money, we discover the grimy and dirty hands of the Secret Brotherhood groping around in the piggy banks of the world's largest financial institutions. For years now, from the Watergate and ITT scandals of the Nixon era to the savings and loan and banking fiascos of the Bush administration, the key to the whole sordid game plan of the elitists has involved international banking interests.

Are We Getting Close to the "Grand Finale?"

Yet another respected authority who seems to have finally caught on to this is Meg Greenfield, who writes a monthly opinion page for *Newsweek* magazine. Greenfield wrote an eye-opening piece for the magazine back in 1991. She noted that since the days of the ITT scandal during the Nixon era decades ago, an incredible array of "government creeps and pomposities . . . marginal characters and duped celebrities and misbehaving personages" have darted in and out of the news.[2]

Moreover, Greenfield keenly observed, the lives of these men and women, which at first glance seemed to be disparate and far afield from each other, "seem, unaccountably, to keep intertwining."[3]

Whatever the tragedy that befronts us at a given time, says Greenfield, whether the ITT scandal, the Watergate burglar incident, or now the BCCI banking affair and scam, the same "miscreants" seem to be involved. The same "improbable cast of characters" has become all too familiar. Greenfield characterized the recurring slate of bad guys as:

> . . . between jobs sleuths, spooks and troublemakers, bigshot financial figures, a genuinely eccentric female or two, government appointees with terminally bland expressions and (one had thought until one learned of their villainy) minds to match, political leaders who should have known better—all in all, your basic scandal package.[4]

What Has Been Going On?

"No one ever quite explained how that all came together," wrote Greenfield, "but, importantly some of them have turned up again and again."[5]

Greenfield finally was led to cry out: "This opera has been going on too long . . . from ITT to BCCI, *what the hell has been going on?*" "Tell us," she implored, "Get it over with whoever you may be. I think we'd all be grateful to be done with it and never hear from you again. I think we might even offer amnesty."[6]

Now before you make a too hasty decision that Meg Greenfield is jumping to conclusions, listen to what she had to say about the BCCI scam, only one of the many scandals and hazy yet crooked operations that has befallen the world recently:

> Only consider: Any scandal that has mixed up among its innocents and guilties and in-betweens (Panamanian dictator) Manuel Noriega, (Arab terrorist) Abu Nidal, (former Secretary of State) Clark Clifford, (President Carter's financial advisor) Bert Lance, the Mafia, the Colombian drug cartels, the CIA, and in a stunning walk-on part, Princess Anne, is coming about as close as we're going to get to the *Grand Finale*. And of course, there are characters involved in this one who took part in some of the infamous others.[7]

Newsweek's astute Meg Greenfield suggested that the incredible saga of BCCI and the other scandals may well constitute *one great thriller*. She notes that the BCCI affair appears to have in common with operas "a gigantic cast of characters you can never keep straight, all of whom are hiding something and at least half of whom are in disguise most of the time."[8]

Penetratingly, she also observes that:

> In our world it is the laundered money, the hidden bank accounts, the camouflaged ownerships and involvements . . . These are not so different from the endless deceptions that the characters in operas are perpetrating on each other and the audience most of the time. And, as in that art form, it is also the case in modern political reality that bizarre, unexpected connections among the unconnected (or so it had seemed) keep turning up.[9]

Significantly, Greenfield writes that the continuing and somewhat crowded trail of weird and strange events has done nothing to promote American confidence in either the honesty or "even the sanity of our leaders." But what has Greenfield really upset is that unlike the opera, in the strange and fantastic real world that confronts us, "the ends are always left loose:"

> The statement is usually uttered that these leaders simply didn't know what was going on, but that they will admit some sort of 'mistakes in judgement.' So the whole thing

> passes—until the next outbreak when some of the same low-lifes and the same issues reappear in an enormously enlarged cast.[10]

"What we never know," she says, "and what that great last scene on stage could tell us, is exactly what has been going on all these years and how all these seemingly unrelated folks got so weirdly and incriminating entangled with one another."[11]

The Financial Masquerade That Ends in Bloody Wars

Those of us who are by now aware of the reality of the great world conspiracy agree with Meg Greenfield. It is, indeed, time to pull down the curtain and end the masquerade of the would-be masters of the universe. But to do so, we must first believe, understand, and accept that a great charade and spectacle is occurring in the first place.

This charade involves bloody wars and notorious acts. For example, consider the case of the the Persian Gulf conflict. We were told that America fought in the Gulf to bring freedom to Kuwait, but the totally decadent reign of Kuwait's despotic Emir, al Sabah allows no freedoms. He's the Christian-murdering tyrant whom President Bush reinstalled on the throne after some of America's finest young men and women shed their blood in the victorious Persian Gulf battle.

It was disgraceful that this indecent Arab Sheik, his tyrannical family bullies, and their Arab cronies were allowed once again to seize power.

Predictably, pro-democracy elements inside Kuwait were very quickly cruelly suppressed as the Emir's more hardened loyalist soldiers rounded-up dissenters, raped women and children, and callously carried out assassinations.

Worse, with the BCCI bank failure comes the disclosure that all along it has been Kuwait's Emir who has been bankrolling Abu Nidal, the most notorious Arab terrorist in the world. According to the bank fraud investigators, in 1987 alone Kuwait's government deposited $60 million in Abu Nidal's secret BCCI account. Then, in 1989 some $500 million was put into Abu Nidal's account by the Kuwaiti and other Arab sources.

Incredibly, *our own CIA knew of these transactions.* Thus, even as President Bush cried crocodile tears over Saddam Hussein's overthrow of Kuwait's Emir and even as he welcomed the Emir back on the throne, *President Bush was keenly aware that this wicked Arab potentate was greatly responsible for such terrorist atrocities as the high-jacking of airliners and ships, and for terrorist bomb attacks around the world.*

Snickering at the Conspiracy "Theorists"

Interestingly enough, if there is a world conspiracy that has existed for decades or more, and if the conspirators do control the media—TV, magazines, newspapers, radio and so forth—would it not make sense that they would first of all seek to convince us that *there is no conspiracy*? After all, a conspiracy occurs in secret and the thugs who perpetrate it always do their best to keep their hideous acts under concealment. Naturally, they would attempt to downplay and discredit any talk of a conspiracy. They would also stamp out, to the best of their ability, any rumors or gossip that they are colluding behind our backs.

They would encourage the media to snicker at the conspiracy "theorists" among us. They would teach the media to proclaim that all of this is simply "wild talk." Crazy stories invented by strange people who need such mind games for entertainment during long, lonely, cold winter nights or steamy, hot summers.

That would be the minimum that the conspirators would do to keep the lid on things and to keep the masses hoodwinked. But I believe, after reading this book, many of you will pull off the masks and run up the window shades and again peer with 20/20 vision into the clear rays of sunlight.

The Ranks of Believers Swells Daily

Certainly, the ranks of those who recognize a conspiracy at work are growing fast. Jonathan Vankin, the news editor for the *San Jose Metro* newspaper in California, journeyed for two years into the world of grand-scale conspiracy theories. The result was his 1991 book, *Conspiracies, Cover-ups, and Crimes: Political Manipulation and Control.* At first Vankin was reluctant to admit that such events as the John F. Kennedy assassination were the result of conspiracy. "I went into it curious" and with an open mind, he states.[12]

Once he became immersed in a score of intricate plots whose origins can be traced back centuries to the Bavarian Illuminati, the medieval Knights Templar, and ancient mystery groups and secret societies, Vankin began to "recognize a definite kind of logic in the unanswered charges and hints of duplicity that footnote history."[13]

How, he wondered, could Robert Kennedy be killed by gunshot from inches behind his head when the convicted assassin, Sirhan Sirhan, was several feet in front of him?

"I consciously decided to question things like, what was the CIA doing at Jonestown?" says Vankin. "The more you think like that . . . the way you see things start to change, and it all looks a lot different than before."[14]

Meanwhile, at the American Psychological Association's convention in San Francisco in 1991, Sacramento psychologist Terence Sandbek delivered a research paper which attempted to take an objective view as to whether a world conspiracy actually exists. Yet, Sandbek noted that in light of current events, it may well be healthy for citizens to be skeptical of governments.

"You read non-fiction about the inner workings of the CIA and it's unbelievable," says psychologist Sandbek. "You figure it has got to be only the tip of the iceberg."[15]

Spies, Spooks, and the Secret Brotherhood

The frequent mention of CIA involvement in the world conspiracy is not happenstance. My own investigation reveals that the men who run the networks of the Secret Brotherhood have for decades controlled America's Central Intelligence Agency as well as spy agencies in Great Britain and other countries. Thus, it is not accidental that George Bush, Skull & Bones class of '47, was magically chosen in the late 1970's to be director of the CIA. Nor was it a mere coincidence that William Casey, Reagan's appointee to be chief of the CIA, belonged to yet another brotherhood-linked secret society, the Knights of Malta.

Lady Queensborough, in her highly acclaimed, two-volume work, *Occult Theocrasy*, had this to say about the Illuminati takeover of international spy organizations:

> Ancient and Accepted Scottish Rites (Freemasonry) runs its own Secret Service which cooperates with the national secret services of all countries, thus serving the aims and purposes of internationalism.[16]

In a separate book I'm now working on, I hope to unmask the Secret Brotherhood's clandestine control and manipulation of the CIA, the Russian KGB, the FBI, and the British intelligence agencies. I am convinced that I will be able to conclusively prove that George Bush was himself a key CIA operative even before he became CIA director.

Moreover, it can be proven that Bush was given his earlier CIA position by contacts in Skull & Bones. He used his Texas oil businesses as a cover for his clandestine activities in the 1960's. George Bush was even involved in the Cuban Bay of Pigs invasion, but his role in the JFK assassination especially deserves scrutiny.

Unraveling the Mysteries of the JFK Assassination

In a November 29, 1963 memorandum from J. Edgar Hoover, then head of the Federal Bureau of Investigation and himself a 33rd degree Mason, to the U.S. State Department, the "George Bush connection" was mentioned. In the memo, Hoover stated that on November 23, 1963, while accused assassin Lee Harvey Oswald was in police custody and being interrogated about his then unknown undercover role with the CIA, FBI, and other governmental agencies, the FBI's Dallas, Texas, special agent W. T. Forsythe, briefed "Mr. George Bush of the Central Intelligence Agency" about "problems" related to the assassination. Forsythe was accompanied in his briefing of the CIA's George Bush by a Captain William Edwards of the Defense Intelligence Agency.[17]

This startling memo was (I believe, inadvertently) released to the public along with tens of thousands of other, mostly unusable and innocuous documents that had been previously stamped and classified "Top Secret." These documents were released only after dozens of researchers availed themselves of the Freedom of Information Act and repeatedly threatened to take reluctant and unenthusiastic government agencies to court. Of course today, the bulk of documentation regarding the Kennedy assassination still remains under lock and key.

Strange Alliances of Greedy Bedfellows

Did the Secret Brotherhood order hit men to finish off President John F. Kennedy? If so, it would not have been the first time that these evil men have used the ultimate weapon—assassination and murder—to cover up their tracks and get their way. And if all this seems too preposterous to imagine, then consider the cautionary words of Russian dissident and Nobel Peace Prize recipient Alexander Solzhenitsyn, who noted the amazing fact that the conspiracy is not only of a money nature, but that its perpetrators could care less from whom their money came.

> There also exists another alliance—at first glance, a strange one, a surprising one—but if you think about it, in fact, one which is well grounded and easy to understand. This is the alliance between our communist leaders and your capitalists.[18]

In 1913, U.S. President Woodrow Wilson also spoke of the corrupt men who make up the international money power: "There is a power so organized, so subtle, so watchful, so interlocked, so complete, so pervasive, that prudent men better not speak above their breath when they speak in condemnation of it."[19]

It was Thomas Jefferson who once trumpeted the famous line, "Power to the people!" But it was the Secret Brotherhood that developed the occult understanding that the root of all power is money and with enough money a small band of men can greatly influence a huge mob of fools. They were and are the "power" about which Woodrow Wilson warned.

Confessions of A Money Insider

In a recent book by Jacques Attali, special advisor to France's President Mitterrand and one of the top leaders of the European Community, the author shares his considerable insight into the financiers of the Secret Brotherhood, and into their mind set concerning the power of money.[20] Attali is no enemy of the conspiracy. In fact, he is a part of the great system of money and power that pervades the world today. Therefore, he vindicates the use of super-capitalist techniques and devious methods employed by the Brotherhood to develop their schemes.

It is for this reason—the fact the Jacques Attali favors world government and the unity of all things under the direction of a global Brain Trust or World Mind—that we should pay even closer attention to his writings.

In describing how the international financiers are organized, Attali shows that the financiers are "linked together in a close-knit, almost dynastic network." He says that they "constitute a parallel aristocracy planted within the very heart of every regime." He further describes them as "an elite both of wealth and culture, behaving like a dynasty."[21]

Their power to influence history and to organize themselves together, and their use of *rituals* to further their aims is recognized by Attali when he states:

> Pioneers of capitalist rationality, founders of and witnesses for the Mercantile Order, financiers are essential links in the chain of our history . . . they organize themselves finally into a strange aristocracy, a sort of austere Order with its implacable moral code and ferocious rituals; the Name is its primary riches and the Land its ultimate vanity.[22]

Can this much power really be wielded over the common man by the international financiers? Attali provides astonishing information, consistent with all the research that I have done on the conspiracy, that the men at the top actually have such vast, encompassing power and influence that they become superintendents of all other men on this planet. Attali reveals that it is the money men who pull the strings of power by direct control over heads of state.

A "Power Over Power"

What's more, Attali writes, the financiers have organized themselves into an *Order* and recognize each other by a certain "Name." They possess a magnificent *"power over power."* Their fantastic success has permitted them to set-up on a global scale a "Mercantile Order" in which, because of their ability to create and distribute money to whomsoever they please, they are therefore able to discreetly exercise an incredible form of "power over the holders of power."[23]

Ominously in my view, Jacques Attali presents to us a "vision of the world that is about to be born." He notes that we have witnessed the death through exhaustion of the Soviet empire and now we are witnessing the triumph of democracy. Next on the horizon, according to Attali, is a New World that will be based on this Mercantile Order. It will be altogether different from anything we have ever seen before in history and it will be ruled over by a small clique of power brokers—the financiers who have this "power over power."[24]

How Mighty is the Rockefeller Klan?

While Jacques Attali is an insider of the conspiracy, Emanuel M. Josephson, author of a number of enlightening books on the Rockefeller dynasty and the Federal Reserve conspiracy, most definitely is not. In one of his thoroughly documented exposé books, Josephson says of the conspirators that their accomplishments could be written up in a bestselling fiction novel. Such a novel, he suggests, would be more provocative and thrilling than Ian Fleming's *Goldfinger*, the fictional tale that was made into a James Bond 007 blockbuster movie.[25]

The truth, said Josephson, is much stranger than fiction:

> The truth, in this instance, is stranger, more menacing and frightening than fiction. The key characters are not as ostentatious in their criminality. They are far more ruthless, though cowardly, gangsters. They pose as "philanthropists" and are unsuspected. They use the U.S. and other governments, their "dis-United" Nations, and kings and queens as pawns in their games. Millions of humans have been slaughtered in an endless series of wars they have engineered to expand their empire and increase their loot. Their grandiose objective is

"internationalist," "One World" dictatorship, genocide and enslavement of mankind.[26]

For those who suspect Josephson guilty of overstating the case, of some form of literary hyperbole, I can only refer them to the wording of the U.S. Supreme Court ruling of 1911 regarding the high court's decree that the *Rockefeller's Standard Oil Company must be dissolved—at once*! Not mincing words, the majority opinion of the Supreme Court emphatically stated, "For the safety of the Republic we now decree that *the dangerous conspiracy* must be ended by November 15, 1911."[27]

Remember that word, "conspiracy," used with extreme good judgement by the Supreme Court, when people scornfully taunt you and mock you as some kind of a conspiracy theorist or nut. The Supreme Court ruling had to do with the massive plot by John D. Rockefeller to control the world oil business. The Rockefeller family had amassed untold wealth as a result of its establishment of a global network of co-conspirators. This network was greased and facilitated with money and, in turn, it made more money, proving the adage that "It takes money to make money" and adding the little ditty that, to make billions it takes at least several hundred million.

While the Supreme Court of the United States attempted to dismantle the conspiracy put together by the international Rockefeller dynasty, the attempt, unfortunately, did not succeed. Over the years the Rockefellers have grown more and more wealthy and more cunning in the manner in which they employ their wealth to control the affairs of this world. The current head of the Rockefeller dynasty, David Rockefeller (his son is waiting in the wings to take over), was once labeled by *Time Magazine* as "the prime mover in banking that controls the course of world economic affairs and history."[28]

The publication also recognized David Rockefeller as the most important banker in the world. Rockefeller himself, through his press agent, admits that he is "enormously and all but incalculably rich."[29] Not only is he rich, but such world notables as Japan's emperor and the monarch of Thailand have astutely said that he "outranks royalty."[30]

The Financial New World Order

Though David Rockefeller may be the most visible of the Brotherhood, he is joined in his vainglorious scheme by a handful of others with huge money resources. In a recent newsletter, former Congressman Ron Paul of Houston, the man who first exposed the plot to give us a "new money" (see my book *Millennium: Peace, Promises, and The Day They Take Our Money Away*), wrote about the financial aspects of the New World Order and the plans of the money men who are its architects:

> The Financial New World Order is the creation of an elite system of interconnected governments and bureaucrats, which conspires to tax, regulate, and inflate away the wealth held by the middle class peoples of countries around the world, in the name of global democracy.

Congressman Ron Paul has made it plain that, in his view, the United States has taken the lead in imposing this Financial New World Order. My own investigation makes clear the fact that this is a conspiracy of *global dimensions*, with only a handful of elitists at the very top pulling the strings of world power. This small group also formulates the policies and sets forth the various battle plans designed to bring all things together as the nations of the world gallop furiously toward the sunset of the 20th century.

FOUR

The Great Work: The Magic of a Thousand Points of Light

What did President George Bush *really* mean when he promised, "I will keep America moving forward, ever forward for an enduring dream and *a thousand points of light*?" And later, during his State of the Union Address, when he mysteriously told the nation that our goal must be "*the illumination of a mankind by a thousand points of light*?"

Is this a coded illuminist message? Is it intended only for a very special, targeted audience? Who first conceived of the idea of a "Thousand Points of Light?" And does this strange phrase have anything to do with the long-cherished *occult plan* for America?

Is there a link between the meaning of the phrase "A Thousand Points of Light" and the New World Order conspiracy?

The public at large seems to be fascinated and enthralled with the dazzling *pageantry and illusion* employed by the Secret Brotherhood to mask their true intentions. Using the universal desire for democracy and freedom as a cover for their activities, the Secret Brotherhood has recently been able to get one of its own elected President of the United States. Other men controlled by its network now hold the top positions in Great Britain, France, Germany, and Russia.

As never before in history, the powers of *money and government* have merged to become one. Thus, the Secret Brotherhood is at the very pinnacle of finally achieving its most cherished objectives. The roadblocks which once impeded its progress have been removed—and now, watch out! The world will never be the same!

Breaking the Illuminist Code

For the most part the Secret Brotherhood operates behind closed doors. Frankly, I had to practically turn the earth inside out—and call down help from Heaven as well—to track these men down and gain access to their unpublished plan for world domination and control. But it was only after I was able to unlock the deepest secrets of their *illuminist code* and decipher their cryptic special language that I first began to make significant progress in my investigative journey to unmask the Secret Brotherhood.

The men of the Secret Brotherhood are not like you and me. *They believe in magic*. Theirs is the strange and bizarre world of *ritual alchemy*, the recitation of *mantras*, of *words of power*, the study of *esoteric* philosophies, and the mysterious display of *arcane New Age symbols*. Yet, in public, they impress us as men who are likeable, intelligent, refined, fair-minded, tolerant, thoughtful, kind, and gentle men who sincerely care about such matters as the environment, the plight of the hungry and starving overseas, the jobless, and the poverty-stricken.

Moreover, they often are recognized as leaders in the legitimate quest for world peace and tranquility. Many are active in church work and charitable organizations. Others give freely to good causes. *No one would suspect for a moment what actually goes on in the deep, dark recesses of their diabolical minds.*

The elitists who comprise the Secret Brotherhood are *without exception* initiates of secret societies. To the average person, the elaborate rituals, secret passwords and hand signs, mysterious symbols, and coded messages employed by the members of the secret societies border on the ridiculous. But to men whose entire lives, from the cradle to the grave, are bound up in arcane, hidden practices, the world is viewed with a far different set of lenses. The earth and everything in it acquires stunningly supernatural magical qualities.

The concealed men of the magnificently powerful Secret Brotherhood are, in fact, blood brothers whose minds have long been immersed and shrouded in a magical paradigm totally incomprehensible to the common man. *It is for this reason that these men are extremely dangerous.*

It is, moreover, most unwise for us to consider them our moral, ethical, and spiritual equals. They are not. The leaders of such groups as the Order of Skull & Bones, the Priory de Sion, the Order of the Garter, the Grand Orient Lodge, and the Rosicrucians are men who totally abhor and find disgusting the plebeian lifestyle and lower class worldview of those of us whom, they are convinced, are their social and spiritual inferiors. The members of the Secret Brotherhood have been taught that the illuminized, superior New Man is not limited by the old world's traditional values. His is instead a pure and spiritual nature that transcends the normal confines of good and evil.

Believe me, the Secret Brotherhood holds you and I in utter contempt. Their deceitful actions well demonstrate their contemptuous attitude toward us. All their lives they have been taught the necessity of *deceiving* the masses. These men are unquestionably the all-time *masters of deceit.*

The Magical Language of the Messengers of Light

To fully understand just how masterful the Brotherhood is in seeding men's minds with illusion and magic, we need only turn to the coded, esoteric speeches of their chief public servant, President George Bush. For years, George Bush has been a primary messenger for the Brotherhood. His messages, though they appear to be full of light, nevertheless are dark and foreboding. What's more, they convey special meanings which can be understood only by those trained in the black magical arts, alchemy, and ritual.

To the uninitiated, these words and phrases act as alchemical processing tools, powerful in their ability to induce visual stimulation. Occult phraseology programs and condition the minds of the masses, and this is its principal purpose.

As Robert Anton Wilson, a notable authority on mass hypnosis and occultic systems, wrote in an article for *Magical Blend*, a major New Age magazine, "Language and hypnosis form the foundation on which humans create worlds of consciousness and of fantasy."[1]

It is remarkably easy to induce at least partial hypnosis in human beings, says Wilson, and "very few people know how to dehypnotize themselves."

This process of hypnosis is strengthened when magical words are used which inject regenerative power into peoples' minds. The best way to do this is to employ *symbolic language*. Thus Ruth Miller, in *The Mystical Origin of the United States*, writes that the secret societies initiated the science of *symbology* in which to clothe their philosophy. Through words of symbolic power, men's minds are "illuminated" and their emotions are "transmuted."

If we examine just two of George Bush's more famous speeches, the coded nature of his illuminist messages easily stand out. The first speech we will look at is George Bush's acceptance speech at the Republican Party National Convention on August 18, 1988. This speech has been considered by many to be the most effective ever presented by the president.

The Mission

First, then Vice President Bush let the thousands of assembled delegates—and the tens of millions of others watching via global television—know that he had a destiny, which he described as a *mission*, to perform. In fact, his speech was peppered *ten times* with the word *mission.* The Secret Brotherhood believes its *Great Work*, the illumination of mankind, is a glorious *mission.* Is this what George Bush had in mind when he remarked:

> I am a man who sees life in terms of *missions* defined and *missions* completed . . . The most important work of my life is to complete the *mission* we started in 1980 . . . Let me tell you more about the *mission.* A nation's leader must be able to define—and lead—a *mission.*

The Ancient Knowledge

To the Illuminati, *ancient knowledge* refers to ancient *occult wisdom* and to the *mystery teachings of the ages.* They also call this ancient knowledge the *perennial philosophy*, the *ageless wisdom*, or the *gnostic philosophy.* How strange, then, to hear George Bush use the term "ancient knowledge" in respect to detente with the Soviet Union:

> We have a new relationship with the Soviet Union . . . It is a watershed. It happened when we acted on the *ancient knowledge* that strength and clarity lead to peace.

The Bright Center

The occult philosophy of the Secret Brotherhood teaches of the *bright, radiant center* within each individual. This bright center reflects the rays of the *Great Central Sun*, the Masonic deity, and is how man expresses the *will* to become awake, to become *illumined.* As Alice Bailey of the Lucis Trust explains in the veiled language so common to the advanced disciples of the secret societies:

> When light illuminates the minds of men and stirs the secret light within all forms, then the One in Whom we live reveals His hidden secret lighted will.
>
> When the purpose of the Lords of Karma can find no more to do and all the weaving and close-related plans are all worked out, then the One in Whom we live can say: "Well done! Naught but the beautiful remains."
>
> When the lowest of the low, the densest of the dense, and the highest of the high have all been lifted through the little wills of men, then can the One in Whom we live raise into radiating light the vivid lighted ball of Earth, and then another greater Voice can say to Him: "Well done! Move on. Light shines!"[2]

According to the occult teachings of the Illuminati, at the bright center is found *energy*, which, the occult philosophy says, is "God energy." This energy within, writes Alice Bailey, is "a point of focused fire, found in the center which permits *radiation* to penetrate to other centers and to other lives."[3]

The "bright center" which is the *individual god-force* radiating out to others is also said to be likened to the sun rays that emanate from the secret societies, or *Orders*. Thus, Gaetan Delaforge, in *The Templar Tradition in the Age of Aquarius*, remarks:

> The aspirations of the Order should be spiritual above all else . . . An Order should strive to be *a center of radiant light* inspiring men and women to join in the redemption of the planet by the example given by its members in their daily lives.[4]

Mikhail Gorbachev and the Bright Center of Man

Mikhail Gorbachev, like Bush a dedicated servant of the Wise Men of the Secret Brotherhood, has also talked about this *bright center of light radiating from within exalted man.* Malachi Martin, obviously a fan of Gorbachev's, describes the political mission of the Russian leader this way:

> He is their (the peoples of the earth) living guarantee that, together, we can reach to the very core of this earth, into every hidden place of this human cosmos. Together we can humanize it all . . .
>
> For Gorbachev will show us how humankind's collective intellect can and will be accumulated within a new form of the present United Nations. On that day of human history, man—the man each one of us is—will be made into a giant, standing as the *center and focus of all our human activities* as nations and as people. That is the beckoning height of Gorbachev's neo-Leninist reach.[5]

Notice, however, that Gorbachev does not beckon us to honor and adore the true *God and Lord* of this universe, whose name is Jesus Christ. No, what Gorbachev, Bush, and other illuminized masters want to do is condition men to accept their own *collective intellect* as divine wisdom. Perfected man shall be a *giant*, whose inner light, given to him by the God of Forces—the great Sun deity, radiates to family and to others.

George Bush made this point clear when he stated:

> An election is about ideas and values, and it is also about *philosophy*. And I have one. At the *bright center* is the individual and *radiating out* from him or her is the family . . . From the individual to the family to the community to the nation.[6]

The Great Invocation and its Points of Light

Could George Bush's phraseology also have come from *The Great Invocation* of the Lucis Trust, a major globalist organization? *The Great Invocation* is an occultic prayer widely used by New Age and liberal church groups. It was even invoked for the opening day ceremonies of the United Nations' environmental Earth Summit in 1992, in which President George Bush participated. A key passage in this occultic prayer reads: "From the point of Light within the Mind of God let light stream forth into the minds of man. Let light descend on earth."

In *Esoteric Psychology II*, Alice Bailey, founder of the Lucis Trust and originator of *The Great Invocation*, reveals that the "Light" or "Mind of God" is the energy that radiates from "the heart of the Sun, which is the inner point of life" in man. It is from the Sun (God), she adds, that man receives spiritual "illumination" and thus becomes a *light bearer* who, through service, "*radiates the light (occult knowledge and power) outward.*"[7]

In *The Beacon*, a journal published by the Lucis Trust and World Goodwill, we find this explanation:

> The sun is a great magnet. So says *The Secret Doctrine*. To esotericists the sun is synonymous with the indwelling higher nature . . . It would seem that we have, each of us, to become sun-like—to become light bearers bringing radiant illumination to the way of all who live on earth . . . Every person is potentially a radiant sun.[8]

In *Mysteries of the Holy Grail*, Corinne Heline, one of the 20th century's most famous occult theologians, echoes this philosophy:

> The *force center* in man . . . when it is fully awake and under the control of the illumined will . . . is able to flood his entire body with the life forces which pour in from the sun . . .[9]

A Pagan Sun God Philosophy

This Masonic-oriented philosophy of the bright center shining from the Sun into the minds of men takes us all the way back to the pagan mystery religion of Babylon. There, writes Alexander Hislop in his outstanding classic work, *The Two Babylons*, the King of Babylon, Nimrod, was worshipped by being deified as the Sun God. As the Sun deity, Nimrod "was regarded not only as the *illuminator* of the material world, but as the *enlightener of the souls of men*."[10]

In Egypt, Hislop records, the disk of the Sun was represented in the temples as it was also in the worship of Baal, Mithras, and Apollo. In each instance, "the image of the Sun which was worshipped was erected *above the altar*."[11] This is today exactly where the Freemasonry lodges place their own sun ray burst and their all-seeing eye of Horus, the Egyptian Sun God—above the altar. And George Bush, as a patriarch of the Skull & Bones Society, is an illuminized Freemason.

The Divine Plan of the Sun God

The Masonic religion—and all ancient mystery religions—teaches that the Sun God represents the exalted and perfected man. Man is himself the deity who, through initiation, service and obedience, and illumination, unites with the Sun force, or energy. That is the Divine Plan.

Thus, John Randolph Price, a prominent New Age leader, writes:

> Has it not occurred to you what the *Divine Plan* is? The Divine Plan for your life *is* the Christ (self) indwelling, *your* spiritual nature, *your* Superconsciousness, *your* LORD . . . The Light of God within you, *your* True Self.[12]

One who has the "higher illumination," Price explains, is he who is blessed by the *solar energy* of the divine Sun:

"It is the sun that does the work . . . my light is not mine but of the Sun . . . God is the Sun."[13]

The Magic of A Thousand Points of Light

Was George Bush referring to the Sun God—the divine, radiant center in each man—in his acceptance speech at the Republican Convention in 1988? To find the answer, we turn to the President's most famous phrase—his reference to "the magic of a thousand points of light."

In his speech in New Orleans at the Convention, George Bush electrified the entire world when he declared:

> This is America: the Knights of Columbus, the Grange, Hadassa, the Disabled Veterans, the Order of Ahepa, the Business and Professional Women of America, the union hall, the Bible study group, LULAC, Holy Name—*a brilliant diversity spread like stars, like a thousands points of light in a broad and peaceful sky.*

First, "a thousand points of light"—what does this cryptic phrase really mean? In occult language, George Bush literally meant *the spread and growth of the universalist Secret Doctrine of Masonry*. This involves nothing less than the success of the "global vision" of the Secret Brotherhood.

This is a phrase well understood by trained occultists. In *Discipleship in A New Age*, Alice Bailey directs occult students to repeatedly make this affirmation: "I am a point of light within a greater light . . . I am a spark of sacrificial Fire, focused within the fiery will of (the Sun) God."[14]

Then, in perhaps the most revealing book Bailey ever wrote, 1957's *The Externalization of the Hierarchy*, she tells us that the "Points of Light" refers to the men who comprise the occult leadership group known as the *New Group of World Servers*. These individuals, she remarks, are in *service* to "the work of the Brotherhood . . . the Forces of Light." They are the ones who are to usher all of mankind from the darkness of outmoded Christianity and faded nationalism into the bright and shining "New World Order."[15]

How amazing that in 1957, 31 years before George Bush uttered those memorable words in New Orleans, one of the world's top occultists, a woman who first named her organization Lucifer Publishing, originated not only the phrase "points of light" but also that vague term said by his closest advisors to be George Bush's own invention, the "New World Order."

It is only fitting that Bailey recognize that it is, in fact, *Lucifer* who is the Sun God. The Bible calls him a deceptive "Angel of Light," but occultists refer to Lucifer as the Radiant One, the Solar Angel and as the Father of Light, who comes to initiate man into the New Age Kingdom, a golden age when perfected man and a cleansed and purified planet earth shall share their own godhood.

The Coming Solar Age: Blending the Points of Light

In his book *Solar Man*, Thomas Ehrenzeller, a director of the World Federalists Association, proclaims that the world and man are soon to reap the vista of "the dawn of the *Solar Age*." This, he ecstatically predicts, "will herald the coming of a new *Solar Race* which will last for centuries, millennia even."[16]

The Secret Brotherhood conceives of itself as the Brotherhood of Light—a functioning *service network dedicated to reconstructing a New World*. Their goal is the spreading of their New Age illuminist gospel to a *thousand points* across the globe. Eventually, all of mankind—except perhaps a few, dim and imperfect souls—will partake of the initiation process. The *Great Work* shall be done on earth as it is now in hell (the spirit world of Lucifer):

> The light shared by and belonging to all, though dimmed by the imperfection of evolving forms, *is the mutual*

> *recognition of many points* and their joining in interrelationship which has created the magnetic aura of the New Group of World Servers.
>
> Through all who identify with this group, seeking to cooperate with its purpose and *blending their little points of light*, the New Group of World Servers will fulfill its purpose and become the planetary lightbearer of the Aquarian age, the radiant torch to light the way for a needy humanity.[17]

The above statement comes from the Lucis Trust's *Beacon* journal, July/August, 1986. In that same issue we are told that, "The keynote of esoteric schools (such as the secret societies) is *service*—service to humanity, service of the Plan, and service of the Hierarchy."

The goal is to produce disciples . . . "who can consciously cooperate with the Hierarchy with intelligence and power."[18] The goal, writes Jane Brewin, is to develop a "group consciousness."[19]

In his presidential acceptance speech, George Bush therefore used coded illuminist terminology, accomplishing two goals: (1) signalling his intent and his loyalty to fellow members of the Secret Brotherhood network across the globe; and (2) conditioning and hypnotizing the minds of uninitiated listeners, inducing visual imagery of the most powerful, magical nature. This process is calculated to desensitize individuals and leave their minds susceptible to even higher stages of magic and alchemical transmutation and processing.

This was not, however, the last time that George Bush used the illuminist phrase, "A Thousand Points of Light." The phrase was regularly used during his campaign for the presidency. Then, in his historic *State of the Union* address on the eve of the invasion of Kuwait and Iraq by U.S. and other U.N. troops, President Bush again emphasized that his goal was "the illumination of mankind by a thousand points of light."

The Points of Light Foundation

So successful was he in capturing the public imagination by repeated use of this phrase that George Bush and his associates decided to establish a *Points of Light Foundation*. Top country singer Randy Travis was recruited to croon a tune entitled "Point of Light," and once each week the White House selected some service group or individual somewhere in America for a "Point of Light" award and certificate.

The Points of Light Foundation was begun with a $5 million grant from the U.S. Congress and the President. Its first chairman was J. Richard Munro, formerly the chairman of Time Warner, Inc., the company whose logo is an all-seeing eye.

Not surprisingly, the logo for the Points of Light Foundation is also of an occultic nature. It depicts the golden sun disk with what at first glance appears to be a torch of light within. But wait, is it not the concealed image of two entities, a male and a female, facing each other? Occultic philosophers can easily recognize these two as the Sun God and his Goddess.

The Points of Light Foundation logo has a hidden, alchemical double meaning.

In an ad produced for the Points of Light Foundation and sponsored by the Coca Cola Company, we find this message:

> The initiative started by the "Points of Light" was one of sharing *the light that is within us* . . . Please join us in creating an *enduring light* for the future and a message for people here at home about the *enlightened* America we want to be.

The Points of Light Foundation is now recognizing deserving cities as "Cities of Light." Orlando, Florida, the community that gave us the "Magic of Disney" and Mickey Mouse with a sorcerer's coned hat, was chosen for distinction as America's first "City of Light." At the grand ceremony, President Bush and Barbara, the Mayor of Orlando, and others were there for the hoopla and to give speeches.

A fancy, illustrated brochure was passed out to the people. Here is just a part of the message printed in the brochure. See if you can decipher the coded, illuminist messages it contains:

> Once upon a time, today and always, there will be people made of magic—as if blessed with a power all their own . . . Their secret rests not in wealth, nor in the trappings of the times, but in the power they have discovered in the gift of giving. Their presence radiates an illumination of spirit in the form of light, creating a glow in the community that if multiplied would be felt across the country.
>
> This energy is meant to be treasured and harnessed in the form of a vision, seen as a "Point of Light." We are calling upon these visionaries to help light the way back home to a place of warmth, to a place of trust, to a place of peace. We are counting on those rich in spirit to lead us back to basic values, where people are acknowledged as being the most special part of life.

If each visionary were to light the candle of just one other, who would in turn share their secret with just one other, we would begin to create what would be called a "City of Light." This flame of love, hope and peace has the power to ignite our country, has the power to change the face of our nation forever.

Please participate in the birth of this creation by joining us at "The Celebration," A Gathering of Community Spirit. Be a part of a movement that has the power to change our community forever. Be part of *Orlando, America's First City of Light.*

The White House: A Lighthouse?

Did Bush's "Points of Light" theme inspire New Age occultist and author Joshua Halpern, who, in his book, *Children of the Dawn: Visions of the New Family*, boasted: "By the year 2000 . . . the White House will be turned into a Light House. Rays of Light will emanate from Washington."[20]

Not possible; you see, Halpern's book was published in 1983—two years *before* George Bush gave his famous speech in which he first used the phrase, "a thousand points of light."

The truth is, the scheme all along has been to illuminate the world by establishing occultic service groups and individuals who are "points of light" in every nation on earth." From such centers, writes John G. Bennett, "there can spread throughout the world—perhaps more quickly than you can imagine possible—the seeds of a new world."[21]

What is shameful is that many groups, if not most, whom George Bush and the Points of Light Foundation nationally recognized as a "Point of Light" had no idea of the occultic meaning. Indeed, most were very honorable and truly worthy of recognition for their dedicated service to their community.

The occultic concept of "A Thousand Points of Light" is thus being masterfully implanted in the minds of millions of receptive but unwitting victims. Some recognize the darkly occult "signal" they are receiving; most do not. It's all part of the New Age and Masonic quest to indoctrinate the world with its humanistic gospel of light. As such, this is a parapsychological, magical *networking* effort:

> Light centers have developed into a worldwide network that purposely link-up telepathically . . . to serve as "superconscious receiving, anchoring and sending stations. Many such groups exist. We have seen their "lights" twinkling across Russia. Some are known this way, intuitively, but many are now consciously aware of each other and are in direct contact.[22]

LaVedi Lafferty and Bud Hollowell, founders of the New Age-oriented "Collegians Universal Church," penned the above words in 1983—about five years *before* George Bush came up with his concept of "a thousand points of light" across America.

The Occult Meaning of the Number 1,000

What does the number "*1,000*" in "a thousand points of light" signify for the Illuminati? There are many reasons why this number is so often used, including:

* The number refers to the astrological sign of Aquarius, connected with the New Age and a New World Order—the New Millennium (1,000 years).

* It mocks the coming millennial (1,000 year) reign of Christ (see Revelation 19 through 22).

* It refers to the *serpent*, or Lucifer. The Hindu version is Sesha, the 1,000-headed "serpent of eternity" who cyclically brings man a "New Age."[23]

* The head of Medusa, the evil Greek Goddess, was said to be covered with a mass of 1,000 writhing, venomous snakes.

* It is a mystical term implying an indefinite and countless number—or simply, "many." One New Age globalist publication recently recommended that the United Nations be given taxing and bond authority to create revenue and "tap widespread public support." This, said the editor, will constitute "a *million* points of light."[24]

* It connotes a new beginning—a new occult cycle and age for mankind. In the Jewish mystical kaballah system, *Alpha*, the beginning, is the number 1. Alpha with a dash (the new cycle) indicates the number 1,000.[25]

* In the pagan Celtic festival of St. John, wrote Alexander Hislop in *The Two Babylons*, devilish fires were lit: "Towards evening one fire is gradually followed by two, three or four; then a *thousand* gleam out from the hilltops till the whole country glows under the conflagration."[26]

* The number 1,000 denotes the "thousand-petaled lotus" of Eastern and oriental mysticism. "With proper sexual exercises," explains Barbara Walker in the *Women's Encyclopedia of Myths and Secrets*, a true sage might achieve the final flowering of revelation described as the *thousand-petaled lotus* of invisible light."[27]

* The Lucis Trust, in the October, 1982 edition of *Reader's Digest* (page 203), paid for a full-page ad for *The Great Invocation.* The thousand-petaled lotus was displayed prominently in that ad, along with the passage, "From the point of Light within the Mind of God let light stream forth in the minds of men."

The Mysterious Order of Ahepa

George Bush's mention of the *Order of Ahepa*, along with the Knights of Columbus and other "service" groups, was not accidental—it was extremely significant. Few Americans have ever heard of this group, so why would it be mentioned in Bush's speech? Here's the secretive reason why—this is another coded illuminist message: the *Order of Ahepa* is a Masonic order for Greek Americans! In the enlightening book, *The Axis of Death*, Dr. D. C. Yermak reveals these facts about Ahepa:

> As soon as a Greek immigrant arrives in the U.S.A. and before a week or two elapses, he is informed by friends or relatives that in order to "progress" and be able to build his new life, he must join a very strong Greek-American organization, which (he is told) is absolutely patriotic and Orthodox-Christian. He will find that this organization is strong politically, too, and even has its people in the U.S. Senate and elsewhere.
>
> Naturally impressed, the Greek immigrant joins the organization . . . But in order to be a "full" member of the set-up, he is invited to some *closed* gatherings . . . He becomes a full member of *AHEPA*! But for us, this supposed organization is nothing else than a MASONIC LODGE that has as its main task to detach our Greek countryman from the Faith of His Fathers, and from his country. But he is already on the "conveyor" and can do nothing to react.[28]

The Illumination of Mankind

What is the meaning of the cryptic term, the "illumination of mankind?" Joseph Campbell, the Hindu and pagan mythologies professor made famous with his TV specials on Public Broadcasting Service (PBS), sponsored by CFR man Bill Moyers with financial aid from Laurance Rockefeller, explains in his and Moyers' book, *The Power of Myth*, that illumination refers to the *transformation and restructuring of the universe.*[29]

According to Joseph Campbell, the Masonic symbol of the point of light within the circle is what is known as the "illumination source." The Illumination of man, says Campbell, is a process in which alchemy and magic are used to transform man and his world. The process is accomplished through *unity* or *synthesis*, the merging of opposites into one whole. As Campbell quotes Chinese philosopher Lao Tzu, "out of many, one."[30]

This is the very same illumination process sponsored over the centuries by Freemasonry and its affiliated secret societies. "Out of chaos, order," is the Masonic motto, and *equilibrium* (unity and synthesis), according to Masonic doctrine, is man's ultimate destiny.[31]

A New Harmony: Equilibrium

We see, then, in this coded language the true importance of *The New World Order*, all wrapped up in a neat, harmonious package. Indeed, *harmony* is yet another word that presidential candidate George Bush used back in 1988. Said Vice President Bush:

> I hope to stand for a *new harmony*, a greater tolerance. We've come far, but I think we need a *new harmony*.

"New Harmony" means sweet surrender—the surrender of all opposition to the ages-old conspiracy of the Illuminati. It means *unity in diversity*, a major New Age theme. A New Harmony means *perestroika*, the end result of illumination, the restructuring of the universe. It means a *new synthesis*, the new working out of the Hegelian and Marxist dialectical process, the final resolution of the continuous conflict of opposites.

A Shining Purpose

No wonder, then, that in his State of the Union address, President George Bush told the nation:

> We have within our reach the promise of a renewed America. We can find meaning and reward by serving some *purpose* higher than ourselves—a *shining purpose*, the *illumination of a thousand points of light.*

The Lord Maitreya, a false "Christ" promoted as the coming New Age messiah by Benjamin Creme and others, has been called "*the one initiator whose light shines forth.*"

And what of George Bush's statement that Americans "can find meaning and reward by *serving some purpose* higher than ourselves?" This must certainly have pleased *Triangles*, a branch of the occultic World Goodwill organization. In its leaflet, *Units of Service*, we are informed that:

> One of the great needs in the world today is the relating of group to group in a worldwide network of light . . . Units of service (groups) are a vital, living part of such a network . . . Through their selfless dedication to the service of humanity they are truly forerunners of a New Age.

In the same promotion leaflet was printed *The Great Invocation*. Its wording includes this pertinent passage:

> From the center where the Will
> of God is known
> Let *purpose* guide the little
> wills of men—
> The *purpose* which the Masters
> know and serve.

Is this the same *purpose* that George Bush is talking about? Evidently so, for the "God" of World Goodwill and Lucis Trust is one who reflects the many "points of light" of occult networkers everywhere. And these points of light, be they groups or individuals, have one and only one *purpose*: the *illumination of mankind*, which is the *Great Work* of all occult societies.

The Pope and the Rays of the Sun God

Pope John Paul II, too, seems to share this same *shining purpose*. In Assissi, Italy, in 1986, the Pope held hands in a circle with Buddhist monks, snake handlers from Togo, Hindu gurus, apostate protestant ministers, Moslem ayatollahs, and African witchdoctors. In his remarks the Pope assured them all that they each worshipped the same "God." That God, said the Pope, is like the mighty and awesome sun. Thus, in all religions can be found "the seeds of the Word, the rays of one truth."[32]

The Serpent and the Sun

Freemasonry's leaders likewise rejoiced over Bush's clever occultic wording. In the *Royal Arch Mason* magazine, in an article and speech entitled, "Let Your Light Shine Forth," Masonic brother R. S. Sagar states:

> Freemasonry is the world's oldest, largest and greatest fraternal society. To have become that way, it has obviously had a burning core of light to attract its members . . . Freemasonry should be like a *lighthouse* . . . You as individual Masons are the lamps or source of light . . . It is for us to recreate the bridge and unfurl the flag of Freemasonry.[33]

The 28th degree of Freemasonry is called the "Knight of the Sun." In earning that degree the initiate learns of the "points of light" concept that George Bush now has publicly and enthusiastically propagandized to the world. In the Masonic textbook, *A Bridge To Light*, Rex Hutchens, 32nd degree Mason, comments that, "The greater light comes from the sun and the transparencies (man) provide lesser light . . . Symbolically, the sun or great light is the Truth and the lesser lights are man's symbolic representation of Truth."[34]

Now for a shocker, listen to what Hutchens reveals as the one great Masonic symbol which represents this "great light" of the secret societies, this sun of the Freemasons. It is, says Hutchens, "the Gnostic worm ouroboros, which is a simplified *dragon* or *serpent* biting its tail."[35]

"God," then, the Masonic God according to this textbook published in 1988 by the Supreme Council, 33rd degree of the Ancient and Accepted Scottish Rite of Freemasonry, the largest Masonic organization on earth, is none other than the *serpent*! In the lecture for the 28th degree, the initiate is told this secret:

> There is a Life-Principle of this world, a universal agent, wherein are two natures and a double current of love and wrath . . . It is a ray detached from the glory of the Sun . . . It is the Holy Spirit, the universal Agent, the serpent . . .[36]

Regardless of what Freemasonry teaches, any Christian—or any non-Christian for that matter—can readily identify the serpent. And I assure you, he's *not* God!

According to Hutchens, "the serpent biting its tail is symbolic of all cyclic processes, and in particular of time."

In other words, it is now time for the great serpent, or dragon to return. That it is the devil, or Lucifer, to whom Hutchens refers, is made clear in the very next page of *A Bridge to Light* where he tells readers that, "The visible is the manifestation of the invisible" and "what is above is like what is below."[37]

"Thus," Hutchen reveals, "the black and the white, dark and light must merge to become one." He uses the Latin term *Lux E Tenebris*, which means "Light in Darkness," and says that the pentagram, or *star*, is the symbol of this new type of light.[38]

The Stars: A Brilliant Diversity

How appropriate, therefore, that George Bush, too, used this term, "stars" in his 1988 speech. His exact words were:

> A brilliant *diversity* spread like *stars*, like a *thousand points of light* in a peaceful sky.

During the Christmas season the following year, the President and Barbara Bush pulled the switch and exactly 1,000 pentagram-shaped stars twinkled and lit up. The number was no accident, nor was the term "stars" in George's speech.

The Bible describes the Evil One "as a 'star' fallen from heaven." Indeed, the Bible often refers to angels, dark and otherwise, as "stars." It is also noteworthy that the great goddess of Babylon was called Astarte and Ishtar, the "star goddess." In the French Revolution the Masons made her popularly known as the "Goddess of Reason," and Joseph Campbell, who discusses the aims of Freemasonry in *The Power of Myth*, says that this Masonic star goddess is the divine Goddess of restructuring and transformation. In sum, she is the goddess of enlightenment, or illumination.[39]

In the mystery religions, it was paramount that the peoples serve, honor, and adore this star goddess. Through *service*, the disciples of the deity were told that they were *empowering themselves* and earning through good works their own illumination. In turn, they could potentially earn the right to become deities themselves—little, twinkling points of light!

Pursuing the Better Angels

Occult philosophers have long taught that the rich have the luxury of time. They are therefore better able to pursue the study and practice of magic, symbols, alchemy, and other occultic subjects. The idle rich have always become more deeply involved in satanic pursuits and sinful passions than the busy, everyday laborer and worker, who has bills to pay and mouths to feed.

The corrupt monks, gnostics, pagans, and medieval occult philosophers often used the term, "pursuing the *better angels*" to describe these dark spiritual endeavors. Many occultists mistakenly believe that there are two types of magic—black and white, so to pursue the *better angels*, they believe, would be to discover the secrets of white magic and to communicate with the "good" spirits.

What a revealing thing for George Bush, in his New Orleans acceptance speech, to make positive mention of "pursuing the better angels:"

> The fact is prosperity has a purpose. It is to allow us to pursue the "*better angels*," to give us time to think and grow.

Malachi Martin, in his interesting book about Pope John Paul II, *The Keys of This Blood*, proposes that Mikhail Gorbachev, because he supports globalism and other New World Order objectives, is also pointing the way toward the "better angels," and is, in a sense, himself one of those "angels." Martin writes:

> Gorbachev may be the *chief attendant angel* in this globalist effort. But he points to *other angels* we all must obey. He points to the objective (historical) processes that . . . form global channels for history's progress.
>
> As a simple example, the environment of our world is threatened . . . Similarly our planet cannot support too great a population. If that means we must have fewer people, then the iron logic of history demands that we practice conception, abortion, and even euthanasia.[40]

A Socialist Dictatorship is the Goal

A Catholic theologian and priest, Malachi Martin, claims to speak for Pope John Paul II. Stunningly, he adds: "John Paul agrees with Mikhail Gorbachev's view that such global processes as these are every day gaining a new momentum." These global processes, Martin reveals, are "*dialectical materialism*, . . . elaborated and adapted by Karl Marx."[41]

So, what we have here is a statement by Martin that the same, horrible Marxist system that claimed "historical inevitability" and massacred and butchered over a hundred million people in the 20th century, is the "angelic" system that both Gorbachev and the Pope now promote. It is their "new way of thinking!"

The Secret Brotherhood has always used a system of conflict of opposites, dialectical materialism—communism—to promote their goals. Crisis after crisis, conflict after conflict has been caused by this system. This is what has been called "systems theory"—the notion that *thesis*, attacked by *antithesis*, produces *synthesis*. In today's world, that simply means that the century long conflict of two opposites—capitalism and communism—now shall produce *socialism.*

The Secret Brotherhood intends to preside over a world socialist, so-called "democracy." Theirs is to be a socialist dictatorship run by them "for the good of humanity." The elite and their occult doctrines are the "better angels." Their ancient and *enduring dream* has been to keep America and the world moving forward, always forward, in a grand, historical, dialectical process of conflict and resolution, conflict and resolution.

Evolutionary synthesis through continuous, perpetual motion is at the essence of the occult philosophy and goals.

The *mission* of the Brotherhood has been to achieve the universal spread of the ageless wisdom philosophy—the attainment of "*a thousand points of light.*" The "thousand points of light," metaphorically and symbolically, is the spectacular universe of stars (peoples) to be ruled by the men of the Secret Brotherhood.

That is the burning, fiery mission of the conspirators—not to promote a thousand volunteer service groups, but to have all of humanity serve *them*, the better angels, and their occult dream.

As H. G. Wells, an open advocate of the world conspiracy once wrote, "This idea of a planned world-state is one to which all our thought and knowledge is tending . . . It is appearing partially and experimentally at a *thousand points* . . . its coming is likely to happen quickly."[42]

Forward, Always Forward for an Enduring Dream

The capstone of George Bush's speech in 1988 was a resounding affirmation of the Illuminati's occult philosophy and goals. In an incredible, carefully coded illuminist message, the Vice President concluded with these glaringly frank words:

> I will keep America *moving forward, always forward* for a better America, for an *endless, enduring dream*, and a *thousand points of light* . . . This is my *mission* and I will complete it![43]

As Alice Bailey writes in *A Treatise on the Seven Rays*, the superior, illumined man has a mission and a destiny set out before him from birth. That has been true for George Herbert Walker Bush. "The emphasis," said Bailey, should be "laid upon the determining of a man's life purpose."[44]

George Bush says he has a "mission" and he is determined to complete it. Unfortunately, I believe him. But whether or not he will complete it is not up to him, nor in the final analysis can the Secret Brotherhood influence whether that occult mission will be completed. God alone—the *true* God of the Bible—will make that judgement and decision, and in His good timing.

Ronald Reagan's Sunlit New Age

If Satan himself had written the speeches of George Bush and Ronald Reagan at the Republican National Convention in 1988 in New Orleans, he couldn't have done a better job. President Reagan, a 33rd degree honorary Mason who is often called the "great communicator," charmed the vast audience with his illuminist-laden talk. First, he assured the approving crowd that:

> With George Bush, as we approach the *New Millennium* . . . we'll have a nation confidently willing to take its leadership into the uncharted reaches of a *New Age*.[45]

Since George Bush has publicly stated his intention to be in Egypt at the Great Pyramid on December 31, 1999 at the stroke of midnight to welcome in the *New Millennium*,[46] it could just be that Ronald Reagan's words packed important, hidden meaning.

Masons and other Sun God worshipping secret societies measure calendar years beginning in the year 4000 B.C. The year 1999 is therefore 5999 AL (AL stands for "*Anno Lucis*," in the year of light.") In 6000 AL (2000 AD), the dawning of the *New Millennium*, the long awaited New Age, is to burst into radiance, transforming the whole world. The dominance of Lucifer, known by the occultists as the "Light Bearer," the bright morning star, shall then come into full being.

What a new day that will be for all Sun worshippers, the perfected and illumined men who conceive of themselves as "points of light!" In fact, expressing this type of sentiment was exactly how Ronald Reagan enthusiastically and dramatically concluded his speech: "That's a new day," said the outgoing President, *our sunlit new day*.[47]

Manly P. Hall, 33rd degree Mason and occult philosopher, once told us that illuminist-coded language is purposely intended to conceal the truth from the profane and the vulgar (the average citizen). But how concealed can Reagan's sunlit words be? To those of us who understand the hideous and grotesque hidden language of occult double-speak, the light seems to have shined straight through the darkness. *We understand. We get the message, but we utterly reject it.*

The True Light of the World

The intent of the Secret Brotherhood is to create a system of magical belief in which men and women willingly support the New World Order. They come disguised as ministers of light. The Bible warned us in advance of these men and their dark schemes: the apostle Paul called them "ministers of unrighteousness" and branded the one whom they secretly serve as a false "angel of light." (see II Timothy 3:12-13; 4:1-8.)

But the Bible also reveals to us the True Light, the One whom the conspiracy refuses to acknowledge:

> Then spake Jesus again unto them, saying, *I am the light of the world*; he that followeth me shall not walk in darkness, but shall have the light of life.

Secret Words of Magic to be Unmasked

As we have seen, the conspirators believe themselves to be powerful magicians who are able to deceive through illusion and sleight-of-hand. They also believe in verbal alchemy—that their coded language possesses magical, supernatural powers. As Alice Bailey once cryptically stated, "Through the Words of Power, the worlds came into being, and the Lord of the Ray of Ceremonial Magic brings about the organization of the divine organism."

Well, I have news for these men. The vast majority will, indeed, fall victim. But those who trust in God are not going to be deceived by illusory magic and shadowy "word power." Daniel 12:10 says of the last days, "The wise *shall* understand." That is the reason why I wrote this book—so that the wise would understand.

And God Himself is the revealer who is unmasking the hidden, occultic secrets of the Illuminati. In Luke 8:17, we read, "For nothing is secret that shall not be made manifest, neither any thing hid, that shall not become known and come abroad." Moreover, in Daniel 2:20,22, we have this calm assurance:

> Blessed be the name of God . . . He revealeth the deep and secret things: He knoweth what is in the darkness.

FIVE

The Bilderbergers and Other Conspirators

In June, 1991 in the secluded Black Forest resort town of Baden Baden, Germany, a very special group of influential men met to map out their grand strategy for the coming year and possibly beyond. Called the *Bilderbergers*, each of these well-known world leaders had come by special and exclusive invitation. The general public was not invited and, in fact, was locked out. Fortunately, an account of what transpired at the meeting was leaked, and we are now in possession of some of the details of the conspiratorial plans of the Bilderbergers.[1]

Banking czar David Rockefeller, former head of New York's Chase Manhattan Bank and founder of the Trilateral Commission, gave the opening address to his fellow Bilderbergers at Baden Baden. He started off by telling the assembled elitists, "We are grateful to *The Washington Post, The New York Times, Time* magazine, and other publications whose directors have attended our meetings, and respected their promises of discretion for almost 40 years."[2]

Rockefeller explained: "It would have been impossible for us to develop our plan for the world if we had been subject to the bright lights of publicity during these years."[3]

Bush and Clinton: Bilderberger Twins?

In my audiotape *The Secrets of the Bilderbergers*, I explain how the Bilderbergers' manipulate *both* the Democrat and the Republican national political parties and their candidates.

To prove this point, all that's necessary is that we identify *who* is pumping the money into the political campaigns of the top presidential contenders for each political party.

George Bush *Bill Clinton*

Investigation reveals that the same money men are supporting *both* President George Bush and Arkansas Governor Bill Clinton. This in spite of the fact that the two are *theoretically* opposing each other as Republican vs. Democrat. In fact, the election will be a sham. The Order controls *both* Bush and Clinton!

Just follow the money trail. One of Clinton's top money men is internationalist banker and investor Jackson Stephens. Stephens, who operates out of Little Rock, Arkansas, has reportedly given Bill Clinton access to at least $2 million.

But wait! Stephens has also recently donated $100,000 to George Bush's campaign! Moreover, Stephens' wife, Mary, was co-chairwoman in 1988 of the national "Bush for President" organization.

As it turns out, elitist financier Stephens is reportedly also one of the founders of the criminally corrupt and now defunct BCCI bank.

Bush and Clinton are in reality co-actors in the grand charade and side-show of U.S. presidential elections. *No matter who wins the November national election, it is the Bilderbergers who will come out on top.*

Reprinted from Texe Marrs' newsletter, Flashpoint (May, 1992).
For a free subscription to this monthly publication, simply write to:
8104 Caisson Circle, Austin, Texas 78745 or phone toll free 1-800-234-WORD.

And so it is that the top guru of the Bilderbergers gives credit to the publishers of America's greatest newspapers for their cooperation. They have cooperated in hushing up and keeping from the American citizenry the inside story of a hideous future that has been plotted behind our backs for over four decades.

Following Rockefeller's welcoming address, the Bilderbergers reviewed their agenda for the unity of Europe, including their plans for a common European currency and a central European bank organized along the same lines as the U.S.A.'s corrupt Federal Reserve Bank. The Bilderbergers also laid out a blueprint for how they wanted the U.S. presidential primary contests to proceed.

Arkansas Governor Bill Clinton Passes Test

Invited secretly to Baden Baden was key democratic party contender Governor Bill Clinton of Arkansas. Clinton was questioned and auditioned by the conspirators. He passed with flying colors. It was then decided that huge transfusions of campaign cash would be shuttled to Clinton. It was also approved that these Democratic Party regulars in all 50 states controlled by the Bilderbergers would get in step and line up behind Presidential candidate Bill Clinton.

The Bilderbergers always hedge their bets, sponsoring one or more presidential candidates from *each* U.S. major political party. George Bush is, of course, their "boy wonder"—their in-house establishment representative. But, if Bush falters or stumbles during the campaign election, the Bilderbergers well know they need an alternative.

Remember, the Bilderbergers are philosophically neither Republican *nor* Democrat. Their only "party" is filthy lucre—spelled *M-O-N-E-Y*! Money, in turn, brings them *power*, and these folks have a never satisfied appetite for raw power.

Dan Quayle—A Bilderberger Favorite

Vice President Dan Quayle is another fair-haired boy of the wealthy Bilderberger supermen. Quayle was there in person last year at the gathering. Reportedly, David Rockefeller and fellow big-wigs were duly impressed at what they saw. "He's our man—for '96 or sooner!" one Bilderberger exclaimed.[4]

Exposing the Bilderbergers

Like their counterparts, the Skull & Bones Society, the Bilderbergers try to keep what goes on at their meetings hidden from public scrutiny. If the American people were to discover the truth about how they are being sold down the river by these arrogant and treacherous plotters, all hell would surely break loose.

These two clandestine organizations, the *Skull & Bones Society*, and *The Bilderbergers* have much to hide or else their procedures would not be kept behind closed doors. What these cynical and powerful men are doing to damage America, take away our freedoms, and undermine Christianity, is *criminal*. It's high time we expose them for the despicable traitors and sham artists that they are.

In his historically important book *The Occult Conspiracy*, Michael Howard, a man by the way who is actually not at all opposed to the secret societies, discusses the Bilderbergers. "The Bilderberger group," says Howard, "was originally founded as an anti-Communist organization with a predominantly right wing membership."[5]

But then he says something very interesting that I haven't been able to find in any other resource. Michael Howard writes: "However, in 1976, *15 representatives from the Soviet Union attended* one of the Bilderberger conferences that was held in the Arizona desert."[6]

If true, the implications are tremendous. If representatives from the Soviet Union, as far back as 1976—nine years before Gorbachev took power in 1985—and began to make the changes that resulted in the breakup of communism in the Soviet Union—many questions are answered about the sudden collapse in the Soviet Union of communism and imperialism.

Russell Baker, a political commentator whose column can be found in newspapers across the country, was asked one time what he thought of Mikhail Gorbachev. How, Baker was asked, was Gorbachev able to do what he did, and why did the Russian leader seem to be so much in favor of a New World Order and a world government? Baker's answer was stunning: "All I can figure out," he said, "is that Gorbachev must have been a CIA mole."

In other words, the suggestion is that Gorbachev was a secret agent of the CIA. Could Mikhail Gorbachev have been there in the desert in 1976 at that Bilderberger meeting? Was he one of those 15 Soviet representatives, and did he make a commitment that someday, he would do what he could to bring about the New World Order. I believe it is extremely possible that this is the case.

Now we turn to another book by researcher Nicola M. Nicolov: *The World Conspiracy: What The Historians Don't Tell You*. Mr. Nicolov has this to say about the secretive Bilderbergers group:

> The Bilderbergers organization is comprised exclusively of the international elite. It owes its name to Hotel Bilderberg in Oosterbech, Holland, where its first meeting was held in May of 1954. The meeting was chaired by the organization's founder, Prince Bernard, the husband of Queen Juliana of the Netherlands and member of one of the richest European families.[7]

Nicolov goes on to say that in the last 34 years the media has mentioned little about the meetings and activities of the Bilderbergers. Only a few small religious publications in the United States and *Spotlight*, the populist newspaper published by Liberty Lobby, closely follow the activities of this group. Nicolov appropriately asks, "Why do the big newspapers like the *New York Times*, *The Washington Post*, and *The Minneapolis Tribune* neglect to inform their readers about the Bilderbergers' conferences?"[8]

His answer: "Because all these big newspapers directly or indirectly belong to this organization." So, he says, "The world receives no pictures, no agendas, no information about this group—even their name is hardly ever mentioned."[9]

Regardless of the news blackout, prominent people who are members of the Bilderbergers, have been photographed going into the meetings by reporters and photographers who camped out across the street or in hotel rooms with telephoto lens. They were able to note the people going in and out of the Bilderberger meetings. In addition, other information has been published about the membership. Here are some of the people who are Bilderbergers: former U.S. President Gerald Ford; President Nixon's former Secretary of State Henry Kissinger; President Carter's former Secretary of State Cyrus Vance; Robert MacNamara, former head of the World Bank and former Secretary of Defense in the Kennedy administration; David Rockefeller, founder of the Trilateral Commission and former chairman of the Chase Manhattan Bank; and Helmut Schmidt, the former Chancellor of Germany.

Other members of the Bilderberger organization have included the late Baron Edmund de Rothschild. His successor, the Lord J. Rothchild, is a member today; Margaret Thatcher was a member, but she evidently fell into disfavor among the Bilderbergers.

There's also Laurance Rockefeller. It was Laurance Rockefeller who gave the money to Matthew Fox that made possible the publication of the heretical, ungodly book entitled *The Coming of the Cosmic Christ*. Fox is a Catholic priest who's pro-homosexual, pro-witchcraft, and pro-New Age; in fact, he's the head of Holy Names College, a Catholic college in San Francisco that has on its faculty Miriam Starhawk, one of the world's best-known witches.

In his book, *The Coming of the Cosmic Christ*, Mr. Fox gives thanks in the acknowledgements to Laurance Rockefeller for giving him the financial means to publish the book.

Laurance Rockefeller owned the very inn, Woodstock Inn in Vermont, where the Bilderbergers had one of their meetings. Also, a famous resort in Williamsburg, Virginia, owned by the Rockefeller family was yet another site of a Bilderberger conference.

The Bilderbergers seem to specialize in meeting at exotic European locations. Once the group met in the French Alps. In Sweden they were hosted by the billionaire Wallenberg family.

Now we go to another source, the interesting book written by William Sutton, entitled *The Illuminati 666*, in which Sutton writes of the Bilderbergers: "The chairman of this secret society of the elite is one Prince Bernard of the Netherlands, the royal consort of Queen Juliana, reported to be the richest woman in the world. Queen Juliana and Lord Rothschild are the principles stockholders of Shell Oil Company, while the Rockefellers, also Bilderbergers, control Standard Oil Company."[10]

The latest information is that Prince Bernhard, though still a Bilderberger, is no longer the chairman. That honor goes to Britain's Lord Carrington, a very wealthy banker who's on the board of the huge money center, Hambros Bank. Lord Carrington was joined in 1991's Baden Baden, Germany conclave by Giovanni Agnelli, the owner of the Fiat Automobile Company in Italy and many other bankers and industrialists. At that meeting, the members focused on finance and economics. They reviewed events in the Middle East. In one session, they discussed the status of Eastern Europe and its economic prospects, and addressed the developments in the Soviet Union and their impact on "The Alliance."

In Baden Baden, the Bilderbergers referred to their group as "The Alliance." Some used the code-term, "The Relationship."

Economic and Financial Planning

The most important session at the 1991 conclave looked at the topic of the "Economic and Financial Threats to The Relationship." The two speakers were, first, American Michael Boskin, who is chairman of President Bush's Council of Economic Advisor's, and Carl Otto Pohl, president of the central bank of Germany, the Bundesbank.

How intriguing: The top financial man from the White House, Michael Boskin, and the top financial man from Germany, Carl Otto Pohl, together informing their fellow Bilderbergers of the status of the world's economies and finances.

U.S. Treasury Secretary Nicholas Brady was also there in Baden Baden. He's the man that President Bush has put in charge of a plan to reform our banking system. What they have done is proposed to our Congress that the banking system in America be changed. Huge national banks are to become larger and gobble up the smaller local banks across this country. We're going to have a consolidation and a centralizing of the American banking system if Nicholas Brady of the Bilderbergers gets his way. He's now our Secretary of the Treasury so, obviously, George Bush knew of his attendance at the Bilderbergers conference.

Other Big Shots at the Conclave

Also in Baden Baden were Theodore L. Elliott, Jr., the honorary secretary of the North American Bilderberg group. Elliott worked in the U.S. State Department as a Soviet expert, was U.S. Ambassador to Afghanistan during the conflict there, and has financial ties with powerful Wall Street financier John Train. Others attending: Wilfred Martin, Belgian's Prime Minister; Theo Sommer, Editor in Chief of the German publication *Die Ziet*; Emilio Collado, Executive Vice President of Exxon Corporation; and Conrad Black. Conrad Black is chairman of a corporation known as the Hollinger Corporation. On its board are such people as Lord Carrington and Henry Kissinger, both of whom are fellow Bilderbergers. Hollinger Corporation just happens to own the *London Daily Telegraph* newspaper and *The Jerusalem Post.*

John Gavin, the supreme allied commander for Europe (SHAPE) was present, as was Manfred Woerner, Secretary General of NATO. Jacques Fontaire, the Luxembourg Prime Minister; Queen Beatrix of the Netherlands; Queen Sophia of Spain; and Ludd Lubbers, the Dutch Prime Minister.

A very interesting man, Christopher Cogg, who is the chairman of the Queen of England's portfolio—in other words, he controls the purse of the Queen of England—was there. You may not know it, but the Queen of England has a net worth of some $18 billion. That's Billion with a capital "B."

Katharine Graham, head of the liberal *Washington Post* newspaper was in attendance. Katharine Graham is said to be an arrogant woman. In fact, she's been called "Katharine the Great." There was even a book about her entitled, *Katharine the Great.* It was the *Washington Post* that came out with the Watergate story that brought down Nixon.

In Germany at the Bilderbergers conference, Katharine Graham evidently became enamored with Dan Quayle, Vice President of the United States, who was also at the Bilderberg meeting. Dan Quayle is the "fair-haired boy" of the Bilderbergers. He has been chosen by the Bilderbergers for bigger and better things. He's already vice president, so where else can he go but up? In 1996 we may see Quayle seeking the Republican nomination. He will have the support of the Bilderbergers, I am convinced, unless he falters between now and then.

Is it any coincidence that within months of the June, 1991 meeting in Baden Baden, Germany, the *Washington Post* newspaper, whose chairwoman is Katharine Graham, a Bilderberger member, decided to write a surprising series of articles, syndicated across America praising Dan Quayle.[11] Maybe you saw some of those articles in your local newspaper. Dan Quayle has been sort of a fall guy for the media all this time, but suddenly here is the *Washington Post* saying wonderful things about the man. The newspaper proposed that Quayle was selected as vice president because of his great abilities. The articles suggested that Dan Quayle had been recognized as a political genius by his former colleagues in the U.S. Senate. The *Post* attempted to make Dan Quayle into a hero.

Some of the other people at the Bilderberger meeting were John Reed, the chairman of Citicorp, the largest banking corporation in the United States; U.S. Senator John Chaffee, Republican of Rhode Island; Arkansas Governor Bill Clinton and Virginia Governor Douglas Wilder.

What is the Bilderberger Agenda?

What is the agenda of the Bilderbergers? There are *three basic goals* of the Bilderbergers: First, a *New International Economic Order*. That is going to be followed by the *second* goal, the *New Political Order*. And then we complete the third side of the pyramid, the third side of the satanic triangle—*New World Religious Order*.

So we first have the goal of controlling the world economy, something that these men pretty well have in hand. Then comes control of the political order, and they are on their way to accomplishing that. The United Nations is being strengthened. George Bush is a key person behind that move. And then we have the new religious order, which is also being rapidly put together.

To achieve these three goals, I am convinced that the Bilderbergers seek first of all to destroy our monetary system. That is objective one. Objective two is to destroy our faith, our love, and our admiration and respect for nationalism and patriotism. They want no man to have any loyalty to his country, so they're promoting globalism. The third objective of the Bilderbergers is to destroy the Christian church—of that I am absolutely convinced. To attack the church, they now actively use the media and the education establishment. They are working to destroy legitimate Christian ministries and are meanwhile bankrolling some of the worst of televangelists.

Now, a fourth objective of the Bilderbergers is to destroy the traditional family. They hope to do this by promoting homosexuality and lesbianism. No wonder we have the National Endowment for the Arts here in the United States, getting 170 million dollars funding by President Bush, the White House, and our Congress. Many pro-abortion lobbyists are getting money from the Bilderbergers. The Planned Parenthood people no doubt are getting money. The Gay and Lesbian Task Force was recently invited to the White House—they met with Rob Mosbacher, President George Bush's top campaign manager. Together they mapped out a strategy as to how the gays and lesbians could help George Bush win office again.[12]

George Bush is their man—he's the only president that has ever invited the gays, the lesbians, the homosexuals to the White House. He did so during the signing of a so-called "Hate Crimes Act."[13] He's the only man that has insisted on full funding and no censorship whatsoever for the National Endowment for the Arts, with its pornographic, blasphemous "art." Is it any wonder that George Bush is a member of the Bilderberger group? Or that he's a member of the Skull and Bones, that he was a director of the Council on Foreign Relations, and a member of the Trilateral Commission? All these groups are linked together.

Is it any wonder that George Bush was the ambassador to the United Nations, that he was director of the Central Intelligence Agency?

The Role of the Media

The use of the media to accomplish their objectives is very primary, very important for the Bilderbergers. In *Meditation Magazine* there was a very interesting interview with

Jose Arguelles.[14] He's the man who masterminded the Harmonic Convergence, the big, New Age planetary meeting of August 16 and 17, 1987. Jose Arguelles said some very interesting things. He said that what the New Age planners are working on is the formation of a *"mediarchy."*

What is a mediarchy? Well, Arguelles tells us that if the New Age community can take over our media—that's our television networks and our cable systems—if they can take over our publications, our magazines, our newspapers, children's books and adult books. If they can take over all of these media outlets, they can control the forces of all of planet earth.

The mediarchy, Jose Arguelles reveals, will help process the information necessary to propel man into the New Age. Through the media, he says, mankind can demilitarize the planet. We can clean up the planet. Through the media, Arguelles brags, New Agers can network together. He noted that already, the New Age is at the completion stage of bringing it all together—thousands of groups and organizations and secret societies and churches. They're at that point, and it is through the use of the media that they're going to be able to complete the job.

Is this why the *Washington Post*, the *New York Times*, and the three TV network news organizations have covered up the clandestine meetings of the Bilderbergers?

A Coming Democratic World Order?

The goal of the Bilderbergers is to create a pretense, *democratic* World Government, controlled by them. Only a few years ago, the development of a New World Order seemed an impossibility. The superpower blocs—the Soviet Union and the United States—and the existence of the Third World bloc of nations appeared set in concrete.

True, it was feared that Soviet Russia might just seek to take over the planet with brute military force and a preemptive nuclear attack on the American continent. But that, so the experts reasoned, would have triggered World War III—a bloody Armageddon with no outright victor. No, it was deemed suicidal and therefore, unthinkable. So for decades, a One World Order has been considered neither practical nor imminent.

What a revolution we have experienced! The seeming dissolution and freeing up of Communist Eastern Europe, as well as Gorbachev's *Perestroika* and *Glasnost* policies inside the Soviet Union have resulted in a euphoric mania of One Worldism. Finally, exclaim gleeful globalists, finally we can have a unified and harmonious One World Order. The *democratic* revolution in communist East Germany, Czechoslovakia, Russia, Romania, and elsewhere, they contend, enables such a political and economic entity to be forged.

In effect, the appealingly deceptive proclamation has gone out: a Democratic World Order is now not only practical, it is inevitable! Utopia is at hand! That is the clarion call of the Bilderbergers—the establishment of a World Democratic Government.

The theoretical base for the globalist view was recently set forth by Morton Kaplan in the influential journal, *The World and I*. Kaplan, professor of political science at the University of Chicago, presented an important paper, "Steps Toward a Democratic World Order," to colleagues at the Professor's World Peace Academy Conference of Liberal Democratic Societies. His proposal in *The World and I* was a summary of that paper.[15]

Undoubtedly, the folks who have sold out to such New Age-oriented organizations as the United Nations, the Council on Foreign Relations, and the Trilateral Commission, will trumpet the supposed "wisdom" of Kaplan's proposals for a new democratic world order. In truth, these elitists do not want democracy so much as they want to build and organize a World Order controlled by *them*.

Morton Kaplan's intriguing proposal for what the Bilderbergers and globalists are now calling a *Global Democratic Community* starts with his observation that "One of the most urgent tasks facing humanity is the construction of a *democratic world order*."[16]

The job of creating a *democratic world order* is important, says Kaplan, for a variety of reasons. "Matters of urgency such as the possible greenhouse effect (on earth's environment)," he emphasizes, "require international management."[17]

Kaplan writes that there can be no more important prelude to the building of a *democratic world order* than the uniting of all of Europe "and the integration of the Soviet Union into the new world order . . ."[18]

What authority would Kaplan and his globalist pals confer on this New World Order? "The new Europe," he writes, "in cooperation with the new Soviet Union and the United States, would have to take responsibility for preventing new . . . wars and deterring or controlling tyrannical states . . . from the use of nuclear or chemical weapons."

Only a New World Order, Kaplan assures us, can permit the degree of cooperation that is needed to serve the joint interests of the major states.

Therefore, he advocates a *Global Democratic Community* to support this end, while retaining the United Nations for those tasks for which it *temporarily* remains the most suitable body.

According to Kaplan, this is a *global age* marked by new conditions that can best be met by the establishment of a World Order. He further proposes that this Global Democratic Community be rigidly organized. It would have "a Secretariat . . . a Court of Human and Political Rights . . . and . . . a World Future Committee."[19]

As you can see, the globalists hope to seize this historic opportunity to implement their revived Plan for an unholy One World Order. They would prefer to call it a *"Democratic World Order,"* yet, there is still no guarantee of true democracy in the republics once controlled by the Kremlin—only promises and more promises by the ruling elite. The eventual governments may not at all be "democratic" in the constitutional sense that Americans think of democracy. Moreover, in Eastern Europe countries once subject to the iron rule of communist overlords, the present movement toward democracy could well end up in disorder, turmoil, and anarchy if economic conditions continue to sour, as they may well do.

Those people who are now exclaiming, "Isn't peace breaking out all over?" could be very, very surprised.

What seems to be forgotten in all the euphoria over the momentous events in Eastern Europe and Russia is the Bible's strong prophetic warnings. Daniel prophesied of the last days world ruler, "By *peace* he shall destroy many" (Daniel 8:25). Moreover, the apostle Paul prophesied that "when they shall say, *Peace and safety*; then sudden destruction cometh upon them and they shall not escape" (I Thessalonians 5:3).

Today, as the military threat of Soviet Russia seems to be receding, many are crying out "Peace, peace." Others preach that we are on the threshold of a One World Democratic Order. But, there will be *no peace* until Jesus returns. And even in a democratic society such as the United States, the vast majority of people *choose* evil over good. Exercising their democratic rights, they are choosing the devil and his destructive ways over Christ and His righteousness.

AIDS, abortion, pornography, occultism, promiscuity, adultery, alcoholism, drugs—all these present-day epidemics are based on *pro-choice* alternatives in a godless democratic society.

Democracy may indeed be the best that man has to offer. But in the end the democratic governments of this globe will be converted into a hellish dictatorship ruled with an iron hand by an Antichrist, the Son of Perdition (II Thessalonians 2).

Peace and democracy will ultimately fail, because it is built on the vain greed and ambition of men such as the Bilderbergers.

SIX

International Network of Light

There are thousands of groups acting either knowingly and in concert with or unwittingly supporting the Secret Brotherhood. Consider a recent book published by Doubleday and Company entitled *Networking: The First Report and Directory*, by Jessica Lipnack and Jeffrey Stamps. This resource book, 398 pages in length, is billed as "a comprehensive report on networking and a directory of over 1,500 networks."

Notice that we're not just talking here about 1,500 groups, but instead *1,500 networks*! Indeed, there are so many organizations, groups, and associations pursuing the same aims as the Secret Brotherhood that an organization called the *Networking Institute* has even been set up to keep track of them all.

In a recent bulletin from World Goodwill, a major occultic organization promoting the Brotherhood's blueprint for the world, we read about a directory, a two-volume, 2,140 page book, the *Encyclopedia of World Problems and Human Potential*, which covers topics deemed important by the Brotherhood for the world's peoples to study and comprehend. This encyclopedia, published by a group called the

Union of International Associations (UIA), is now in its third edition.

According to World Goodwill, "The first volume of this encyclopedia looks at 13,167 world problems that are of concern to international groups." The array of problems covered, says World Goodwill in its review, is impressive—"ranging from such topics as shortage of urban land, political torture, and illiteracy to entries on suppression of creativity and innovation, superstition and fanaticism."

Volume 2, we are told, "is concerned with ideas about humanity's potential to build an independent world." The aim of the encyclopedia is "to present as broad and complete a view as possible of human perceptions of development." The publisher itself notes that one section of the encyclopedia "contains 64 entries on concepts implicit in the Chinese classic, the *I Ching*." Another section contains "a valuable index to thousands of references in the encyclopedia to religious and esoteric concepts related to numbers" (in other words, occult numerology).

25,000 Networking Organizations of Light

The Union of International Associations is billed as "an organization that links international, voluntary, and nongovernmental organizations." Formed in 1907, it publishes a growing list of guides and directories that it says are "indispensable reference tools for anyone who wants to track down addresses and details of international organizations" working for one world unity.

The Union of International Associations is also publisher of a massive, three-volume directory called *The Yearbook of International Organizations*. This annual directory, says the publisher, "gives authoritative information on over 25,000 international organizations based in 200 countries."

Certainly, an investigation of the strangely mysterious Union of International Associations needs to be launched. But whatever we can find about this group and where its source of money comes from, our minds have to be boggled that any group could actually publish a two-volume, 2,140 page book that is a subject reference guide for action and study by internationalist-oriented groups supporting the aims of the Brotherhood. What is even more phenomenal is *The Yearbook of International Organizations* and its stupendous listing of 25,000 different international groups based in 200 countries.

For anyone who refuses to believe that there is a conspiracy and that like-minded groups are working closely together to accomplish the same ends, all I can advise is that you please get your head out of the sand. *Someone* is behind these 25,000 groups. They didn't just spring up spontaneously overnight. There is a design and a purpose—and scads of money—that has made these groups possible and continues to assist their performance.

Dark Angels of Light

Fortunately, I am finding that more and more people are understanding that a conspiracy of unimaginable proportions does truly exist in the world today—and has existed for much longer than we might realize. Recently I was reading an interesting book written by a good friend of mine, David Allen Lewis. The book, *Dark Angels of Light*, briefly discusses the existence of what Lewis calls an "International Network of Light." He writes: "Since 1954 we have been preaching and teaching that there was a loosely-knit world conspiracy, a so called Network of Illuminists."

Lewis traces this network all the way back to Adam Weishaupt, who began the Order of the Illuminati (Lightbearers) in 1776. He further explains:

> Whether the Illuminati has one special organization that is its organic descendant . . . we can be very sure that its philosophical torchbearers are represented by literally

> hundreds of organizations and individuals in many diverse realms.[1]

Lewis goes on to state: "I have never doubted that such a network existed."[2]

Like my friend David Allen Lewis, millions of Americans have become aware that something is amiss. They know that the history books don't tell the whole story, and historians today willingly distort the facts. They also now realize that our biased media also regularly reinterpret the news and that most of our books and magazines must be "politically correct" and go through some kind of process of censorship to be published in the first place. It takes money, organization, networking, and design to accomplish such a massive black-out of the facts and present a false rendering of human history.

However, *knowing* that there is a conspiracy and tracking down and tracing the *one group of men at the top who are directing it* are two different things. The Secret Brotherhood has over the years erected thousands of roadblocks and impediments to the dedicated researcher and American patriot who would attempt to unmask its highest council and its dirty works. Perhaps I can give you just one personal example of the incredibly complex process that is involved when one concerned citizen sets out to purposely investigate and expose the illuminized leadership of the Secret Brotherhood.

The Priory of Sion: In Search of Christ's Bloodline

Not too long ago, another friend of mine, J. R. Church, published a very interesting book, *Guardians of the Grail*. In that volume, J. R. unmasked the existence of a group called "The Priory of Sion," a shadowy secret society in Europe tied in with the Hapsburg dynasty of Austria-Hungary. The Priory of Sion is an alleged secret society that's been hard at work for over 800 years influencing world affairs and events. According to J. R.—and my own investigation confirms what he discovered—the occultist cadre of this fervent but somewhat strange and totally unscriptural secret society believe that Jesus actually married Mary Magdalene.

Supposedly, Jesus and Mary Magdalene had children and the descendants of Christ are said to now be alive. They live in Europe and comprise a "holy bloodline." Someday, the Priory of Sion teaches, the Priory's own leader, a direct descendant of Jesus, will step forward onto the world scene and will take over the reigns of world government.

If the members of the Priory of Sion want to believe such a fantastic tale, that's one thing. But if such a group has over the centuries accumulated vast powers to *carry out and effect this scheme*, to put one of their own on the throne of world power, that is an entirely different matter. Therefore, I decided to investigate the claims of the Priory of Sion to see where this group fits into the overall goals of the Secret Brotherhood.

What I found was a virtual labyrinth and maze of fact and speculation. I first accumulated about 100 books and articles, many published overseas. These books and articles were a great help to me, but then I had to go deeper than the books by contacting certain people in organizations that will remain nameless here, to establish facts and to further investigate the trail that opened up to me after closely examining these publications.

My investigation lasted about three years. It took me through some of the most amazing experiences. I discovered that the Priory of Sion controversy has definite connections and tie-ins with such groups as the Bohemian Club, the Bilderbergers, the Vatican Bank, the Grand Alpina Lodge of Switzerland, the Grand Orient Lodge of Freemasonry in Paris, France, the P2 Black Masonic Lodge in Italy, numerous British-Israel groups, the traditional Catholic hierarchy, the Knights of Malta, goddess worship covens, witchcraft sects, mystery teaching groups, the Ordo Templi Orientis, the

Hermetic Brotherhood of Light, Islamic Sufi groups, and on and on.

A Strange Cast of Characters

I also discovered that many famous named individuals appear to be involved in the Priory of Sion cult in one way or another. I came across such names as the late Emperor Joseph von Hapsburg; his modern-day descendant Otto von Hapsburg, now a member of the European Parliament; Ludwig the Mad, who was King of Bavaria in the last century; the composer Beethoven, who supposedly once wrote a musical concerto for the Illuminati; Prince Bernhard of the Netherlands, a founder of the Bilderbergers; Pope John Paul II, who played a strange role in the cover-up of the Vatican-P2 Masonic Lodge banking scandal; the late Catholic Archbishop Lefebvre, who was a dogged opponent of the modernization carried out by recent popes; and Mino Pecorelli, editor of the muckraking newspaper *L' Osservatore Politico*. (Pecorelli was killed by assassins in Rome after sending over to the Vatican a list of Cardinals and other church officials who were secretly members of Freemason secret societies.)

My inquiry also turned up information on a shadowy French official named Pierre Plantard de Saint-Clair, who, until quite recently, was the head of the Priory of Sion.

In my investigation of the Priory of Sion I came across numerous assassinations, a half-dozen accusations of slander and libel; and numerous plots within plots. My studies took me into a compilation of genealogy after genealogy and sent me on fascinating but sometimes not so fruitful chases into dusty bins and infrequently-used shelves to examine ancient manuscripts and old, rare books. I interviewed former CIA and FBI agents and talked with various other intelligence and law enforcement agencies and officials. My search also put me in touch with embassy officials and consuls of various foreign countries.

Slowly, I was able to build a composite picture of what the Priory of Sion really is and what it is up to. I also put together a dossier of some of its key officials and a documentation of their activities. Just as important, I was also able to throw out a lot of the diversionary disinformation that was shuffled to me and to finally gain a straightforward understanding of the true goals of this unseemly, yet powerful, secret society.

The Illuminati and its Network: A Gigantic, Greedy Octopus

My adventure in investigating the Priory of Sion, coupled with years of research tracing the money connection of the Secret Brotherhood with hundreds of other New Age cults and organizations, has assisted me in comprehending the true dimensions of the Secret Brotherhood. There can be no doubt that the Brotherhood is like some kind of gigantic, greedy octopus. It has spread its tentacles across the globe and operates in many facets and mysterious ways.

To help readers to understand the leadership structure of the subtle yet astonishing global network that now exists, I provide on the next page an incomplete, but highly informative organizational chart. It depicts, at the top echelon, a handful of directors for the Secret Brotherhood. I call them by the name the *Illuminati*, though they themselves do not use such a term.

The Banking and Money Group

Directly underneath this small group of key leaders, the Illuminati, are the men and organizations who comprise the *Banking and Money Group*. These are the controllers. They have possession of billions of dollars they use annually to bribe, influence, and seduce men and women on a global

ILLUMINATI

BANKING AND MONEY GROUP
- International Money Center Banks
- Central Banks
- International Monetary Fund
- World Bank
- International Bank of Settlements
- World Conservation Bank
- Multinational Corporations
- Foundations

SECRET SOCIETIES GROUP
- Freemasonry
- Skull & Bones
- Grand Orient Lodge
- Grand Alpina Lodge
- Knights Templar
- Royal Order of the Garter
- Priory de Sion
- Rosicrucians

POLITICAL GROUP
- National Government Leaders
- United Nations
- Bilderbergers
- Trilateral Commission
- Council on Foreign Relations
- Club of Rome
- Aspen Institute
- Bohemian Grove
- Regional Federations (NATO, EEC, etc.)
- International Labor Unions

INTELLIGENCE GROUP
- CIA
- KGB
- FBI
- British Intelligence
- Mafia/Organized Crime
- Drug Cartels
- Interpol
- Communist Party

RELIGIOUS GROUP
- World Council of Churches
- National Council of Churches
- World Parliament of Religions
- Vatican/SMOM
- New Age Cults/Groups
- Liberal Protestant Denominations
- Unity Church
- Unitarian/Universalist Church
- Baha'i
- Temple of Understanding

EDUCATION GROUP
- UNESCO
- World Peace Groups
- Planetary Congress
- World Federalist Association
- World Constitution and Parliamentary Assoc.
- Environmental Groups
- Lucis Trust
- World Goodwill
- World Union
- Esalen Institute
- Media Establishment

scale in order to accomplish their purposes. In the Banking and Money Group we find the international money center banks—Chase Manhattan, Morgan Grenfel, Bank of America, and the now defunct Bank of Credit and Commerce International (BCCI). We also find the central banks of nations, such as the Bank of England, America's Federal Reserve Bank, Germany's Bundesbank, and the European Monetary Institute now being formed.

Also in the Banking and Money Group are the institutions of financial control—organizations operating strictly for the benefit of the Illuminati that are designed to supervise the whole world's financial networks. Among these institutions is the International Monetary Fund, the World Bank, and the International Bank of Settlements.

Included in the Banking and Money category are the largest of the multinational corporations—giant business empires set up by such men as the late Robert Maxwell (an empire now dissolved by the Brotherhood), the Rockefellers, the Rothschilds, and the many corporate chieftains involved with such groups as the CFR and the Trilateral Commission.

We also should not forget the World Conservation Bank, a unique institution set up to grab hold of the wilderness lands of the world in the name of conservation. Moreover, there are the monied foundations—the Rockefeller Foundation, Carnegie Institute, Ford Foundation, and so forth. With their grants and allotments, the foundations are able to control vital elements of thought and action throughout society.

The Political Group

The Banking and Money Group is the most influential but there is also the Political Group, which includes the heads of state of many governments, Britain's Royal Order of the Garter, America's Council on Foreign Relations, the Royal Institute of International Affairs, the Aspen Institute for Humanistic Studies, the Club of Rome, the Trilateral Commission, the Grand Alpina Lodge, the Bilderbergers, the

United Nations (and its 39 directorates), international labor unions, Freemasonry, and regional federations such as NATO and the EEC.

The Intelligence Group

In the Intelligence Group we find a number of organizations and groups that are affiliated with and operate under the direct command of the Illuminati. There is our own CIA; the Russian KGB; the FBI; the British Secret Services; the Mafia, which has its own global intelligence network; the Vatican, which likewise has a surprisingly capable stable of global watchers and intelligence operatives; and the drug cartels, whose agents operate across national boundaries.

The Religious Group

Whereas the Intelligence Group guides, assists, suppresses, conceals, destabilizes, and carries out dirty tricks and even assassinations for the Illuminati, the Religious Group has a wholly different aim. It is the spiritual unity arm of the Illuminati, being composed of groups, organizations, and churches which are promoting the Illuminati's goal of world religious unity. Among the religious groups which I believe are now affiliated with the Illuminati are the National Council of Churches; the World Council of Churches; the World Parliament of Religions; the World Assembly of Religions; hundreds of groups and cults affiliated with the New Age Movement; various Protestant front groups and some TV evangelists; Alcoholics Anonymous (funded from the beginning by the Rockefellers); and numerous other cult groups (for example, the Unification Church, "the Moonies").

The Vatican also now can be firmly listed as a server group of the Secret Brotherhood's Illuminati. This includes such worldwide Catholic organizations as the Knights of Malta (formerly called the Sovereign Military Order of Malta) *Opus Dei*, and the Jesuits.

The Educational Group

In the Educational Group, which is the propaganda arm, we should list the various world peace groups; Planned Parenthood; the government-funded National Endowments (for the Arts; for the Humanities, etc.); the Peace University; Planetary Citizens; Planetary Congress and other New Age-oriented groups; hundreds of environmental and ecological groups; transpersonal and humanistic psychology associations and groups; global forums; various people and corporations in the media; globalist groups; holistic health groups and organizations; and occultic international groups and cults such as World Goodwill and Lucis Trust. Also in the category of educational groups is President George Bush's Points of Light Foundation.

An Alliance of Conspiratorial Interests

These five major groups—Banking and Money, Political, Intelligence, Religious, and Educational—are under the immediate direction and control of the small band of men who lead the Illuminati. We should realize that many of these groups are closely allied together. In some cases the same man may simultaneously serve as either president or on the board of directors of a banking and money institution, a political group, an intelligence organization, a religious denomination or organization, and a foundation or educational group. The members of the Illuminati themselves often directly participate in the various organizations and groups that are funded and operate to support the goals of the Secret Brotherhood as a whole.

We should also realize that at least some of these groups have no idea whatsoever that they are being controlled and manipulated by the Illuminati. Some leaders of various groups believe themselves to be in control of their own destiny. They foolishly believe that their group can take its own independent course of action. Everything goes well as long as they support the goals of the Illuminati. But if they ever run afoul of the ambitions and objectives of the big boys, watch out.

I've also discovered that the Illuminati are quick to discipline leaders of organizations and groups who formally are subordinates in their global network. When a scandal breaks out and a person is unmasked as, say a homosexual, an embezzler, or in the field of intelligence, a double agent, that person is usually immediately cut off. He or she is replaced or simply disappears and the Illuminati move quickly to cover up the fiasco or scandal using their friends in the media.

With their control of such powerful institutions as international banks, national government office-holders, the giant foundations, and the CIA, KGB, and other intelligence agencies, and considering their close working relationships with the Mafia and the drug cartels, the Secret Brotherhood has the capability of either directly or indirectly influencing almost everything that happens to us each minute of our waking and sleeping hours. It is easily proven that the Illuminati funds almost all anarchic and revolutionary movements throughout the world. Its hit men have pulled off mind-boggling assassinations, and governments have fallen because of Illuminati-sponsored coups.

The Illuminati also run an international ring of terrorists whom they use for maximum benefit in creating crises and then offering solutions to resolve the crises that benefit the Secret Brotherhood.

Keeping Secrets "to Baffle the Vulgar"

It is a tribute to the leadership of the Secret Brotherhood that their conspiracy has remained concealed from the majority for so long. Increasingly, men and women of discernment are discovering the facts, but the system is designed to make detection of the conspiracy extremely difficult. As I will later explain, this is an *occult* conspiracy, and one in which its perpetrators have demonstrated their knowledge of how alchemy and Masonic magic can be effectively used to process and condition humanity.

Conspiracies which utilize occultic alchemy and Masonic magic are always the hardest to penetrate because of their use of such tactics as disinformation, coded and veiled illuminist language of a double-speak nature, and intentional campaigns to produce error, lies, and falsehoods in the minds of the deceived. As one technological expert in sorcery and magic explains: Alchemy is a science "based on a secret reserved for only a few privileged adepts possessing the intellectual and moral qualities requisite for obtaining it."[3] To confuse and cover-up their criminal and conspiratorial activity, the arrogant elite trained in the use of alchemy and magic purposely create disinformation traps and mental obstacles and fruitless paths which, they believe, the uninitiated cannot navigate:

> Difficult and narrow is the way, and many are those who stray into wrong paths, where they are to find only deceit, error, and falsehood, which will beguile them into expending vast sums in sheer waste . . .
>
> Alchemists conceal in order to baffle the vulgar.[4]

Obviously, you and I are the "vulgar" whom the elite believe they are entitled to lie to and deceive. But the men who comprise the upper ranks of the Illuminati conspiracy also have no reluctance about deceiving and misleading their own subordinates, either. The whole, interlocking network of the Secret Brotherhood is based on half-truths; concealed goals; hazy, symbolic meanings; and distorted aims.

For example, in Freemasonry, the average Mason—especially those in the Blue Lodge, the first three degrees—is lied to, and this lie is a part of a great deception planned in advance. As Albert Pike, former Grand Sovereign Commander of Scottish Rite Masonry, once wrote, "They do not know because we lie to them."[5]

The initiates of the secret societies rarely know what they're getting into when they first join. Most are never let in on the secret. This is true also for those who are seduced into joining the Secret Brotherhood network at other entry points, such as the intelligence agencies, various educational institutions, religious, and peace organizations and groups. The same alchemical techniques employed by the Masonic lodges are widely used throughout the vast conspiratorial system.

In Albert Pike's *Morals and Dogma*, a book that the Lodge encourages every Mason to consider as their basic guide for daily living, we find this revealing passage:

> The Blue Degrees are but the outer court or portico of the temple. Part of the symbols are displayed there to the Initiate, but he is intentionally misled by false interpretations. It is not intended that he shall understand them; but it is intended that he shall *imagine* he understands them. Their true explication is reserved for the Adepts, the Princes of Masonry."[6]

Regrettably, most Freemasons do not bother to read their own Masonic textbooks, philosophy textbooks and guides. If they did, they might just come across such revealing passages. For example, they might find extremely enlightening the works of the late Manly P. Hall. Hall, a 33rd degree Mason and one of this century's most authoritative experts on secret societies, disclosed how the masters of the secret societies are able to conceal their anonymity and hide the truth from not only the masses but even the lower-level initiates:

> Freemasonry is a *fraternity within a fraternity*—an outer organization concealing an inner brotherhood of the elect . . . It is necessary to establish the existence of these two separate yet independent orders, the one visible and the other invisible.
>
> The *visible society* is a splendid camaraderie of free and accepted men enjoined to devote themselves to ethical, educational, fraternal, patriotic, and humanitarian concerns. The *invisible society* is a secret and most august fraternity whose members are dedicated to the service of a mysterious arcanum acandrum (defined as a secret; a mystery).
>
> In each generation, only a few are accepted into the inner sanctuary of the Work . . . The great initiate-philosophers of Freemasonry are masters of that *secret doctrine* which forms the invisible foundations of every great theological and rational institution.[7]

Purpose: To Mislead and Cover-Up

The men at the top levels of the Secret Brotherhood pride themselves on their "secret knowledge" and on their ability to divert and mislead those whom they consider their spiritual and mental inferiors. In this way they hope to dilute the strength of and neutralize all who might otherwise effectively oppose their conspiracy.

By the time the initiates of a secret society such as Freemasonry or the Skull & Bones advance in their knowledge of what is actually occurring behind closed doors, they have already compromised themselves beyond redemption, usually to acquire monetary and financial rewards, but also for reasons of prestige and status.

In addition, at each step up the ladder, those chosen for higher leadership roles are required to commit themselves to *obey* their superiors in the Brotherhood. An example of this is found in the ritual for the 30th degree of Freemasonry. In the official *Scottish Rite Masonry Illustrated*, Vol. II, p. 259, we find that the candidate, after a bizarre and somber ceremony in which coffins, skulls, and other occult symbols are employed, hears these words voiced by the Grand Master: "Kneel down with me." The Grand Master then continues:

> Hitherto you have seen in Masonry nothing but emblems and symbols. Now you must see in it nothing but reality. Are you determined to repudiate all prejudices and *to obey, without reserve, all that you will be commanded to do for the good of humanity*?

Thus, the man who aspires to the highest offices of this secret society must make a covenant vow to "obey without reservation" his superiors, those who supposedly possess greater "light" and "understanding." The prejudices he must repudiate, as it turns out, include the morality system of Christianity, the patriotism of nationalism, and the principle that all men are equal in value before God. Meanwhile, the words "for the good of humanity" are simply a code-phrase of the Illuminati which are interpreted in only one way: that the people of planet Earth are to be ruled *for their own good* by a superior and more noble class of man.

SEVEN

The Supermen of the Imperial Brain Trust

In their quest, they picture themselves as supermen and as philosopher-kings who must take on the brutal but necessary task of restoring the world to its natural order. They seek to create a new paradise, a rebuilt Garden of Eden. The great ones of the Secret Brotherhood are so exalted that their underlings refer to them in awe-inspiring tones. When these high-level men are described by lower-level initiates, they're often referred to using such veiled terms as:

The Council of All Beings
Wisemen
Torch-bearers
The Brain Trust
Crusaders of the Green Cross
The Lords of Compassion
Guardians of the Grail
Masters of Wisdom
Society of Illumined Minds
World Mind
Council of Masters
Order of One
Invisible Order
Invisible College
Custodians of the Plan
Great White Brotherhood
Seekers on the Threshold
Modern Knights Templar
The Illumined Ones
Great Ones
Hierarchy

Rarely are such terms as the "Illuminati" or the "Secret Brotherhood" used. That is because those terms clue-in the public to the true, hideous purpose that the supermen represent. But whatever term is used, it is clear that the men at the highest level of the Secret Brotherhood consider themselves to be indescribably superior to the average man and woman. Indeed, they believe themselves to be as different from the man on the street as man is to a barnyard animal.

Other Men are "Half-formed Creatures"

As one of their propagandists, Alice Bailey once arrogantly bragged, the superheroes of the Illuminati consider themselves "too great for narrow creeds of right and wrong." They are not bound by the limitations of morality as are we, but have the right to determine their own code of conduct. Compared to them, she says, other men and women are simply half-formed creatures:

> Such men (supermen) are even now upon the earth,
> Serene amid the half-formed creatures round,
> Who should be saved by them and joined with them.[1]

The supposed superiority of the Brotherhood was discussed by Laurence Shoup and William Minter in their 1977 book, *Imperial Brain Trust*. According to Shoup and Mentor, the Brotherhood has been especially active in Britain, the former nations of the British Commonwealth, and the United States. They're following a script laid down by Cecil Rhodes, the founder of the Rhodes Scholarships that are awarded to favored American sons. Governor Bill Clinton, the democratic nominee for President in 1992, is a Rhodes Scholarship recipient—he attended England's Oxford University, courtesy of the scholarship. *Imperial Brain Trust* tells us that these Rhodes Scholarship men make up a network of secret and quasi secret organizations. Isn't it interesting that Bill Clinton was a secret participant at the 1992 Bilderbergers conclave in Baden Baden, Germany.

The Council of "Wise Persons"

Yet another indication of the egotistical spirit of the elitists is their incarnation as the "Council of Wise Persons." From all quarters of the earth now, we are hearing cries from certain quarters for the creation of such a group. For example, in the *International Herald Tribune* in 1992 was this report on a call by former Soviet communist party boss Mikhail Gorbachev for a "Brain Trust" of wise men:

> Mikhail Gorbachev has called for the U.N. to set up a "Brain Trust" of the world's elite to push global politics towards detente. He claims the Brain Trust should include "nobel laureates, diplomats and churchmen."[2]

The *International Herald Tribune* also gave a rundown on others promoting the concept of a Council of Wise Persons: "Likewise, the United Nations Association of the U.S.A. has called for a 'global watch committee' of prestigious leaders to lead the international community." Continuing, the *Tribune* stated:

> In reaction to Black Monday (the Stock Market crash) back in October of 1987, Paul Streeten at Oxford University called for "a surrender of some national sovereignty and a transfer of sufficient power to decision-makers who can manage this system . . . a Council of Wise Persons."[3]

It's interesting to note that the Bible (Revelation 17) says that in the last days there will be such a Council of Wise Persons. Bible prophecy indicates that there will eventually be ten such world leaders who sit on the Council and that these ten will all be "of one mind . . . for they will give all of their strength and power unto the Beast."

How intriguing that the Club of Rome and other semi-secret organizations who have served as front groups for the Secret Brotherhood have made proposals for dividing the world up into *ten regions*, each to be headed by a governing body and leader. Those secularists who so quickly dismiss Bible prophecy as utter nonsense may well want to reconsider their opinion.

Mikhail Gorbachev, who in mid-1992 was sponsored in his trip to the United States by the Esalen Institute, a New Age think tank in California, has long been a leader in calling for the creation of a Council of Wise Persons. Not only did Mr. Gorbachev suggest such a group when he spoke before the United Nations, but several times in the past he has mentioned publicly that he is willing to sit on such an august group. Gorbachev has suggested that the Council of Wise Persons, also to be known as the Brain Trust, include such other notables as former British Prime Minister Margaret Thatcher and former U.S. President Ronald Reagan.

On his recent visit to the United States, according to press reports, Gorbachev met privately with former U.S. Secretary of State Henry Kissinger. No doubt they worked out plans for the Council of Wise Men to "go public." What

When Mikhail Gorbachev visited the United States in May, 1992, he made sure he had time to stop by to see the powerful Henry Kissinger.

Gorbachev, Kissinger, and the others do not reveal, of course, is that such a group *already exists.* But the time is soon coming when a "Council of Wise Men" will be made known to the world. That time will come after a series of incredible, debilitating crises afflict humanity and the globe, making all the world's peoples cry out in unison for such a group to be set up to present solutions to end the bloodshed, carnage, and chaos.

Precursors to the Coming "Council of Wise Men"

Already, each year, at a different site around the globe, a number of world leaders in all areas of human endeavor get together at a gala "Global Conference of Spiritual and Parliamentary Leaders on Human Survival." Another name this group gives itself is the "Global, Spiritual, and Parliamentary Forum on Human Survival." These men and women have met in Moscow and in England at Oxford University, bringing together not only politicians and financiers, but also spiritual representatives from Buddhism, Christianity, Hinduism, Islam, Judaism, and tribal witchdoctors.

Representatives from over 60 countries have attended these global conferences, and Mikhail Gorbachev and the Dalai Lama, among others, have been keynote speakers. But this group, as well as others on this scale, appears to be icing on the cake, mere window dressing. Still, they generate public interest and a steamroller type of public mentality that a Council of Wise Persons *must* be appointed by the world's governments if solutions to mankind's increasingly desperate problems are to be found.

The Council on Foreign Relations (CFR), which has among its elite membership Governor Bill Clinton, David Rockefeller, Henry Kissinger, General Colin Powell, former Presidents Gerald Ford and Jimmy Carter, and just about every other major political and social leader in America, has also been at the forefront in calling for a Council of Wise Persons. Its recommended name for such a group is

"Global Watch." The CFR says that it wishes to give "increasing political authority" to this group, adding that the group must "be composed of the world's intellectual leaders." The CFR's push for the creation of this group has come through its subsidiary organization, the United Nations Association of the United States.

In the *New York Times* of January 15, 1988 appeared a full-page advertisement with the headline "Facing the 21st Century: Threats and Promises." The ad was significant in its call for a "World Council" to be set up in which all Nobel Prize winners would gather together to solve world problems. The key organizers of such a group were listed as Francois Mitterrand, the President of France; and Elie Wiesel, a man who has been a leader in many world peace and unity movements. In 1988, such a meeting of Nobel laureates in fact was held and drew some 76 Nobel Prize winners.

Meetings of such groups as the Nobel winners and the various global conferences fulfill an interesting propaganda purpose. What is more interesting, however, is the fact that the call by Mikhail Gorbachev and other world leader and groups for a "Council of Wise Persons" to be established appears to be a little belated. Back in 1982, in the initial issue of *Initiator*, billed as "the network newspaper" for the influential globalist organization, The Planetary Initiative for the World We Choose, was printed this announcement:

> THE WORLD COUNCIL OF WISE PERSONS. Simultaneous with the occurrence of the culminating Planetary Congress, the first such Council will be convened at the headquarters of the United Nations in New York City, U.S.A. Its purposes include facilitating input into the Planetary Congress from this group of widely respected individuals. They are expected to share not only their concerns for the state of the globe, but their vision and insight into moving humanity over the next threshold.

Endorsers and Luminaries of the Council of Wise Persons

The Planetary Initiative for the World We Choose is a New Age, globalist organization which numbers among its luminaries such notables as Reverend James Parks Morton, dean of the New Age-oriented Cathedral of St. John the Divine in New York City; political organizer Donald Keys; and science fiction writer Isaac Asimov (now deceased). On the staff of this organization is Gerhard Elston, former executive director of Amnesty International. Elston has also been a member of the board of directors of such groups as Bread for the World, Clergy and Laity Concerned, and the ultra-liberal American Civil Liberties Union (ACLU). Elston is active in the Lutheran World Federation and previously served on the staff of the National Council of Churches.[4]

Other endorsers of the Planetary Initiative for the World We Choose include Glen Olds, a Methodist church official who is pushing a "Mother Earth" theology; Linus Pauling, Nobel laureate scientist; Aurelio Peccei, president of the Club of Rome; Rusty Schweickart, former astronaut; Reverend Theodore Hesburgh, president of the University of Notre Dame; Erwin Lazlo, a noted teacher of dialectics and so-called "systems theory;" Saul Mendlovitz, director of the Institute for World Order; Douglas Roche, member of Canada's House of Commons; and Professor George Wald of Harvard University.

Also affiliated are author Norman Cousins, who, until he recently passed away, was head of the World Federalists Association; Arnold Fraser, former U.S. congressman and mayor of Minneapolis, Minnesota; George Brown, professor at the University of California; and the Tibetan Buddhist spiritual leader, the Dalai Lama.

The involvement of all of these world-acclaimed leaders in a scheme to set up a Council of Wise Persons certainly lends credibility to the warnings and "red alerts" that have been sounded over the years that the leadership of the world revolution was about to come out of the closet.

When it does someday publicly and openly assume the reins of world government, what the Secret Brotherhood wants to do is to insist that its leadership role of this globe was *invited* by the peoples of earth. The Brotherhood wants to maintain the myth that everything it does is simply done in response to the desire and longing of all of humanity. The Secret Brotherhood wants us to believe that it is a *democratic* group which will come up with *democratic* solutions and policies designed through a *democratic* process.

But the awful truth is that the entire democratic system—euphemistically called *The New World Order*—now being set up and organized by the Brotherhood is to be a dictatorship of the worst kind.

A New Religion Called Networking

At a symposium in Ashville, North Carolina, with the theme, "Toward a World Global Economy," globalist leader Donald Keys, head of the Planetary Initiative for the World We Choose, trumpeted to an ecstatic audience:

> We're at the final stage now of putting it all together. It's a New Religion called "Networking" . . . the New Age Wave is now entering social change.[5]

Keys also told the group: "Don't anyone think for a moment that you can run a planet without a head . . . this planet has to be managed."[6]

What is this new religion called *networking* that globalist New Age leader Donald Keys has so strongly endorsed? Networking, of course, is a word found in our dictionary. It is a term often employed by job counselors, and the term is even used by such companies as Amway and other pyramid-type marketers. We can really define networking as "the synergistic collaboration or collusion of a number of people or organizations or secret societies working together to fulfill common goals." Naturally, there can be secret networks as well as public, open networks.

The Secret Brotherhood has developed the social and political art of networking to a fine science. *World Goodwill*, in its newsletter of 1986, No. 2, listed a number of groups that have participated in its World Service Forum. Such groups include those that are connected with World Goodwill's centers in London, New York, and Geneva. The list is absolutely mind-boggling in its scope. In London, groups that have actively participated include the United Nations Association, the Teilhardt Center, the International Broadcasting Trust, the Buddhist Society, the Scientific and Medical Network, St. James' Church (Picadilly), Emerson College, International Health Research Network, Habitat International Council, the Shumacher Society, the New Economics Foundation, World Health Organization, Peace Through Unity, the British Holistic Medical Association, the World Wildlife Fund, and United World Colleges.

You might wish to note that the World Wildlife Fund is headed-up by Prince Phillip, Queen Elizabeth's husband, and that Prince Bernhard of the Netherlands is also involved with this group. Both gentlemen have been closely affiliated with the Bilderbergers. Meanwhile, United World Colleges has had on its board of directors two former prime ministers of Great Britain, as well as Prince Charles. United World Colleges is also supported by a U.S. group, the Millennium Society, which has been warmly praised in the past by President George Bush.

In New York, World Goodwill gives credit to the following organizations for their involvement in its work: the Earth Society Foundation, Clergy and Laity Concerned, Waldorf Education, UNICEF, Emmaus, Hale House, the United Nations Association, the Peace Corps, the U.S. Mission of the United Nations, the Better World Society (CNN founder Ted Turner's group), the Foundation for Global Broadcasting, Fellowship and Prayer, the Institute of Cultural Affairs, Physicians for Social Responsibility, the Bank for Social Responsibility, Habitat for Humanity, The

Christophers, the Institute for Community Economics, Women's World Banking, Tibetan Buddhist Learning Center, Environmental Action Coalition, the Catholic Worker, the Nicholas Roerich Museum, the International Center for Integrated Studies, the Sri Aurobindo Society, and the Mead Institute for Human Development.

In Geneva, Switzerland, we find the following groups to be participants in the programs of World Goodwill: The International Commission of Jurists, Pax Christi International, Transnational Prospectives, Amnesty International, the United Nations University for Peace, and the Bureau for the Affairs of Non-Governmental Organizations of the United Nations Organization.

Religion, Peace, and Networking

Obviously, Donald Keys meant exactly what he said when he triumphantly declared that *networking* is the *religion of the New Age*. The process of networking has become successful for the Secret Brotherhood's implementation of its plans in every realm—political, economic, religious, education, entertainment, medical, etc. In the religious realm, for example, it might be enlightening to look at one small group alone that is closely associated with the plan of the Brotherhood: The Reorganized Church of Jesus Christ of Latter-Day Saints (RLDS—Mormons who are not affiliated with the larger Salt Lake City, Utah sect).

As I demonstrate in my book *New Age Cults and Religions*, the RLDS has become a hotbed of New Age activity in recent years. This church group is a major promoter of globalism, peace, and disarmament organizations, many of which are funded covertly by the Brotherhood. Many have a Marxist connection and some received financial aid undercover from the communist government of the former U.S.S.R.

In the RLDS instructional manual, *Youth Ministries Ideas 2*, readers are told that to learn more about "the ways of peace," they might wish to seek out the following organizations recommended by the hierarchy of the RLDS church: American Friends Service Committee, Council for a Lovable World, Educators for Social Responsibility, Greenpeace, Nuclear Weapons Freeze Campaign, Physicians for Social Responsibility, and Sane.

Meanwhile, in a RLDS study book, *Becoming Makers of Peace*, the following groups were recommended as "a few of the many excellent groups in the United States who are working for peace:" Center for Defense Information, Clergy and Laity Concerned, Council on Economic Priorities, Council for a Lovable World, Fellowship of Reconciliation, Positions for Social Responsibility, Friends of the Earth, Interface Center on Corporate Responsibility, Peace Links, Sane, Union of Concerned Scientists, Women's International League for Peace and Freedom, and World Policy Institute.

Education for the New Age Globalist Agenda

The organizations listed above are not just empty titles. These are legitimate organizations. Some have budgets in the tens and even hundreds of millions of dollars. They use this money to educate the world on the wisdom of a New World Order, the unity of all religions, and the United Nations goal of a "New International Economic Order." Consider, for example, one organization alone: *Planetary Citizens*, located at 325 Ninth Street, San Francisco, California. Recently, I received a form letter from this group addressed to "Dear Friend of Peace and the Planet."

My research into the membership of Planetary Citizens provides startling evidence of the enormous influence and capability of such organizations. Let me list just a few of the more prominent officials and persons involved actively with Planetary Citizens. Keep in mind that this group is only one of thousands of front organizations set up by the Secret Brotherhood, endorsed by it, or which perhaps unwittingly sponsor agendas that are virtually identical with that of the Secret Brotherhood.

First, we discover that the honorary chairman of Planetary Citizens is Norman Cousins. Listed as "first endorsers" are, from Australia, Conrad Moritz; from Belgium, Maurice Bejart; and from Canada, Maurice Strong. (Strong is the mastermind of the United Nations Environmental Program and was the chief organizer and head of the Earth Summit held in Rio de Janeiro in June, 1992, in which most of the world's leaders participated.)

Continuing, other "first endorsers" of Planetary Citizens are Martin Niemoller, Germany; Marcel Marceau, France; Jean-Francois Revel, France; Archbishop Angelo Fernandez, India; Princess Juliana, the Netherlands; Sir Edmund Hillary, the famous explorer, New Zealand; Thor Heyerdahl, Norway; Gunner Myrdal, Sweden; the Dalai Lama, the god-man of Tibetan Buddhism; Peter Ustinov, famous actor and political commentator; and the list goes on and on.

Among the endorsers of Planetary Citizens from the United States, are these persons: Leonard Bernstein; Kenneth Boulding; Coretta Scott King, widow of the assassinated Reverend Martin Luther King; Linus Pauling, Nobel Prize winner in medicine; Victor Reuther, international labor leader; Pete Seeger, musician; Professor George Wald of Harvard; best-selling novelist John Updyke; novelist Kurt Vonnegut; and humanist psychologist Rollo May.

The list above is impressive enough, but wait . . . there's more. Let us continue our examination of the impressive number of dignitaries and people of influence connected to this one New Age, globalist organization. On its advisory council and listed on its letterhead are famed science fiction writer Isaac Asimov; Noel Brown of the United Nations Environmental Program; George Brown, of the environmental group World Watch; Peter Caddy, co-founder of the Findhorn New Age community in Scotland, often called the Vatican of the New Age; Britain's Lord Exeter; American Hindu advocate and guru Ram Dass; Sri Chinmoy, another Hindu guru who has been identified as the spiritual advisor to former Soviet communist party boss Mikhail Gorbachev; David Steindl-Rast, a Catholic Benedictine Order brother; Theodore M. Hesburgh, president of Notre Dame University; Edgar D. Mitchell, a NASA Astronaut; and Michael Murphy, founder of the Esalen Institute, which sponsored the recent visit of Mikhail Gorbachev to the United States and also one of Boris Yeltsin's visits to America.

The list continues: Englishman Sir John Sinclair; New Age theologian David Spangler; Sierra Club writer William Irwin Thompson; scientist Willis W. Harman of the Stanford Research Institute; René Dubois, a French author who promotes the New Age belief in the "god within" (Dubois is the spiritual mentor of former Tennessee Governor Lamar Alexander, now the Secretary of Education under President George Bush); Archbishop Makarios, top official in the Greek Orthodox Church; England's Lord Phillip Noel-Baker; Lester Pearson, former prime minister of Canada; Jean Piaget, a French child psychologist of worldwide renown; General Carlos Romulo, the Philippines; Paul Henri Spaak, former secretary-general of NATO; U Thant, former secretary-general of the United Nations; and acclaimed British historian Arnold Toynbee. (A few of the persons listed are now deceased and are recognized by Planetary Citizens as being "emeriti.")

All in all, the distinguished leadership cadre of Planetary Citizens is nothing short of amazing. These men constitute the greatest number of movers and shakers I have ever seen affiliated with any one organization. So when people doubt the influence of New Age groups such as Planetary Citizens and its affiliate, the Planetary Initiative for the World We Choose, I can only say that the doubters are ignorant. We must recognize the enormous power wielded by these groups. Therefore, a key question is, what is the *agenda* backed and endorsed by Planetary Citizens?

The Agenda of Planetary Citizens

The major concerns and interests of Planetary Citizens are a mirror image of those of the Secret Brotherhood. When we realize that this group is merely a propaganda front, witting or unwitting, of the Secret Brotherhood, we're aided in our understanding of the blueprint drawn up by the Order. For example in the letter from Planetary Citizens I have in my files addressed to "Dear Friend of Peace and the Planet," its author, Donald Keys, president of Planetary Citizens, mentions that a task force of 40 members of Planetary Citizens is taking a trip to Central America to work on solving the guerrilla wars that beset that region.

Also favorably mentioned in the letter is the University for Peace, an organization set up by Robert Mueller, former assistant secretary-general of the United Nations, who serves as the chancellor for this institution, which is located in Costa Rica, in Central America.

We also find in the letter the reference to the Brotherhood's goal of ending American national sovereignty. Keys writes, "A disarmed world cannot just be 'disarmed.' It must also contain some new elements. 'Global Patriotism' . . . is one of them." The letter goes on to explain that national sovereignty must give way to a form of *global citizenship.*

The letter from Planetary Citizens also discusses the group's establishment of a subsidiary group, the Independent Commission on World Security Alternatives. This group, says Keys, is putting out a report which will be distributed in over 10,000 copies to world leaders. It is the report's contention that mankind must make a rapid transition to "world security," that we must carry through and complete "a *design*, a *plan*, and a *process* which achieves sustainable peace."

Indicating the power broker role that Planetary Citizens provides in support of the Secret Brotherhood, the letter remarks that this report by the so-called Independent Commission on World Security Alternatives, "will be rightly timed (in the United States) to play a role in the Presidential election campaigns and in the redirection of global policies."

We see, then, that merely one organization, operating worldwide across national borders, can exert an astonishing influence in our lives. Yet, Planetary Citizens is only one of thousands of such active groups and organizations. My study and investigation has convinced me that almost all of these groups have been established and are now being funded behind the scenes by the Brotherhood.

Some of them are also receiving money under the table from the Central Intelligence Agency or from other national intelligence groups closely allied with America's CIA. In this way, because the CIA budget is kept secret and classified accordingly by the U.S. Congress and the White House, the money can be doled out privately without attracting public attention to these organizations.

EIGHT

Strange Glory: What Are They Hiding Inside That Tomb?

The Skull & Bones Society—secretive, influential, powerful, made up of the super-rich, the upper class, the elite of the United States and perhaps the world. Is it an evil group? Why is it a *secret* society, a *secret* organization with *hidden* initiation rituals, *hidden* membership lists, *hidden* doctrines, and *hidden* goals and objectives? Is it unbiblical, is it unholy, is it of the devil? Is it un-American? *Who* belongs to the Skull & Bones Society? *How* do they become a member of this group? *Why* did they become a member of this group? *How many members* of the Skull & Bones Society are living today? *What positions* do they hold in our government, in banking and finance, and in education and religion? These are some of the questions we'll be discussing in detail in this and subsequent chapters as we examine one of the most bizarre of the secret societies: *The Order of Skull & Bones.*

In *Dark Majesty* and in my previous books, including *Millennium: Peace, Promises, and the Day They Take Our*

Money Away, I disclosed information about a number of the secret societies and organizations that exist in America and around the world. There are a number of such groups. Yet, I'm convinced from my research and the evidence that God has allowed to come my way over the last six years that, although there are many organizations, secret societies, and groups dedicated to the triple goals of world government, a unified world economy, and a one world religious system, today as never before, these groups are linked together. They are networking. Moreover, there is, in fact, an elite, a clique, at the very top. You can call it an *invisible college*, you can call it an *invisible order*, some have called it the "hidden hand;" but there *is* a powerful and centrally located leadership unit.

Now, of all the influential secret societies and orders that I have come across, the Skull & Bones Society seems to enjoy unusual prominence and authority. The Skull & Bones has infiltrated and penetrated almost every area of our society. For example, some of the members of the Skull & Bones have moved into the oil industry, many have been and are diplomats, others are railroad magnates, banking and finance czars, heads of lumber and forestry combines, and on and on. President George Bush is the best known member of the Skull & Bones, but he is not the only president to have been a "bonesman."

The Founding of the Order of Skull & Bones

The Skull & Bones originated at Yale University in 1832, being founded by a man named General William H. Russell. Today, actually, the Skull & Bones is formally known as "The Russell Trust" and is incorporated in that name. William H. Russell visited Germany in the year of 1832 and while there was introduced to a German secret society which was a successor of the Bavarian "Illuminati" of Adam Weishaupt.[1]

Germany has been the home of many secret societies. In fact, they existed all the way up until the time of Adolf Hitler and still operate today. Hitler himself was a member of two secret societies, the *Vril Society* and the *Thule Society*, and he believed himself to be a Teutonic Knight.[2] Upon his return to the United States in 1832, General Russell and some associates determined to establish a similar group in America. Yale was then one of the Ivy League colleges, was perhaps the top school, along with Harvard and Princeton in the United States at that time. It was therefore Russell's intention—he and his very wealthy, rich friends—to make sure that they and their sons could become members of a secret order which would have favored, privileged status in society.

At the time, Freemasonry was in disrepute throughout the United States. A Captain William Morgan, a Mason, renounced the group and published a volume in 1829 unmasking most of the secret rituals, handshakes, and symbolism of Freemasonry. So enraged were Masons that Captain Morgan was murdered. This violent act became a rallying cry against all Masonic lodges everywhere. So great was the public outcry that an Anti-Masonic political party was even established.

So when General Russell and his Masonic friends decided to found their secret society at Yale, they avoided the Masonic name. However, the Skull & Bones is, in fact, nothing less than a black lodge of Freemasonry and its rituals are almost carbon copies of the highest level ceremonial rituals of Freemasonry.

It was decided that 15 juniors at Yale would be chosen each year from among the "upper crust," the upper classes, the rich, the famous, the privileged, the influential. And so they set up this secret society to be known as Skull & Bones. They also constructed an impressive, windowless building that came to be dubbed "The Tomb," adjacent to the campus of Yale University.

Interestingly, the esoteric motto of both the Skull & Bones and Yale University itself is the one inscribed on certain campus buildings and is also to be found inscribed in Latin on the $1 bill of our currency. The words of this motto, in Latin, are: *Novus Ordo Seclorum*. That is also the Yale slogan; translated in English, the words mean *New World Order*.[3]

Thus the members of the Skull & Bones perceive themselves as the men who are to bring in the New World Order.

A $54 Million Endowment for Pampered Rich Boys

At Yale, then, we have this secret society in which only 15 students are inducted each year. They live in a building, the Tomb, that resembles a combination library and mausoleum and are cared for by paid servants, cooks, and attendants. The Russell Trust is endowed by $54 million in alumni grants. Imagine, $54 million for the welfare of these 15 pampered initiates! These 15 students are obviously chosen, special people. They are called Knights while they are at the university, but when they graduate, they are called Patriarchs of the Order.

It has been the case that since 1832 the Patriarchs, also calling themselves bonesmen, continue to meet together frequently. The new graduates are also mentored by older patriarchs and are rewarded with jobs, loans, grants, and favored treatment throughout their lives. "Once a bonesman," it is said, "always a bonesman."

Behind the Closed Doors of the Tomb

In 1873 some Yale students wanted to know the secrets of the Tomb, the building where the strange, arcane ceremonies and rituals are held to induct the chosen new Skull & Bones members. A group of Yale students therefore decided to break into the Tomb, to discover what goes on in the inner sanctum. What they found there was quite shocking. They came upon actual skulls and bones—not only the insignia logo of the group—*real* skulls and bones. Many evidences of occultism were found in the Tomb.

Some of those students later wrote of their experiences and revelations in the Yale newspaper, the *Iconoclast*.[4] Evidently, sentiment was then against the bonesmen, as a result of their arrogance and their unfair actions in consistently favoring their own, regardless of merit.

We can be sure there have been many fine, brilliant and hard-working students inducted into the Yale secret society known as the Skull & Bones. But in fact, it does not matter what merit a man may have, by virtue of his being a member of this secret order, he is always favored, not only by fellow bonesmen, their blood brothers at Yale, but later in life by the alumni. It is the alumni who actually control the Order of Skull & Bones.

That Cryptic Number: 322

The logo of the Order of Skull & Bones is a skull with crossed bones and underneath a strange and mystic number "322." At Yale the Order is known as *Chapter 322*. What does the "322" stand for? There seem to be many explanations suggested. The most prevalent theory is that the number 322 has a connection with Demosthenes, the famous Greek orator. And so, because of this small clue that the number has a connection with Demosthenes, I decided to research the life of Demosthenes and find out more about him.

As it turns out, Demosthenes was a great Greek orator and patriot. He lived from 384 to 322 BC. He died in 322 BC, so if in the Skull & Bones Society the "Chapter 322" designation comes from a link with Demosthenes, it would indicate the year of his death, 322.

Now, historians tells us that Demosthenes poisoned himself—he committed suicide in 322 BC. He did so because the Greeks were ruled by Philip of Macedonia.

Demosthenes, a politician, a leader, and a patriot of Greece was extremely depressed. He and others had instigated an uprising against Philip but their efforts had failed. Therefore, Demosthenes committed suicide by poison.

Today, a statue of Demosthenes stands in the Vatican, in St. Peter's Cathedral in Rome. Could there be a connection of the Skull & Bones with the Catholic Church? Possibly. In any case, what we have here is a situation in which the historical legend of the death of Demosthenes seems to have been the inspiration for the founding of Skull & Bones Chapter 322. It could be that what the Order of Skull & Bones is saying is that its members prefer death to giving up freedom and liberty—so much so that they would rather be dead or poisoned than not to have this freedom, this liberty. It is significant for us to understand that for the secret societies, words such as "freedom" and "liberty" have no meaning as we know them, nor does the word "democracy."

To the secret societies, such words refer to the concept that the human spirit, the human soul, can win freedom and divinity for itself through achieving higher consciousness, the *gnosis*. "Gnosis" is defined as higher wisdom and knowledge. There is no God, no personal God to whom the men of the secret societies must pledge allegiance; no religious system, no Bible that they must adhere to. Instead, they are convinced that they possess a divine, inalienable right to seek *perfection* in themselves and literally to become "*godmen*," divine beings in their own right. This has always been the principal core, the mysterious secret doctrine, of such esoteric groups as the Freemasons, the Knights Templar, the Knights of Malta, and the Skull & Bones Society.

Initiation and 322

Not too long ago a gentleman proposed to me that the *real meaning* of Chapter 322 of the Skull & Bones was not to commemorate the death of Demosthenes, but instead, could

This is the actual logo of the Skull & Bones Society, complete with the number "322."

One of Kaiser Wilhelm's field marshals in his black uniform and death's-head headpiece, called a "busby."

be found in Chapter 3, verse 22 of the book of Genesis in the Bible. Now, in turning our attention to Genesis, chapter 3:22, a fascinating revelation comes into focus. What Genesis 3:22 is all about is *initiation.* Just as each of the candidates for Skull & Bones membership must pass through an initiation process, so Genesis 3:22 is talking about the ordeal of a man who passes through ritual initiation into perfection and godhood.

Here we have recorded the story of Adam and Eve and their fall from grace. You see, before they sinned and disobeyed their creator, Adam and Eve were immortal creatures. They would not die unless they transgressed against God. And so God put them in the garden, with the prohibition against the eating of certain forbidden fruit. But they did eat of that fruit of that tree which they should not have, which they were ordered not to by God. And so God, in Chapter 3 of Genesis, verse 22 says this: "And the Lord God said, behold *the man is become as one of us. To know good and evil.*"

But God continues: "And now lest he put forth his hand and take also of the tree of life and eat and live forever, let us banish him from the garden!" Thus, in verses 23 and 24, we find that God sent Adam and Eve out of the Garden of Eden; he drove out the man and woman from paradise, and he placed at the East of the Garden of Eden guards known as the cherubim, and a flaming sword to keep inviolate, sacred, and untouched the *Tree of Life.*

In other words, Adam and Eve were driven out of the Garden because God said: "He has already eaten of the one fruit. He knows he's almost like us. He's become one of the heavenly hosts. He knows the difference between good and evil and now let's drive him out of the Garden or he'll take of his hand and eat of the other tree, the Tree of Life, and he'll be an immortal god and live forever.

If man *had* eaten of the Tree of Life, he would have become an immortal, a divine being: a god. So the Lord said, "let us drive him from it."

Therefore, the number of Skull & Bones Chapter 322 may be a veiled reference to unredeemed man's inner desire and yearning to become a god—to partake of the Tree of Life. Through initiation, the secret society candidate does, in fact, partake of the fruit from the Tree of Life—he symbolically returns to the Garden and is made perfect and divine!

Indeed, my investigation demonstrates that, metaphorically speaking, *the goal of every secret society is to have man, the initiate, eat of the fruit from the Tree of Life, to become immortal, to become a god.* This is also the goal of the New Age. And I think it makes perfect sense that it could, indeed, be that account in Genesis 3:22 which inspired the Skull & Bones founders to utilize this number.

The Meaning of the Skull & Bones

What is the symbolic meaning of the *skull* and *bones*? Now, I think anybody with common sense would know of the occultic legend of the skull and bones. The pirates of the high seas had their black flags, on which they would paint a white skull and crossbones. So we know that this symbol has an evil and corrupt, outlaw type connotation.

It is, therefore, a fascinating fact that when George Bush (Skull & Bones, class of '47) first went into the business world, he and his associates (also "bonesmen") named their new, upstart company, Zapata Petroleum, after the Mexican outlaw and badman, Emilio Zapata.[5]

Throughout the years, a number of sinister groups have used the skull and bones as symbols of death and as artifacts for occultic, Satanic rituals. We know that witches, sorcerers, shamans, witchdoctors, and devil worshippers make use of the skull and bones. These symbols of death have often been used by medieval knights and orders and by 20th century dictators. Kaiser Wilhelm II of Germany, who was a member of the Order of the Teutonic Knights and other secret societies, chose the skull with crossed bones as a military insignia for one of his World War I units. The *Death's-head Corps* wore a fur cap in which was embedded a scary and frightening skull and crossbones.

The "X" Factor: A Mark of Satan

In ancient Egypt, the mark of "X" and the symbol of crossed-bones in the form of an X was very prominent in religious contexts. You can find the X on the walls of a number of ancient Egyptian temples and pyramids. The meaning of the X is simply this: it is the sign of Osiris, the great sun god, who, it was said, sends forth his "thousand points of light" to earth to do his work—meaning his disciples, his organizations, and his temples throughout the world.[6]

Now it began to be said among the peoples of ancient Egypt that if you were illiterate and could not sign your own name, then it would be acceptable to simply sign your "X." And so today, a lot of people, when you're going to sign a document, will say, "sign your X here," "put your X right here." Legally, if you can't write, you can put your X mark, witnessed by others who sign their name which indicates that you did attest to the document.

This practice came from the ancients who were, in effect, swearing and affirming to Osiris the sun god, of the authenticity of their X mark.

The ancient pharaohs, when they were buried, had their legs crossed in the form of an "X" as a sign of devotion to Osiris. And it is true, too, that during the medieval period in Europe, many of the Knights Templar and later the Freemasons also had their legs crossed in the casket. They may well do so today, because for the Freemasons, the skull and crossbones is considered a most important symbol.

Keep in mind, too, that the skull is also the symbol of Baphomet, the androgynous (male *and* female) goat-headed god who represents Satan. The skull represents for occultists the head or center of the universe, a universe ruled by Satan.

The Nazi Swastika and the Skull & Bones

The Yale students who in 1873 illegally entered the Skull & Bones Tomb alleged that inside were a number of human skulls. More recently, in 1979, several Yale women co-eds also infiltrated the Skull & Bones sanctuary. Evidently, according to their eye-witness report, things haven't changed much since 1873. The co-eds found some amazing things; for example, on one wall was a triangle-shaped black pirate flag emblazoned with the skull and crossbones. They also found an entire skeleton on display in a standing-position coffin. They reported seeing a painting of a sinister man with a dagger. A number of skulls were discovered. The co-eds also allege that they observed Nazi-like swastikas, the swastika being the eternal sign of the sun god.[7]

Throughout history, swastikas have been used in pagan rituals, not only among Hitler and the Nazis, but in Buddhist temples and Hindu temples. Today the swastika is often displayed in Hindu temples in India and Shinto shrines in Japan. It is the sign, the great swirling spokes, or wheels, of the great sun god.[8]

The skull is also considered by the occultists and by the devil worshipers as representing the demonic spirit known as *Asmodeus*, who is considered to be the guardian of the treasure of Solomon. All Freemasons proclaim as their objective the rebuilding of the great Temple of Solomon. Is there a connection?

When the Knights Templar, in 1314, were charged with blasphemous and devilish crimes by the Catholic Church and French authorities, leader Jacques de Molay was accused of drinking blood and wine from a human skull in ritual ceremonies. De Molay was also accused of sodomy, and of urinating on a cross or a crucifix. He was therefore condemned by a court to be burned at the stake.[9]

Today, the Freemasonic order for young boys is called the *Order of DeMolay*.

The most important symbols of Freemasonry are shown above. Note the skull and also the all-seeing eye inside a triangle. The sun rays coming from the eye and triangle are called the "blaze of glory." (Reprinted from a Greek book on the Masonic Lodge.)

The Skull and the False Christ of Freemasonry

Possibly the most grotesque meaning of the skull in Freemasonry is that it represents a false Christ, or Antichrist who is the enemy and counterfeit of the real Christ, Jesus. In the lowest degrees of Freemasonry, the initiations include rituals in which participants play out, or role play, the part of a heroic character named *Hiram Abif*. Now Hiram literally means, "he ram," in other words, the "Lord Ram." The goat-headed god. And so we have an incredible connection with the blackest aspects of occultism.

In the Masonic ceremony is acted out the killing of the builder of Solomon's temple. The legend is that this Hiram Abif was the King of Tyre. Solomon invites Hiram, the King of Tyre, and his craftsmen and stone masons to Jerusalem to build the great Temple of Solomon, the Temple of the Lord. According to the Masonic legend, the master builder, Hiram Abif, goes to the temple one day to inspect the temple construction and see how the work of his artisans is progressing. But, upon arrival at the site, he meets up with and is confronted by three "criminals." (I believe these three criminals portrayed are, in fact, the Father, Son, and the Holy Ghost, the true deities of this universe, Jesus Christ being Lord.) These three criminals demand from him the magical and supernatural Lost Word of Masonry—they want to know the most sacred secrets of Freemasonry. Hiram Abif says no, he will not tell, so they smash him over the head with a club, and of course, his skull is crushed. And thus, we have the symbolic significance of the skull in Freemasonry.

The skull and bones of the Skull & Bones Society therefore has to do with Hiram Abif, the Freemason, the builder and false Christ figure, who built the great Temple of Solomon, but, in its last stages of construction, was murdered and assassinated. This is why, in the 30th degree ceremony of Freemasonry, the candidate enters a tomb, hung with black, adorned with skulls and a crown.

The Wicked King Solomon and His 1,000 Wives and Concubines

It is very important to recall that, as recorded in I Kings and II Chronicles in the Bible, we find that Solomon did, indeed, send a message to a Hiram, the King of Tyre, requesting Hiram to come, he and his skilled workers, to build the temple. They were to help in the engraving work and the bronze and the iron. But why did Solomon ask for help from Tyre, a city where heathen gods were worshipped? Well, in his old age, the Bible tells us, Solomon had grown wicked, he had disobeyed God, and so Solomon, even though he had hundreds of wives, was not content to have Jewish wives, but he also wanted to marry the beautiful women of the neighboring tribes and cities and nations. These women, however, were worshippers of the false goddesses and gods. Solomon took for himself a total of 1,000 wives and concubines and some were from Tyre.

The Bible does not inform us about the name "Abif." But Abif literally means "father," so the Masonic story refers to Father Hiram. Also in Tyre during the days of Solomon the people worshiped the mother goddess, *Astarte*. Astarte, also called Ashtoreth and Ishtar, was bequeathed the title of the "Queen of Heaven," the goddess from the sea.

At first, the temple built by Soloman was a holy place. But eventually it became an evil abode of the demonic goddess of the pagans. The priests of the temple also were wicked during the days of Solomon. They brought in the Asherah totem poles in honor of the goddess. This was the image of jealousy, the abomination that maketh desolate in the temple. And Solomon himself was given a pagan offering by the priests of the temple. Each year they gave him 666 talents of gold.

Solomon angered God when he attempted to blend worship of Jehovah with the adoration and veneration of the heathen goddess. Solomon sought to mix the things of

God with the things of evil. Hiram, King of Tyre, brought darkness with him to Jerusalem.

In the Freemason ceremony, this Hiram Abif is literally honored as a Christ-type. It is the goal of all Freemasonry to rebuild the great Temple of Solomon. Hiram is to be resurrected and worshipped in a glorious new, reconstructed Temple. This is the ultimate objective of Freemasonry—the worship of a false Christ (the Antichrist!). This false Christ must, naturally, rule over a Kingdom. The whole world is to be that Kingdom.

George Bush and the Goals of the Secret Societies

Since George Bush's roots came from Freemasonry, as exemplified by his initiation and continuation in the Masonic Skull & Bones Society, we can gauge the goals and objectives of esoteric Freemasonry best by examining George Bush's actions. We know, for example, that George Bush was at one time the United States Ambassador to the United Nations. As president, he has called for a stronger United Nations, to be fitted with a standing military police force. He is therefore in favor of a United Nations able to enforce its rule around the globe.

As strange as it may seem, George Bush also is linked with pyramid powers, another occultic symbol. There is a group called the *Millennium Society*, founded in 1979 by Edward McNally, a New York attorney. Every year it gives a huge party or a celebration in different cities around the world. This gala event is said to be for the benefit of students selected to attend colleges affiliated with the New Age organization, *United World Colleges*. United World Colleges was founded and is headed on an honorary basis by Britain's Prince Charles.[10]

The *Millennium Society* says that in the year 1999, in fact on New Year's Eve, on the very precipice of the year 2000, the next millennium, they plan to conduct a great ceremony and ritual in the Great Pyramid of Egypt. And according to the *Los Angeles Times* (January 3, 1989), George Bush says that he and his wife, Barbara, will attend. According to the *Los Angeles Times* report, the President wrote a personal letter to the *Millennium Society* and assured the group that he and Barbara "fervently support the *Millennium Society's* dedication to education, international understanding, and world peace."

George Bush also stated that he had committed himself to being there in Egypt in person, to help usher in the new millennium. The time and date is thus set at the stroke of midnight, 1999, on New Year's Eve.

The New Money and a Strange New U.S. Mint Building

As president, George Bush has also implemented a plan for a *New Money*. Eventually, our currency is to change dramatically. To print the new money, a new U.S. Mint facility has been constructed in the Dallas/Ft. Worth area. This U.S. Mint is built using the principles of occultic, sacred architecture. It is constructed in the shape of a circle with a great pyramid in the very center of it. In fact, when you go in the front gate of this U.S. Mint facility, constructed by the way with your tax dollars, you pass through two great pillars. At the top of each pillar is also a small pyramid.

The pyramid (or the triangle) within the circle has long been a satanic symbol. It is the very symbol that the Rajneesh, the corrupt Hindu guru who came to America during the 1970's and built a New Age community in Oregon, used to represent his work. If you visit the Rajneesh's community in India today you will see this symbol displayed.

It is also the symbol of Alcoholics Anonymous, because AA was founded with money from John D. Rockefeller. Although many people erroneously believe that AA is a Christian organization, and although some drunks do get sober through its 12-step method, AA in fact, was designed by its founders to support occultic goals. Observe, for example, the fact that the name of "Jesus" is forbidden at AA meetings. And while reference is made to a vague "God," the God of AA is defined simply as a nebulous, unnamed "higher power"—he is God as *you* understand him to be. The witch, the satanist, the Hindu, the Buddhist, and the deceived "Christian" all can worship and celebrate together in harmony at an AA conclave.

The Skull & Bones Initiation Ceremony

What happens when a person is inducted into the Skull & Bones Society? What I'm going to describe to you is the initiation ceremony for all new "bonesmen." It is exactly what George Bush and many other prominent political, media, and financial leaders have gone through.

First, as part of this ritual of initiation, the new man is placed in a coffin, in a casket. He is then carried into the central part of the Tomb, the Skull & Bones building. The other members of the society, dressed in bizarre, occultic costume and wearing masks or hoods, stand solemnly around the coffin, chanting and moaning, invoking the powers. They are chanting, evidently, for familiar spirits to facilitate the "rebirth" of the candidate. The rebirth is said to transform the candidate from ordinary human status into a "superman"— a god-like being.

The individual next is removed from this coffin and given a robe with certain Masonic symbols on the robe. Evidently, in at least some of the initiation ceremonies, one of these symbols is the Maltese cross with eight points (eight is the occultic number of new beginnings).

Finally, a bone with the man's new name on it is tossed into a bone heap. Initiates have also commonly taken part in a ritual in which they plunge naked into a mud pile. The purpose is that the initiate takes on filth and is then cleansed and purified.

Now you say, Texe, all this is ridiculous. A man lies in a coffin, they chant over him, they remove him from the coffin, he's given a robe with occult symbols on it, then there's wallowing in a mud pile, followed by tossing a bone with the initiate's name on it into a bone heap. That's absurd!

Well, I agree. It *is* absurd. I can only tell you that this is exactly what goes on. There have been a number of secrets revealed--this is one of them. You can find this not only in Roger Javin's paper that I am privy to,[11] but also in Antony C. Sutton's book *America's Secret Establishment.*[12] The initiation rite/ceremony was also discussed by Ron Rosenbaum, who wrote an article in 1979 for *Esquire* magazine. In fact, Rosenbaum described exactly this initiation ceremony.[13]

A Ritual of the Mystery Religions

The initiation rite is a throwback to Masonic rituals (particularly the ritual for the 30th degree) and is modeled after the similar rituals conducted in ages past by the mystery religions of the Greeks, the Romans, the Babylonians, and the Egyptians. Its purpose is occultic: the new member of the Skull & Bones Society supposedly dies to the world and is born again into The Order. The Order is considered a world unto itself. The man has a new name and 14 new blood brothers. Moreover, he joins an elite few numbering in the hundreds—chosen from among the 5.5 billion inhabitants of planet Earth!

There is not only this elitist element, but also a *spiritual dimension* to the initiation ceremony. This is a counterfeit of the Christian act of being "born again." Jesus Christ said in John 3:3, "You must be born again." As a Christian, a person is not reborn as a result of some arcane and sinister initiation ceremony with bones and skulls, and coffins and mud piles. He or she is reborn through faith in the precious and redeeming name of Jesus Christ.

That is the rebirth for the Christian, but not so for the secret society. Not so for the Skull & Bones initiate. Instead, these individuals pass through the ordeal and tests of a satanic ritual. Elder members of the society, during the ceremony, are assembled in black hooded robes with lit candles, and the member shares his life story as he lays in the coffin. He is required to recount and confess his sexual experiences. He is bonded and soul-linked with the other members of the society. They know about his innermost secrets—everything he has done of a wicked nature. He confesses and tells it all right from the coffin.

This has been known to be a most powerful and emotional experience for Skull & Bones members. It is what ties them together emotionally. It is a psychological conditioning process and can be very traumatic. It is also an intense form of peer pressure—a type of sensitivity or encounter group training.

The new man's inhibitions, his defense mechanisms, are broken down. Some people have told me of other things. Some claim that acts of sodomy have taken place during the rituals, but I have not been able to really confirm this.

But what I have told you is, indeed, very factual. It's an interesting thing that as far back as 1873, the Yale students who broke into "The Tomb" discovered some of these secrets. They warned in their school newspaper at the time that, "Year-by-year the deadly evil of the Skull & Bones is growing." The Society, they wrote, is not just obnoxious and arrogant, it fancies itself superior. Moreover, the students suggested that the true goal of its membership was to endeavor to rule in all things and to clutch tightly its power.[14]

NINE

The Pleasant Adventures of a Bonesman...Or How George Bush Made it all the Way to the White House With Just a Little Help From His Friends

George Bush's association with the Brotherhood—the men who have long guided his destiny and fulfilled his worldly ambitions—actually began before he was born. Bush's father, Prescott S. Bush, was himself a bonesman. Son of an affluent manufacturer, Prescott S. Bush graduated from Yale University in 1918, having been initiated into the Skull & Bones Society the previous year.[1]

The Skull & Bones class of Prescott S. Bush's blood brothers at Yale was an illustrious one. Every one of the 15 who were initiated at the Tomb in May of 1917 went on to become *more* rich (they were *already* of the wealthy aristocratic class) and join the ranks of the global elite. For example, Prescott Bush's fellow initiate Henry Peter Isham was the epitome of monied success in the 1930's and 1940's, being associated as director with Marshall Fields department stores, the First National Bank of Chicago, and Dresser Industries (more on Dresser Industries in a moment).[2]

Then there's Artemus Gates, head of the investment banking firm, New York Trust Co., and later to become under Secretary of the Navy; John Farrar, who became a publishing magnate; Frank Parsons Shepard, of both the Guaranty Trust and the Banker's Trust Companies; Knight Wooley, also with Guaranty Trust, and E. Roland Harriman, a partner in one of the greatest global money machines ever put together—the investment banking firm of Brown Brothers Harriman.

Prescott S. Bush, George's father, also linked himself with Brown Brothers Harriman as well as with other incredibly powerful financial combines, such as Union Banking Corporation. But it was as a partner at Brown Brothers Harriman that Prescott S. Bush and his fellow bonesmen and secret society brothers made their greatest contribution to the world revolution conspiracy.

Help to the Nazis and Communists

There is a mountainous, unquestionable body of evidence that, directly or indirectly, the investment and banking firm of which George Bush's father was a major figure gave early financial backing to Adolf Hitler and his Nazi henchmen such as Rudolf Hess. Earlier, in the 1920's, they had seen fit to finance the communist dictatorship and regime of Vladimir Lenin in Soviet Russia. As Antony Sutton writes in his insight-filled book, *The Two Faces of George Bush*: "The conclusion is that the Harriman firm and Prescott Bush were intimately associated with financing both Nazis *and* Soviets . . . both extremes of the political spectrum."[3]

The dialectical plan of the Secret Brotherhood was to fund, arm and build up two great powers, Nazism and

Communism, and watch as these two ferocious, blood-thirsty monsters tore, chewed, and blasted each other into oblivion. The net result of such a strategy was that once Germany and Russia had foolishly and needlessly exhausted themselves and ravaged their nations in their vain campaigns for global dictatorship, a third world power, greater than they, could eventually emerge to fill up the world scene of authority: a New World Order ruled by the Brotherhood.

At the same time, Japan, an Asian tiger, outsider, and threat to the world conspiracy, had to be declawed and tamed.

Without a doubt, from the ashes of the flames of World War II ascended a new phoenix of world power—the international commercial cartel I have identified in this book as the *Secret Brotherhood.*

George Bush and the Skull & Bones Dynasty

George Bush's father, Prescott, was at the center of the conspiratorial planning and strategizing in preparation for the upcoming great struggle for world domination. But because the world revolution is an intergenerational battle, a series of ongoing conflicts all aimed at the final, ultimate objective of total dictatorship and control of planet earth, it was necessary that Prescott S. Bush and his fellows choose, train, and groom yet another generation of leaders from among their ranks. And what better choice than to keep it all in the family?

Thus it was that George Bush was chosen for tapping by the Skull & Bones even before he left the cradle!

Like his father, young George Herbert Walker Bush would be given the best of everything. No obstacles would be allowed to obstruct his path. His mentors and guides—the alumni, the elder patriarchs of Skull & Bones—would see to it. After all, had the word not gone out, as early as 1873, when an anonymous Yale student, distraught at the favoritism shown the Knights of Skull & Bones, had written:

> We offer no objections to their existing plan. No one disputes with them this right, we question but the *plan* on which they act, *that only he who wears upon his breast their emblem, he for every post shall be considered best.*[4]

I have tracked George Bush's professional career and family history from that dark evening in 1947 when, in the Tomb at Yale, he threw a bone on the pile and proudly acknowledged his new name of "Poppy," a name known at present only to his closest friends and associates. The results of my investigation are fascinating, to say the least.

The history of George Bush's life is proof positive of the almost unbelievable influence and ability of a small band of rich and powerful co-conspirators to create a pliant company man perfectly fit and trained for their own sinister purposes, and to actually propel that man to the very seat of world authority as head of the United States of America, the mighty military arm of the Secret Brotherhood's New World Order.[5]

The Rewards of Membership

Newsweek magazine published an interesting article in its April 29, 1991 issue about the Skull & Bones. Entitled "God, Men and Bonding at Yale," *Newsweek* noted the staggering ability of the Skull & Bones to take care of and promote its own. Why, the magazine asked, would a man want to be a part of a "club with a name like a heavy metal band and a ritual of mumbo-jumbo straight out of the Raccoon Lodge?" The answer:

> Well, there's the clubhouse (or "tomb") itself, rumored to contain among other treasures, the skull of Pancho Villa. There's the tax-free gift of $15,000 that members are widely believed to receive on joining . . .
>
> Most of all, there's the prestige of belonging to a 159-year old organization that counts among its alumni the

> President of the United States, three U.S. Senators, and luminaries of the American establishment ranging from McGeorge Bundy to William Bundy.
>
> Membership in Skull & Bones has often been portrayed as entreé to the inner sanctum of the American elite.

However, though there have been a number of articles written on the subject, the establishment news media has only the dimmest understanding of the incredible opportunity conferred on a person by virtue of his initiation into the Skull & Bones. *Newsweek*, for instance, suggested that, "no one can specify exactly what benefit it conveys in later life."

Nonsense! We need look no farther than the history of one man, *George Bush* (though we can recite that of many others) to discover "exactly what benefits it (Skull & Bones) conveys in later life." What follows, then, is a brief but enlightening sketch of what it can mean to the individual and to the Secret Brotherhood when the right man is tapped by the bonesmen of Yale.

The Myth of the Old Studebaker and the Struggling Entrepreneur Oil Man

By many accounts, including his own, upon graduation from Yale, George Bush and his young wife, Barbara, herself a member of an aristocratic, wealthy clan, the Pierces of New York, struck out for Texas in an old jalopy of a Studebaker. Once in Midland, the heart of Texas' oil country, young, plucky George Bush first signed up in an entry level job at a drilling company where he learned the basics of the oil industry.

Then, unsatisfied with working for someone else, the fledgling and ambitious young man soon joined up with like-minded entrepreneurs. They together founded Zapata Oil Company, an oil exploration outfit and—Presto! They hit pay dirt! Their wildcat wells struck black gold and the money came rolling in.

Emboldened by this astonishing, fast-paced success in what is known by one and all in Texas as the rough and tumble, highly competitive oil business, the astute new businessman named George Bush next sought to extend his good luck by establishing an oil drilling and service company, Zapata Offshore Drilling. Again, bang! Success was to be lucky George Bush's amazing lot in life.

By then, the young man from New Haven, Connecticut was worth millions. He followed up his breakthrough in the oil stakes arena by running for a seat in the U.S. Congress. George Bush was successfully elected to the House of Representatives in 1966.

A Rising Political Star

Then, following two brief setbacks when his two Texas campaigns for the U.S. Senate fell flat, George Bush regathered his inner forces and plunged dizzily headlong into an awesome series of career successes. The dazzling young oil entrepreneur and congressman successively became U.S. Ambassador to the United Nations (1971); Chairman of the Republican National Committee (1973); Special Envoy to the communist People's Republic of China (1975); Director of the Central Intelligence Agency: the CIA (1976); Vice President of the United States (1980); and President of the United States (1988).

Now consider: What possible justification could there be for a totally unqualified oil man and freshman Congressman from Houston, Texas, who is a twice failed senatorial candidate, to be selected for the highly coveted diplomatic post of Ambassador to the United Nations? This post is typically reserved for a man or woman with a track record of excellence after decades of proven experience in public service, preferably in diplomatic circles. But the resumé of bonesman George Bush needed some puffing up, so . . .

Then, about George Bush's taking over as Chairman of the Republican National Committee—another position of untold power. The holder of this position is in charge of the entire apparatus of the Republican Party. He holds the purse strings, hob-knobs with big contributors to party coffers, and controls the direction of party policy. His support—or opposition—can make or break a person's political campaign for any one of thousands of political offices, from mayor and state legislator to U.S. Senator and President, across America. What a coup for a young man like George Bush to be given this plum position!

The Chosen Few

And who put the unqualified George Bush in these powerful, coveted positions? Richard Nixon, President of the United States, appointed him. My investigation shows that Nixon did so at the insistence of Henry Kissinger, his National Security Advisor, and David Rockefeller, the man who bankrolls most Republican candidates for the office of President and who personally mentors the chosen few young men deemed worthy to aspire to that high office. George Bush was one of those worthies.

Very few are aware that it was Richard Nixon, a puppet of the Rockefeller-Kissinger monied interests, who became George Bush's undercover "Godfather" in the early 1970's. But in the *New York Times* national edition of June 11, 1992, we learn of just how much George Bush owes his success in politics to former President Richard Nixon and certain well-heeled money men. The *New York Times* feature article revealed that Bush, then a congressman, was given a financial boost from the same Nixon folks who funded the Watergate break-in scandal:

> In the early 1970's, even as President Richard Nixon became enveloped in the Watergate scandal, he helped elevate George Bush, then an obscure Texas Congressman, to national prominence.

Now, as the June 17 break-in at the Watergate approaches its 20th anniversary, a review of thousands of files—many made public in the last few years—offers interesting new historical details of Mr. Bush's connections to the Nixon presidency . . .

The documents in the National Archives shed new light on the benefits Mr. Bush received from a 1970 campaign financing arrangement by the Nixon White House, known as the "townhouse operation" because it was operated out of a townhouse in Northwest Washington, D.C., that later came under the scrutiny of Watergate prosecutors. And they provide new evidence of blackmail efforts . . .

The documents from the Nixon White House detail plans to distribute . . . cash to selected candidates, including Mr. Bush, then a Congressman from Texas who was running for the Senate . . .

In 1970, Mr. Nixon and his aides supervised a secret $3 million campaign slush fund run out of the Washington townhouse. The operation funneled money to selected Republican candidates including Mr. Bush, who received more than $100,000 . . .

On September 24, 1970, President Nixon met with two Texas oilmen . . . as a result of that meeting, the oilmen put (an additional) $25,000 cash into Bush's campaign in Texas . . .

Former U.S. Senator Llowell P. Weicker, who is now Governor of Connecticut, recalled in an interview last week that he had a telephone conversation with Mr. Bush in July 1973 in which Mr. Bush discussed the townhouse records and asked whether the records should be burned. "Bush called Weicker, asked whether he should burn them," say the Watergate prosecutors' notes . . .

Mr. Weicker said he clearly recalled the conversation. "Believe me," Mr. Weicker said, "That is burned too clearly into my mind."

Bush, Red China, and Money-making Schemes

While money was covertly being funneled to George Bush to speed along his political fortunes, other aid was also provided. In 1975 Kissinger, Rockefeller's man on the scene in the White House as foreign policy chieftain, hand-picked Bush to serve as special envoy to Red China. This was an impressive signal to the 1,000 or so at large members of the Secret Brotherhood that this man, George Bush, was the "chosen one" who someday would be President. After all, Red China was an oyster that the international bankers dearly sought to pluck open and plunder.

The Secret Brotherhood's reasoning centered on making more money. A market in Red China of almost one billion human beings must be opened to commercial exploitation—and fast. Following Nixon and Kissinger's 1970's "ping-pong diplomacy" that resulted in diplomatic breakthroughs with the communist war lords in Peking, it was very, very important that the Brotherhood's own man be sent as envoy to Peking. George Bush was chosen to open up the money channels and to create a system whereby the communist tyrants who run that giant, would-be superpower nation could cooperatively work with the czars of world finance, the men of the Brotherhood.

CIA Director George Bush

After only one year, his mission accomplished, George Bush came home from Peking, China. Promptly, the man whose career had long been guided behind the scenes by the Brotherhood, was given another top job. He was assigned to the one position that the conspirators *must* always hold—director of the world's top intelligence agency—the *CIA*. Reporters and observers unaware of Bush's hidden connections were stunned. George Bush had a supreme lack of qualifications (he had no experience in any "official" capacity in the intelligence field) to be head spy for the

George Bush has long had a unique relationship with the communist overlords in Beijing (Peking), People's Republic of China. First appointed as a special envoy (officially, as chief of the U.S. Laison Office), he later returned as Vice President and met with dictator, Deng Xiao Peng.

democratic forces of planet Earth. Nevertheless, his nomination was quickly approved by an approving Senate Intelligence Committee.

In 1977, CIA chief George Bush resigned to devote his energies full-time to a very special, upcoming political campaign some 2-½ years in the future. For the leaders of the Secret Brotherhood it was time. Their man had just the right resumé. He was primed and ready to run for America's highest office: the office of President of the United States of America.

To make sure that their chosen servant would have all the money needed to run an effective campaign, immediately after leaving the CIA, George Bush was appointed as a director of Texas' largest banking corporations and holding companies—International Bankshares, Inc.

In 1980, George Bush went head-to-head with Ronald Reagan in the race to be the Republican Party's nominee for the White House. To the chagrin of the financial wizards who comprise the Brotherhood, George was soundly defeated by the former Hollywood actor from California in the primary campaigns. Reagan, the Great Communicator, was not to be denied. The common people rallied to his side and for a fleeting moment, George Bush's future looked bleak.

Selection as Vice President: A Backroom Deal?

But like every good field general staff, the boys who head-up the secret societies had a new back-up plan ready to go. Surprise of surprises: the high-flying Reagan, a political novice, was quickly brought down to earth by his campaign advisors and managers. Led by William Casey, the persuasive political strategist who had Reagan's respect—and his ear—the future president was told that he "needed" George Bush as his running mate. Why? Well, for two good reasons: First, the big boys, Casey related, wanted their fair-haired boy to have the job; and second, if they didn't get their way, Ronald Reagan was told, the Great Communicator's political campaign against the incumbent president, democrat Jimmy Carter, could become a miserable affair.

"They" are willing to give you their full financial support, confided Casey, but *only* if George Bush is on the ticket.

Besides, the wily Casey argued, George Bush will add some real expertise and credibility to the Republican ticket. Look at that impressive resumé of his. Plus, he hails from one of the biggest states, Texas, a bastion of electoral votes. It's good politics, Casey concluded.

When the Reagan forces announced that George Bush would be the vice presidential choice, conservatives almost fell over. Wasn't this the internationalist who had pumped for the United Nations, the man who, as a Congressman, had voted *for* gun control and who had vigorously supported population control and abortion? How, they reasoned, could Ronald Reagan, a patriotic man supposedly devoted to down-home, conservative policy options, who seemingly was against everything that George Bush and the internationalists stood for, suddenly up and pick this man to be his vice president and sidekick?

The ultra conservatives and grass roots organizers who made Ronald Reagan's surprising nomination possible had no earthly idea of what had occurred behind closed doors in the inner sanctum of Reagan's campaign headquarters. Nor could they have known that William Casey was an intimate and vital link to the upper ranks of the Secret Brotherhood.

William Casey, George Bush, and the October Surprise

In reality, Casey was a Brotherhood mole, a special undercover agent inside the Reagan campaign organization.

It was William Casey who would later see to it that the Reagan Administration was packed with appointees from the internationalist Council on Foreign Relations and the Trilateral Commission. But first, to make sure that his man,

Ronald Reagan, then leading in the polls, would not be defeated in November by incumbent Jimmy Carter, it was necessary that William Casey and his good friend, George Bush, carry out a most important global mission. Thus was hatched the "October Surprise" plot in which Casey and Bush negotiated with the ayatollahs of Teheran, Iran. The objective: to guarantee the release of the U.S. hostages being held by Iranian revolutionaries who had seized the U.S. Embassy some nine months prior.[6]

Flying to Paris in 1987 during the height of the Presidential campaign, Casey and Bush offered a secret deal to the Iranian emissaries: millions of dollars in military arms to the Iranians (then engaged in a bitter and bloody conflict with madman Saddam Hussein of neighboring Iraq) in exchange for the American hostages. But only under one condition—that the hostages *not* be released until *after* the election and Ronald Reagan's inauguration![7]

The essence of the October Surprise plot, therefore, was the strategy that to insure a Reagan victory in November, Jimmy Carter must be prevented from pulling a "surprise"—winning the release of the hostages just prior to the election. That, Casey reasoned, could result in a rapid upturn in Carter's election chances, as an overjoyed and gratified American electorate might well reward the incumbent President who had gotten our hostages out of the evil grip of Iran's Ayatollah Khomeini.

Such an outcome had to be prevented at all costs. So, using their international centers and agents of influence, Casey and the Brotherhood dispatched word to Teheran: they were willing to "make a deal."

The October Surprise predated and set a precedent for the Iran Contra scandal plot of Lt. Colonel Oliver North, John Poindexter, Caspar Weinberger, and associates that was to come later in the Reagan era. This embarrassing "arms for hostages" arrangement was covered up for almost a decade until a few courageous people decided to step forth and tell the whole story. But in late 1979, the plot proved to be an unqualified success. Jimmy Carter was trounced at the polls by Reagan, mainly because of the "wimp" and "incompetent" labels pinned on the hapless President as a result of the unresolved Iranian hostage crisis.

Meanwhile, a victorious Ronald Reagan became an instant national hero when, literally within minutes of the opening of his inauguration ceremony, it was announced that the U.S. hostages had been released!

Reagan's clever advisors and handlers claimed that it was their man's macho Hollywood, gun-slinging cowboy image that won the day. They suggested that perhaps the ayatollahs over in Iran were scared stiff by the prospect that Ronald Reagan had become president. Instead of chancing an "O.K. Corral" shoot-out situation with six-gun Ronald Reagan, the Iranians, they said, had wisely opted to let the hostages go.

The media either fell for it—or simply went along with the charade—naturally, since most of America's media establishment is owned lock, stock, and barrel by the Brotherhood.

The CIA: That "Old Black Magic!"

Once Reagan was in the White House, campaign manager William Casey took for himself the key post of Director of the Central Intelligence Agency, the very same job his pal George Bush had held earlier. In the intelligence driver's seat, Casey, also a member of the Knights of Malta secret society, was able to continue his wondrous working of magic and illusion for the Brotherhood. It was only after his death in the last years of Reagan's second term that Casey's more sinister machinations and maneuvering came to light.

For example, congressional testimony has revealed that CIA Director William Casey supervised Ollie North's contra operation in Nicaragua. Casey also worked undercover with Pope John Paul II and with the Pope's secretive worldwide organizations, the Knights of Malta, the Jesuits, and *Opus Dei*, as well as with the insiders of the Pope's Vatican Chancery—to fund and assist Polish labor leader Lech Walesa (a loyal Catholic) in his successful attempt to subvert and replace Poland's communist military regime led by General Jaruzelski.

Casey not only convinced President Reagan to take the historic step of appointing a U.S. ambassador (the first ever) to the Vatican, but he made sure that the new diplomat selected for the job was a Knights of Malta brother to boot!

"Your Time Will Come," Bush was Told

During this same time period, Vice President George Bush bided his time—and bit his tongue—over at the White House. Administration insiders have reported that in cabinet and other meetings in the oval office, George Bush typically sat, silent and attentive, not actively participating in the goings-on and deliberations. This was George Bush's worst nightmare—a supreme test of patience.

Normally energetic and hyperactive, he was forced to discreetly stay in the background. His mentors gave him very specific instructions not to rock the boat, not to upstage the President.

"Your time will come," Bush was told, "when Ronald Reagan leaves office."

Finally, on January 20, 1989, eight years later, George Bush stood on a platform set up in front of the White House and before a global audience via television, was inaugurated as President of the United States. And ever since, he has devoted every working moment to insure that the long cherished dreams of the Brotherhood for a New World Order, a globally integrated economy, and a unified (if diverse) one world religious system become a reality.

What a dazzling career George Bush has had! Surely, on the surface of things, it appears that he is possibly the most qualified individual ever to run for and win election to the high office of President. Consecutively, Bush has been oilman; congressman; UN ambassador; envoy to Red China (a nuclear power and the World's most populous country); director of the CIA (the world's premier intelligence network); and vice-president of the United States, standby to the top man for eight long years. Wow!

About That Old Studebaker

But nagging doubts remain. A few questions beg to be answered. First, about that old and decrepit Studebaker that the Bushes supposedly drove down to Midland, Texas, after George's graduation from Yale. My own research has uncovered a radically different story. One reliable source claims that it was actually a *new* Studebaker (1948—those were the days before the Mercedes, BMW's, Jaguars, Lexus', and other foreign makes invaded the continental U.S.). It seems that George's dad, Prescott, gave the shiny and sporty new car to son George as a graduation gift.[8]

Then, about that trip down to Texas: Well, my sources allege that George and Barbara *flew* to Midland in an airplane owned by Dresser Industries. As we shall discover, Dresser was then run by a Skull & Bones brother, and it was this same bonesman brother who first set George up in the oil industry. George was enamored of aircraft, having been a bomber pilot for a brief spell in World War II. He would never drive, my sources indicate, when he could fly. What really happened, they explain, is that the new Studebaker followed the Bushes, driven down to Texas by a paid employee.[9]

And that first "entry-level job" in the oil business? Seems that tales take on heroic—and mythical—proportions when chosen members of the Secret Brotherhood are involved. Here are the facts as I've been able to document them:

Months before George Bush graduated from Yale, his father, Prescott Sheldon Bush, arranged with a fellow bonesman, from Prescott's own Yale class, for son George to be mentored by that gentleman in the oil business. It had no doubt been predetermined by the Brotherhood's elite that George's best bet for a political future lay in a large electoral state like Texas. And the oil business offered the young man the perfect opportunity to learn the ropes and to make contacts. In Texas, oilmen have run the show in state politics since the days of the Spindletop oilfield gushers back at the turn of the century.

George Bush's Skull & Bones Mentor and Guide

It was *Neil Mallon*, Prescott Sheldon Bush's fellow bonesman and Yale classmate, who was chosen to be young graduate George's senior guide and mentor as he entered the dog-eat-dog real world. Mallon had stayed in close contact with George Bush's father, Prescott, for some 30 years, since the two had been initiated into the Order on the same night at the Tomb. Like other bonesmen, Neil Mallon had done well for himself since leaving the Yale campus. Eventually, he took over as chief executive officer of Dresser Industries, a giant in the oil service and drilling equipment business.

When George Bush (Skull & Bones, class of '47) went down to Texas to start a career in the oil business, he didn't begin in some low, entry-level job as his public relations writers would have us believe. Instead, his career began in high style, personally managed by Neil Mallon, an elder blood brother (Skull & Bones, class of '17).

To give you, the reader, a little color and a bit more insight into the George Bush-Neil Mallon connection, reprinted below is a story from Walter Scott's "Personality Parade" column (*Parade* magazine, Jan. 21, 1990). Keep in mind as you read this that Walter Scott's columns indicate that he is consistently an apologist for the establishment crowd. Still, his feature in *Parade* is enlightening:

> *Q*. I've heard that the man most responsible for George Bush's wealth—that is, other than what he may have inherited from his father's estate—was Neil Mallon of Dallas. Just what was the connection between the two?

Mallon must have been an important figure in George Bush's life, since one of the President's sons is named for him. Some background on Mr. Mallon, if you can.
J.D.R., Dallas, Texas

A. Henry Neil Mallon (1895-1983) was chief executive officer of Dresser Industries of Dallas. When he died, George Bush, then Vice-President of the U.S., said of him: "Neil Mallon shaped my whole life from the time I was a boy . . . and when I started my first business he was at my side, sharing his vast experience. One of our sons, Neil Mallon Bush, was named for this wonderful man, and he was loved by our whole family." Mallon, a native of Cincinnati, was a member of Skull and Bones at Yale and a crack athlete. Upon graduation in 1917, he enlisted in the U.S. Army, served in the Field Artillery in France during World War I and became a major at 23, reportedly the Army's youngest.

Some 30 years later, young George Bush seemed to follow in Mallon's footsteps. He volunteered for service in World War II, reportedly became the youngest pilot in the Navy at that time and was graduated from Yale, where he too was tapped for Skull & Bones. After the war, Bush and his bride, Barbara, migrated to Texas, where Mallon got him an entry job at an oil-equipment company in Odessa and, with many others, taught him something about the oil business.

Eventually, Bush and a neighbor in Midland, Tex., John Overbey, launched their own business, buying mineral rights from farmers and selling them to larger companies. Subsequently, the two merged with Hugh and Bill Liedtke, founders of Pennzoil, to form Zapata Petroleum Corp.

According to intimates, Bush used Mallon as a role model for many years, convinced that he could find no better one . . .

A Little Help From Yet Another High-Powered Friend

According to the White House's public relations brigade, George Bush followed-up his stint with Neil Mallon's Dresser Industries by co-founding Zapata Petroleum Corporation (sometimes called Zapata *Oil* Company), an oil exploration business. Joining him in this venture, say the White House communications experts, was a man named Hugh Liedtke. Together, this crew made a mint by finding new oil.

What Bush's people *don't* tell the public, however, is far more significant. They don't, for example, volunteer the fact that Hugh Liedtke was not just your average Texas oil wildcatter. *Liedtke was a principal stockholder and founder of Pennzoil Corporation*, a huge oil company on Wall Street's New York Stock Exchange.

In other words, a young novice, George Bush, went into business with an older man who headed up one of America's top oil producing firms! Again we see proof that George's success was never in question. His ticket had already been punched in advance by the good old boys of the Secret Brotherhood.

Was it Shakespeare who wrote that the whole world is a theater, and all of us are but bit players on the great stage of life? George Bush's biography gives evidence that playwright Shakespeare was a man of unusual insight. Some of the richest and most powerful men on earth have been involved in writing the script for George Bush's life. In George's case, that script for success led straight to 1600 Pennsylvania Avenue and residence at the White House.

TEN

The Skull & Bones Lineup: A Rogues' Gallery of Questionable Characters

The Skull & Bones numbers in its ranks some of the world's most powerful men. Known members include U.S. Senators, members of the U.S. House of Representatives, university presidents, ambassadors and diplomats, and corporate CEO's. In this chapter, we'll first take a close-up snapshot of some of the more prominent bonesmen. Then we'll examine the influence of the Skull & Bones on four major components, or areas, of world power: foreign policy, Wall Street and finance, education, and religion. After reviewing *who* the top bonesmen are and *how* they have so vastly affected our society, I believe you will agree wholeheartedly with me: *The Order of Skull & Bones must be unmasked for what it is—a great and present danger to our freedoms and to our constitutional rights.*

Who's Who in the Skull & Bones

J. Hugh Liedtke: Oil Man. One of the founders of Pennzoil Oil Corporation, the elder Liedtke took a young George Herbert Walker Bush under his wings in Midland, Texas, and together they and a few associates set up Zapata Petroleum Corporation. It was with that firm, Bush's press agents claim, that the future President first made his mark as an astute oilman and business tycoon.

In reality, with one of America's top oilmen, J. Hugh Liedtke, watching over his shoulder and pointing the way to "high potential" oil drilling sites, oil wildcatting for young Bush was not so risky and "wild" an occupation after all.

John Kerry: U. S. Senator and Cover-up Artist. This tall, liberal democrat, who is U.S. Senator from Massachusetts, is considered a "publicity hound" by his Senate colleagues. However, having a penchant for getting one's face frequently on television does not always a hero make. Kerry was given the job by his Senate colleagues in 1989 of looking into a slew of allegations that an international bank named "BCCI" was heavily involved in racketeering, money laundering, bribery, terrorism, and a variety of other crimes.

When his Skull & Bones elders and their pals in the Senate, including Utah Republican Senator Orrin Hatch, told him to quietly put the lid on these unsavory allegations and to meekly absolve the bank of wrongdoing, Kerry, always quick to please, complied without a murmur.[1]

Two years later, the lid blew off the BCCI case when the bank went under, filed bankruptcy, and left the taxpayers and unwitting investors holding the bag for some $500 million in losses.

The big boys of the Brotherhood, of course, had already cleared out their accounts, having received a few years advance notice from their front man and good buddy, Senator John Kerry. Then, in 1991, in a weird and surrealistic public relations ploy, the bonesman from New England suddenly announced that his Senate committee would *reopen* its hearings on the failed bank. Sorry, John, but the horses are already out of the barn.

The Tragic Case of the Missing POW/MIA's

The BCCI scandal is not the only shady deal in which John Kerry's tap dancing and cover-up talents have come in handy for the Skull & Bones hierarchy. When U.S. Senator Jesse Helms (R.-NC) and a few others in Congress came out with revelations that some POW/MIA's may still be alive somewhere in Vietnam, the Bush administration, embarrassed over accusations that its officials had sat on their hands and done little to resolve the POW/MIA issue, quickly called on fellow bonesman John Kerry. To the rescue he came, announcing in front of the news cameras that his committee would launch a full-scale investigation.[2]

Kerry's assigned role, obviously, was to take the heat off the President and the Pentagon and to help the Brotherhood in the process. Seems that the Brotherhood has a fond desire and longing to open up the oil and mineral-rich lands of communist Vietnam and its neighbors, Cambodia and Laos, to commercial exploitation. Senator Kerry and his committee quickly went into operation, actively debunking confirmed POW sightings in Vietnam and downplaying the POW/MIA issue. Then came the clincher: In late 1991 Senator Kerry personally flew to Vietnam on a "fact-finding" tour.

The upshot: the photogenic Kerry assured us (on television naturally!) that there were no more POW's being held and that there were no reliable accounts as to what had happened to the missing POW/MIA's. This, even though a Soviet KGB General had openly admitted that during the Vietnam war years, the KGB had callously shipped many of the American servicemen in bondage in Vietnam off to Soviet KGB prisons to be interrogated about their high-tech intelligence and military know-how.

At his news conference, once he had shunted aside the issue of missing POW/MIA's, John Kerry went right to the heart of his *real purpose* in volunteering his committee's time and energy to "resolve" the Vietnam POW/MIA issue. The bonesman Senator recommended that trade links, now prohibited, be immediately opened between the U.S. and Vietnam and that the U.S. diplomatically recognize the communist Saigon government as legitimate. That recognition, and acceptance by the U. S. of Vietnam as a trading partner, had been held up pending resolution of the case of the missing POW/MIA's.

Covering Up the Iran Contra Scandal

It was also Senator John Kerry whose committee conducted hearings on the Iran Contra scandal. Kerry and company handled the matter with kid gloves and it was left to a special prosecutor, Lawrence Walsh, to try to get to the bottom of things and smoke out Oliver North, Caspar Weinberger, John Poindexter, Ronald Reagan, Richard Secord, and a host of other "baddies" involved in perpetrating and/or covering up the bribes paid to the treacherous and bloody Iranian ayatollahs.

David Boren: U.S. Senator and Intelligence Maven. Senator David Boren of Oklahoma is a valuable asset to the occult hierarchy and to the good old boys of Skull & Bones. As head of the Senate's Intelligence Committee, he has oversight responsibility for that out-of-control agency. Thus, in 1991, when fellow bonesman and blood brother President George Bush sent underling Robert Gates down to the Senate for confirmation as the new director of the CIA, Bush and the Brotherhood knew it was a "done deal."

A showy series of public hearings unearthed tons of evidence that Gates was disreputable, dense, incompetent, and a man whose memory (as a long time high-ranking CIA manager) had developed all kinds of snags and gaps. Senator Boren, however, nevertheless threw his considerable weight into a warm endorsement of fellow Skull & Bones "spook" Gates. Following their chairman's lead, the other committee members and then the full Senate promptly opened up their desks and took out their rubber stamps—and Gates took over at the director's desk at the CIA.[3]

Now that the Secret Brotherhood is assured of a continuing lock up on the CIA's voluminous classified files, America may *never* know the truth about the JFK and Martin Luther King assassinations, BCCI, the plot to kill the Pope, the Iran Contra Affair, the Watergate break-ins, the supposed hardliner's coup to overthrow comrade Gorbachev, the October Surprise hostage scam, the Korean Airlines Flight 007 mass murder, the POW/MIA's, and countless other unsolved mysteries.

William Sloane Coffin: Peacenik and Certified Internationalist. Ultraliberal bonesman William Sloane Coffin is best remembered for his infamous leadership of drug-crazed hippies and weirdos in the 1960's "peace" and anti-Vietnam war demonstrations. Coffin is now President of SANE/FREEZE, a socialist, internationalist group pushing for a United Nations military force and general disarmament of national armies, naval, and air forces. Coffin has now added the environmental issue to his left-wing activist agenda. He is also a big supporter of and has been a keynote speaker for the World Federalists Association, the group begun by the late writer Norman Cousins to lobby for a One World Government and the end of American sovereignty and independence.[4]

William F. Buckley: CIA Man and Propagandist. Conservative columnist William F. Buckley is a Skull & Bonesman *par excellence*. Effecting a British upper-class accent and demeanor, Buckley started out years ago as a supporter of right wing causes. With his popular "Firing Line" television talk show, he gained quite a following. But then he veered sharply to the left, and has abandoned any pretense of loyalty to "America First" ideas. William F. Buckley has also been a CIA operative in the past, a fact that has been widely reported.

When fellow columnist Patrick Buchanan decided in 1992 to mount a conservative campaign against George Bush in the presidential primaries, Skull & Bones alumni Buckley went in high gear to do what he had been sworn to do back at Yale—always provide unqualified support for a bonesman brother in need. In his magazine *National Review*, Buckley published a masterful piece of propaganda—a feature article suggesting that Buchanan was "anti-Semitic" and unfit to be President.

Buchanan's political campaign eventually fell apart, not only because of Buckley's attack, but because Bush also called on yet another Yale grad and buddy, televangelist Pat Robertson, for political help. Robertson promptly mailed a campaign letter on his own letterhead to his tens of thousands of Christian "new right" supporters, urging them to vote for George Bush *over* Pat Buchanan in the upcoming "Super Tuesday" primary contests held in the southern states.

This key support from Pat Robertson came just in the nick of time. It also came in spite of the fact that Buchanan had fervently supported the very issues—such as pro-life and the abolishment of the pornography pandering National Endowment for the Arts—which Pat Robertson had supposedly long favored. In addition, whereas George Bush has generally paid only lip service to the conservative Christian community, Patrick Buchanan had earned a reputation for his consistent pro-Christian viewpoint. But evidently, for Robertson, the blood tie of a Yale brother, George Bush, runs far deeper than the compunction to promote the Christian worldview.

We should remember that televangelist Pat Robertson has never been an outsider to partisan politics. Robertson's father was a member of the U.S. Senate and, in fact, served as Chairman of the Senate's powerful Banking and Currency Committee.

Jack and Jill—And Buckley's Son

A postnote: William F. Buckley's son, Christopher, is also a Yale grad and is a member of his old dad's occultic-laced

Skull & Bones Society. This certainly puts the lie to the myth that the alumni do not control the selection process of new members of the society.

Acid-tongued like his dad, Christopher Buckley was once asked by a *New York Times* reporter to reveal some secrets about his Skull & Bones group, and specifically to explain the documented reports that human bones are used in its rituals. Smart aleck Buckley replied: "Yeah, we have Sarah Bernhardt's right leg and we have Peter Stuyvesant's left leg. We keep them in a case and we call them "Jack & Jill."[5]

Gifford Pinchot: Environmentalist. Pinchot is considered the "Father" of the environmental movement. Some say that it was his book, *Breaking New Ground*, that resulted in the establishment of the U.S. Forest Service.

We have seen how the Rockefellers, Rothschilds, Strongs and other banker conspirators are plotting to latch on to the coattails of the "Mother Earth" campaign. They are using the ruse of environmentalism to feather their own financial nests and divide up the world's resource-rich wilderness lands between them. In retrospect, perhaps the true objective of Gifford Pinchot can be more clearly understood.

Amos Pinchot, a blood relative of Gifford, was a key founder of the liberal American Civil Liberties Union (ACLU). Amos Pinchot was also an active financial supporter of Marxism, endorsing Lenin and the Bolsheviks in the early days of the communist regime in Russia.

As far as influence within the ACLU is concerned, the Skull & Bones seems to have quite an inside track. In 1984, the Executive Director of the ACLU was John Shatlack, Skull & Bones class of 1965.

Potter Stewart: Supreme Court Justice. George Bush's pal, the late Potter Stewart, was an Associate Justice of the Supreme Court, a key position at the very apex of the U.S.A.'s judicial system. In 1981, Bush asked Potter Stewart to swear him in as Vice President of the United States at his inauguration ceremony. Stewart was delighted to accommodate his fellow bonesman. Through these two men, the Brotherhood was to send the entire conspiratorial network a powerful symbolic message of harmony and favored status accorded brother elitists.

To reinforce this symbolic connection, the Bible from the altar of the Masonic lodge of New York City, first used in the inauguration of George Washington, was transported all the way to the White House steps so that Bush could lay his hand on it and be sworn in. Unlike other King James versions of the Bible, the Masonic version has an introductory section which meticulously explains that Masonry is *not* a Christian society but, instead, supports *all* religions and creeds.[6]

Thus, George Bush was sworn into office with his hand resting on a Bible that has an added section which attempts to degrade Christianity by declaring a belief in Jesus Christ undeserving of prominence or exaltation above Buddha, Mohammed, Zeus, and all the other false gods and deities.

Would God bless a president or a nation that allowed such an act of defiance against the Truth? Would He look down with favor on a man swearing an oath with his hand resting on a pagan document inserted within the covers of *His* Holy Bible?

William H. Taft: President of the U.S.A. Judge Potter Stewart is not the only high-ranking jurist who has been a Skull & Bones member. The history of the U.S.A. records many bonesmen as federal judges. William Howard Taft was a Supreme Court Justice, *and* he became president of the United States. Taft was also president of his church denomination, the Unitarians. (The Unitarians—now called Unitarian-Universalists—are a New Age church group: see the book by Texe Marrs, *New Age Cults and Religions*.)

In the September, 1921 issue of *New Age* magazine, the official publication of 33rd degree Scottish Rite Freemasonry, the Masonic organization crowed with pride that "a 32nd degree Mason (Taft) has been placed in the Presidential Chair." The article that had this statement in it was entitled, "Freemasonry as a World Power."

Evidently, the Supreme Council of 33rd degree Masonry, which I am convinced is presided over by the invisible college of the Illuminati, felt that the swearing in of their brother, William Howard Taft, would be a big plus for them as they continued their work of subversion and hidden control. Triumphantly, the magazine article boasted that someday, "Freemasonry as a World Power will stand revealed as unconquered and unconquerable."

The Taft family continues today to exert its hideous, anti-Christian influence. Charles P. Taft (Skull & Bones class of 1918) is now president of the financial arm of the ultraliberal World Council of Churches (WCC). The WCC has for decades sponsored terrorist groups overseas. Currently, this apostate "Christian" church group is laboring to bring together all faiths—from Native American Indian medicine men and African tribal witchdoctors to Christians, Jews, Hindus, Buddhists, and Moslems—together under one hideous spiritual umbrella. The directors of the WCC have decided that Jesus is *not* unique and never was really God.

Archibald MacLeish: Founder of UNESCO. Bones Brother MacLeish, class of '15, has held pivotal positions in the U.S. diplomatic corps. He chaired the American delegation to the United Nations London Conference which founded the U.N. subsidiary UNESCO, and he wrote its constitution. UNESCO subsequently became so hatefully anti-American in its sponsorship of Third World terrorism and the communist agenda that even the milk-toast U.S. Congress finally got fed up. For a brief period in the 1980's, the U.S. Congress cut off the millions of dollars (30 percent of its budget) the U.S provided UNESCO. (Later, President George Bush restored the funding and even attempted to *increase* U.S. aid.)

Archibald MacLeish held the important position of Librarian of Congress. Just how important this position is was demonstrated in 1989. According to Fritz Springmeier, a Christian researcher and author, in January, 1989, shortly after he had assumed the office of president, George Bush's aides sent over to the Library of Congress a biographical resumé, as is traditional for new presidents. That resume listed the incoming President as formally affiliated with Freemasonry. However, four months later, the reference to Bush being a Mason was quietly and mysteriously deleted from a *revised* resumé on file at the Library of Congress.

Stevenson M. L. Aronson, Yale '65, wrote an article in *Fame* magazine in August, 1989, in which he reported: "A Bonesman once showed me a letter he'd received from MacLeish . . . that was signed: "With an undiminished trustingness, Yours in—and out of—322, Archie."

Townsend Walter Hooper II: Publisher. Townsend Walter Hooper II (class of '44) is chairman of the Association of American Publishers. The Secret Brotherhood has almost a death grip on all book publishing activity in America and Europe, which is why no books of substance opposing or exposing the Brotherhood are ever published. (Please note that my books are *not* published by the major New York publishing houses, even though there exists a tremendous market and demand for them—over a million books by Texe Marrs have now been sold!)

There is no definitive proof that Townsend Hooper II has used his influence to censor or to keep anti-Brotherhood exposés off bookstore shelves. But as Yale grad and Skull & Bones researcher Roger Javens has suggested, "It could possibly take Hooper only a few phone calls to major publishers to stall distribution of a typeset book."[7]

Hooper was Assistant to the Secretary of Defense for five years, 1948-53, so it would not be plausible to assume that his role as chairman of America's top publisher's association is nonpolitical.

Some Other Notables of the Skull & Bones

It's plain to see that this *one* secret society, the Order of Skull & Bones, packs immense influence in every sphere of our society. In addition to those listed above, below is a rundown on some other bonesmen—alive and deceased—who have greatly impacted our lives and continue to do so.

Henry Luce (Skull & Bones Class of '20). Top man at *Time* and *Life* magazines and a chieftain of the Council on Foreign Relations.

McGeorge Bundy. National Security Advisor for President John F. Kennedy. Bundy, a member of the class of '40, also was a CIA man. *Esquire Magazine* confirmed through a reliable source that Bundy, like other bonesmen, once "wrestled naked in a mud pile as part of his initiation."

John Sherman Cooper. This U.S. Senator from Kentucky was a member of the Warren Commission assigned to investigate the assassination of President John F. Kennedy and determine whether there was a conspiracy. Chaired by Congressman Gerald Ford, a 33rd degree Mason, the committee (predictably) reported that alleged assassin Lee Harvey Oswald acted alone.

Later, Gerald Ford was chosen by Richard Nixon to become his vice president. This was after the then sitting vice president, Spiro Agnew, was disgraced and forced out of office. Then, when Nixon himself was disgraced due to the Watergate affair, Ford assumed the presidency. He was the first unelected president of the United States.

Charles S. Whitehouse (class of '47). Former diplomat to South Africa.

Jonathan Bingham (class of '36). Congressman from New York and a CFR member.

John H. Chafee (class of '44). U.S. Senator from Rhode Island. In June, 1992, within days of his attending a meeting of the Bilderbergers Group in Europe, Senator Chaffee introduced legislation in the U.S. Senate which, if passed, would require every U.S. citizen to immediately turn in their handguns.

Henry Stimson. President Herbert Hoover's Secretary of State. In the 1920's, Stimson made sure that the communist regime in the Soviet Union was aided with money from Marxist Armand Hammer, bonesman Averell Harriman, and other corporate benefactors, many of whom were bonesmen.

Robert A. Lovett. President Harry S. Truman's Secretary of Defense.

John Hersey. Pulitzer Prize-winning book author.

ELEVEN

The Skull & Bones "Good Old Boys" Club—Not Just A Fraternity

The "Good Old Boys" Club of the Skull & Bones alumni have infiltrated every aspect of society. In four areas in particular, their influence is keenly felt—American foreign policy, Wall Street and money, education, and religion. An examination of the "Good Old Boys" network in these four arenas of power should, therefore, be an illuminating experience.

The Skull & Bones has an iron grip on American foreign policy. Its patriarchs have been able to gain impressive positions of influence in the two key Brotherhood groups that dictate U.S. foreign policy objectives: the *Trilateral Commission (TLC)* and the *Council on Foreign Relations (CFR)*. From these positions of advantage, they have been able to grab for themselves high-level positions in Congress, the White House, and the foreign service. They have also been active in places of leadership for the liberal foundations—Ford, Rockefeller, Carnegie, Russell Sage, etc.—which consistently support the aims of the Brotherhood.

Skull & Bones and the Council on Foreign Relations

The bonesmen from the Tomb have especially been adept in controlling the *Council on Foreign Relations*. It is well-known in the Washington D.C. political community that the CFR provides the bulk of executives and politicians for the federal government. Without the CFR stamp of approval, a political candidate, ambassador hopeful, or cabinet post nominee has little chance of selection, appointment, or confirmation.

This power should be kept in mind when we observe that the President of the CFR elite is a Skull & Bones man, Winston Lord (class of '59), of the aristocratic Lord family dynasty. Winston Lord is also on the steering committee of the Bilderbergers and was appointed by President Ronald Reagan as U.S. Ambassador to Red China.

The China connection is important. The Brotherhood has long had its greedy, green eyes on this plum of Asia. Its members get a little giddy and weak in the knees when they daydream of a market of a billion people for their products and when they consider the untapped natural resources of the vast wilderness land areas of China, Tibet, and Mongolia.

With dollar signs in their eyes, the Brotherhood first had President Nixon send Rockefeller associate and CFR/TLC man Henry Kissinger to Red China in the 1970's on a mission to open up diplomatic, financial, and trade relations. He was followed-up by bonesman George Bush, whom President Nixon made a special envoy to Peking. Then, bonesman Winston Lord was chosen for this same, important post.

Columnist William F. Buckley is on the CFR's membership rolls. Buckley, who, as we have seen, is a Skull & Bones alumni, has also been honored as a participant in the secretive Bilderbergers Group.

Two other bonesmen high up in the CFR pecking order are H. J. Heinz (class of '31), who's also president of the

American Friends of Bilderberg, Inc.; and William P. Bundy (class of '39). Bundy is editor of the CFR journal, *Foreign Affairs*.

George Bush was himself a CFR and TLC member until 1980 (his father, Prescott Sheldon Bush, was a co-founder of the CFR). He supposedly resigned from both the CFR and TLC in 1980 during the heat of the campaign for the Republican Party nomination for President, after a concerned group of Americans ran a full-page ad in a Florida newspaper exposing Bush's membership in these two firmly anti-American, pro-New World Order organizations. His resignation was due to political expediency.

But financial magnate and Bilderberger overseer David Rockefeller, in a recent interview, commented that George Bush has kept up his intimate relationship with his Trilateral/CFR buddies. Moreover, Rockefeller revealed that President George Bush continues to maintain an "open door" at the White House for CFR and Trilateral Commission members:

> He (George Bush) has since spoken to the Council and the Trilateral and has been fully supportive of their activities. Even though he has resigned, he hasn't walked away from them.[8]

The Trilateral Commission Link

The *Trilateral Commission* is a very popular stomping ground for bonesmen. J. Richardson Dilworth (Skull & Bones, class of '38) is not only a trilateralist but as president of Rockefeller Family Associates, he manages the day-to-day operations of the vast Rockefeller financial empire. Dilworth operates out of Room 3600 of the famed Rockefeller Plaza building in New York City. As I've mentioned, Dilworth's wealthy boss, David Rockefeller, *founded* the Trilateral Commission.

By holding key positions inside the influential CFR and TLC organizations the men of the Skull & Bones are well-positioned to push forward their New World Order invention. This, plus the Order's current lock on the White House, gives the Brotherhood all the authority it needs to carry out sweeping changes in the international system of governance.

Skull & Bones and Wall Street

The Order's influence in the top ranks of U.S. government is extended into the banking and money community. Bonesmen now hold the purse strings in key positions on Wall Street and have done so for decades. Examples include the investment firm of *Brown Brothers Harriman*, which has an astonishing nine members on the board who are alumni of Skull & Bones; also there's *Salomon Brothers*, whose managing director is Tristan Brooks (class of '62); *Lehman Brothers, Kuhn, Loeb* whose managing director is Stephen Schwarzman (class of '69); *Dillon Read*, whose vice president is Dino Pianzio (class of '50); and *Morgan Stanley & Company*, whose managing director is Vance Van Dine (class of '61).

The Senior Bush and the Financing of Communist Tyranny

Prescott Sheldon Bush (Skull & Bones, class of '17), father of President George Bush (class of '47), was a partner in the Wall Street firm of Brown Brothers Harriman for 40 years. It was Brown Brothers Harriman that helped to finance—incredible though it may seem—the 1917 communist revolution in Moscow and the rise of Hitler and Nazism, through money made possible by it and the affiliated Guaranty Trust Company. For full documentation I refer you to the outstanding books by Dr. Antony Sutton, *How the Order*

Creates Revolution and *America's Secret Establishment.* Sutton especially unmasks the financial shenanigans of bonesman W. Averell Harriman and shows how an associate of Harriman's, Max May of the American Bank Guaranty Trust, actually became the First Vice President, in charge of foreign operations, of Soviet Russia's first commercial bank, Ruskombank.

Meanwhile, Averell Harriman, his brother Roland, and bones brother Knight Wooley (all alumni from Prescott Sheldon Bush's Yale class of '17) used America's Union Bank to keep Adolf Hitler and his Nazi collaborators well greased with money.

W. Averell Harriman, now deceased, was considered the elder statesman of the Democrat Party. During his lifetime a string of Democrat presidents appointed him to numerous prestigious posts, even in spite of (or perhaps *because* of!) Harriman's shady financial dealings with European dictators. In 1941 he was made U.S. Ambassador to the Soviet Union; in 1946, he became our Ambassador to Great Britain. Later that year, he was brought back to the continental United States to serve as Secretary of Commerce by his good friend and fellow 33rd degree Mason, President Franklin D. Roosevelt. In 1955, his money bought Harriman the election and he became governor of the State of New York.

In 1983, "good old Averell" Harriman went to the Kremlin in Moscow to visit Yuri Andropov, the former KGB chief who was by then the Soviet communist party boss. Could it be that it was Harriman, representing the hierarchy of the Secret Brotherhood, who gave the order to Andropov to set in motion the end of communism? We do know that the ailing Andropov, very soon after Harriman's visit, brought Mikhail Gorbachev into high office and groomed Gorby to be his successor.[9]

In 1985, following Andropov's death, Gorbachev assumed his mentor's top party and government posts. Immediately came *Perestroika* and *Glasnost* and the wrenching changes in the Soviet Empire that spelled the end of communism and the opening of Russia and the republics to capitalist trade and influence.

Other Wall Streeters and money men who wear the Skull & Bones pin include C.E. Lord, brother of CFR Chairman Winston Lord and formerly the U.S. Comptroller of the Currency and Vice Chairman of the U.S. Export-Import Bank; and Richard T. Ely, who became the first head of the American Economic Association.

Education for the New World Order

Almost from its inception the Order of Skull & Bones has exerted an almost unbelievable degree of influence on the American educational process. One bonesman, Daniel Coit Gilman (class of 1849) not only served as the first president of two universities in succession—the University of California and Johns Hopkins University—but he also participated in the founding of *four* major foundations known to be linked with the goals of the Secret Brotherhood: the Peabody, Russell Sage, Carnegie, and Slater Foundations.

Although the Skull & Bones was founded at Yale in 1832, it was Daniel Coit Gilman who teamed up with General William H. Russell to officially incorporate the Order as a legal entity in 1856 under the name, "The Russell Trust Association." Again we see the *prima facie* evidence that the 15 students chosen to be tapped each year at Yale for the Order are *not* in charge of the organization. It is the alumni who are the masters of the Skull & Bones establishment worldwide.

Every young man at Yale who is initiated into this devilish society knows full well that his future welfare depends entirely on the handful of much older men who run the Russell Trust Association. The new initiate recognizes that he has two choices: either he can prosper beyond his wildest dreams—or he can become a run-of-the-mill has been. It's up to the Patriarchs, the old men and alumni who minutely oversee and evaluate each initiate's progress throughout his lifetime and who provide rewards or punishments accordingly.

Andrew Dickson White, who was initiated into the Order in 1853, was the first president of a prestigious educational institution, Cornell University, and he was also appointed the first president of the American Historical Society. The rewriting and deceitful misinterpretation of American and world history is one of the main methods used to manipulate and shape public opinion. The establishment of the American Historical Society was no doubt an unprecedented step in instituting this diabolical plan to rewrite the past.

A third bonesman initiate who went on to influence the American educational process was Timothy Dwight (class of 1849). Dwight first became a professor of Yale Divinity School then was selected to serve as the 12th president of Yale University. Dwight, White, and Gilman were sent by the Order to Germany to study at the University of Berlin. It is reasonable to assume that in Berlin they developed a close working relationship with German secret societies that were the equivalent of Yale's Skull & Bones.

General William H. Russell, founder of the Yale Order, was himself reportedly initiated into a German secret society. He promptly returned to New Haven, Connecticut and set to work putting things together for an American Freemason version, which was how the Skull & Bones got started.

Skull & Bones and the Religious Establishment

Religious heresy seems to be a staple of the alumni of Skull & Bones. From the very beginning, the Order's membership was recruited almost solely from the liberal wing of the Episcopal Church and from the New Age-oriented Unitarian Church (now called Unitarian-Universalist). William H. Taft (bonesman class of 1878), who went on to become President of the United States, was at one time the president of the Unitarian Church Association.

The World Council of Churches (WCC) and the National Council of Churches (NCC), both of which are ultraliberal, pro-Marxist, and pro-Eastern religions, were each founded with money from the Secret Brotherhood. John D. Rockefeller even donated the triangle-shaped building that now houses the NCC. An affiliated arm of the WCC, called the American Friends of the World Council of Churches, is headquartered at the liberal Riverside Church at 475 Riverside Drive, New York City, where Vietnam war resister Rev. William Sloane Coffin (Skull & Bones class of '49) pastored.[10]

Another apostate religious organization with close ties to the Skull & Bones is the Union Theological Seminary. Founded in 1835, this seminary has long been a safe harbor and breeding ground for Marxist activists and supposed "Christian" professors who teach that all paths and all religions are the same, and that Christianity is not unique.

When, as president, George Bush became the first resident of the White House to officially invite such groups as the Gay and Lesbian Task Force to "Hate Crime" bill signings, he was thus following in the grand old tradition of his fellow bonesmen. The same is true for George Bush's appointment and support of ultraliberal, pro-pornography spokesman John Frohnmayer to head the National Endowment for the Arts. (Frohnmayer was finally forced to resign in 1992 after years of protest by conservative Christian groups.)

The Brotherhood of Death

We have seen the immense influence of the Skull & Bones in every area of American society. But is this secretive group an integrated part of a *network* of organizations and secret societies founded and controlled from above by a concealed and even more secretive *higher authority*? Fritz

Springmeier, an Oregon researcher who has spent years unraveling the connections between secret societies and internationalist groups, has discovered important links.

In his thoroughly documented book, *Be Wise As Serpents*, Springmeier states conclusively that not only is there close and cohesive coordination between these groups, but they all appear to be supervised by the same elite cabal of overseers. Of the Skull & Bones he ominously writes:

> This group . . . is part of the larger "Brotherhood of Death." Exactly 15 members are added each year . . . There are about 600 members currently. Some members, perhaps exceptions, have been initiated away from Yale. Most are descended from early Puritan families and are tied to the Unitarian/Universalist (church) movement. These older Skull & Bones families have formed blood alliances with wealthy families such as the Rockefellers.[11]

TWELVE

They Worship a God Whose Name They Conceal

Many experts who have studied the political and economic aspects of the World Conspiracy are, unfortunately, totally oblivious to its *spiritual* aspect.

It is important that we recognize the true spiritual nature of the illuminist religion, for only then can we understand the underpinnings for many of the Secret Brotherhood's most closely guarded hidden teachings.

Adam Weishaupt, when he founded the Illuminati in 1776, expressed surprise that he should become founder of a new religion. His was an atheistic and humanistic goal—to destroy the authority of monarchies and the church and thereby to raise his own small clique of men to leadership and riches in their place. The objective was the establishment of a *new, secular order (Novus Ordo Seclorum)*.[1]

Weishaupt's motive was at first a crude and material one; but when he found that his conspiracy had garnered such tremendous support among those who professed a paganistic *spiritual creed* radically divergent from traditional Christianity—and when he discovered that these men could be inspired to fanatically support the Illuminati conspiracy *only* if their arcane (Masonic) religion could find expression, he, Weishaupt, quickly rethought his plan and mission.

He decided that the Masonic philosophy and religion so warmly embraced by his co-conspirators was, in fact, an ideal vehicle to inspire their cooperation and even their fanatical devotion to world revolution. Indeed, he was surprised to discover that their religion, the keystone of which was the enthronement of an elite as gods on earth, was remarkably compatible with his own atheistic tendencies.

Worship of a "God" of Forces

What therefore became entrenched as the essential doctrine of the illuminist spirituality and religion was an overwhelming belief in a "god of forces." This god of forces is impersonal, yet possesses unlimited supernatural powers that can be accessed by illumined men—the gnostics—those who "know" the magical formulae. Such formulae include the powerful use of ritual, symbols, and allegory, all wrapped together with an acceptance of ancient pagan deities and mystery teachings.

At the core of illuminist belief was and is the unshakable conviction that "God," the "Great Architect of the Universe," has established a class and race system which can best be described as the "natural order," or simply "nature." Nature (i.e. *God*), the illuminists teach, dictates that the world be organized into different classes of men.

Similar to the Hindu caste system and Hitler's Aryan race theory (both of which, like the Illuminati religion, are based on ancient Masonic mythologies), this teaching includes the theory that certain men are, by divine prescription, superior to others. Eventually, the doctrine goes, as earth continues its cycles, all men will be found to be equal, to be brothers. But until that glorious day, some men are simply "better" than others—more enlightened, more noble, and more fit to rule.

What is it that marks and distinguishes the men who comprise the superior class of nobility? These men, illuminist doctrine holds, are those who are endowed with something called "Reason." The man whose sole god is Reason has himself become a superman, a type of deity. The rites and initiation process of the Illuminati are all designed to develop this new type of man imbued with Reason. Thus, Adam Weishaupt revealed that in his secret society:

> Reason will be the only code of man. This is one of our greatest secrets. When at last Reason becomes the religion of man, then will the problem be solved.[2]

The Goddess of Reason

It was because of this warped and gnostic belief in divine Reason as the sublime guide for man's own spiritual and moral perfection that the butchers of the French Revolution paraded through the streets their bare-breasted women declared to be exemplars of the "Goddess of Reason." This was the ultimate in synthesis—the combining of the notion of man's reason being enthroned as deity with the ultimate symbol of ancient paganism: the Goddess.

Pictures and paintings of this "Goddess of Reason" proliferated throughout Europe and the United States in the 18th and 19th centuries. During the American Revolutionary War, the Goddess was especially celebrated as a symbol. She became the protectress of the rebellion, Lady Liberty, the One who smashes the tyrants and breaks the chains of bondage. It is she, it was proposed, who gives coequal, enlightened man freedom and liberty.

Today, statues of this Illuminist Goddess of Reason are found throughout the U.S.A.; one stands astride the U.S. Capitol building in Washington, D.C. Another is atop the dome of the Capitol building in Austin, Texas. Her statue has been erected in town squares and city parks. But the most fantastic idol of the Goddess of Reason, the most majestic statue of the pagan lady who bears the torch of light, who illuminates, uplifts, and frees mankind, is found in New York's harbor.

Towering above the shimmering but polluted waters, she holds in her outreached arm and hand a torch of fire and light. A gift of the Masonic Order, the modern inheritors of the Illuminati heritage, the Statue of Liberty was sculptured by Frederic Bartholdi, a member of the Masonic Lodge of Alsace-Lorraine in Paris, France.[3] The statue is an esoteric idol of great significance to the secret societies plotting the New World Order.

The occultic Statue of Liberty is unquestionably one of the greatest hoaxes ever perpetuated on mankind. Her very existence, especially in light of the adoration and veneration she is accorded by Americans, is remarkable. Indeed, she is worshipped as a symbol everywhere. In China, the student demonstrators in Tiananmen Square in Peking paraded about with a crude replica of the Statue of Liberty. In Paris, art books extolling her are brisk sellers.

The plan of the Secret Brotherhood has come a long way when men have such graphic evidence of conspiracy as this immense statue in front of their very noses, but have little or no idea of its true purpose and meaning.

Today's environmental movement reflects this adoration of the Goddess of Reason. Ecological devotees call her by her pagan name "Gaia," after the deity of the ancient Greeks. "We must protect and love Gaia, our mother earth," some preach, "she is alive!" No wonder the masters of the Secret Brotherhood have latched on to the environmental movement as a magical pathway to escalating the emergence of their New Age Kingdom on planet Earth.

The Five Central Beliefs of the Illuminized Brotherhood

Remember, then, these five keys to understanding the spiritual teachings and religion of the men of the Secret Brotherhood:

1) They practice a pagan religion which acknowledges and venerates the ancient sun god; yet they claim that *all gods are the same* and that their ritualistic worship of ancient deities is only symbolic. They further contend that the deity reflected in the illuminist symbol of the All Seeing Eye (on our U.S. $1 bill) atop the unfinished pyramid represents this universalist view of "God."

2) While Lucifer, the "light bearer," is in reality their ultimate deity, most do not directly profess him as Lord. Indeed, most do not even believe in the existence of Lucifer, or in Satan or a personal devil. Instead, they express belief in an evil "principle," a dark and shadowy, but impersonal evil "force" which is but the flip side of good, the opposite of the light.

This is the hidden esoteric (inner) meaning of the double-headed eagle of 33rd degree Masonry and the Illuminati. It represents the doctrine that good and evil coexist as divine principles and are represented by symbols. It is these two forces, the two opposing heads of the eagle, which are both manifestations of the same ultimate reality. Together they shape and mold the individual.

3) The illumined person is considered one who is able to wield the spiritual energies of *both* sides of reality—the good and the evil, light and darkness. Such a man becomes superman. He becomes his own deity, a master magician, a prince among princes, and a king over many.

4) God, being akin to a "force field" or divine principle, is to be worshipped through two means: ritual and service.

> *Ritual* involves the conjuration of symbolic magic and the accessing of the neutral (two-headed—dark and light) powers of the universe. Thus, the adoration of pagan deities during temple ceremonies and initiation rites should not be taken as literal worship but as allegorical

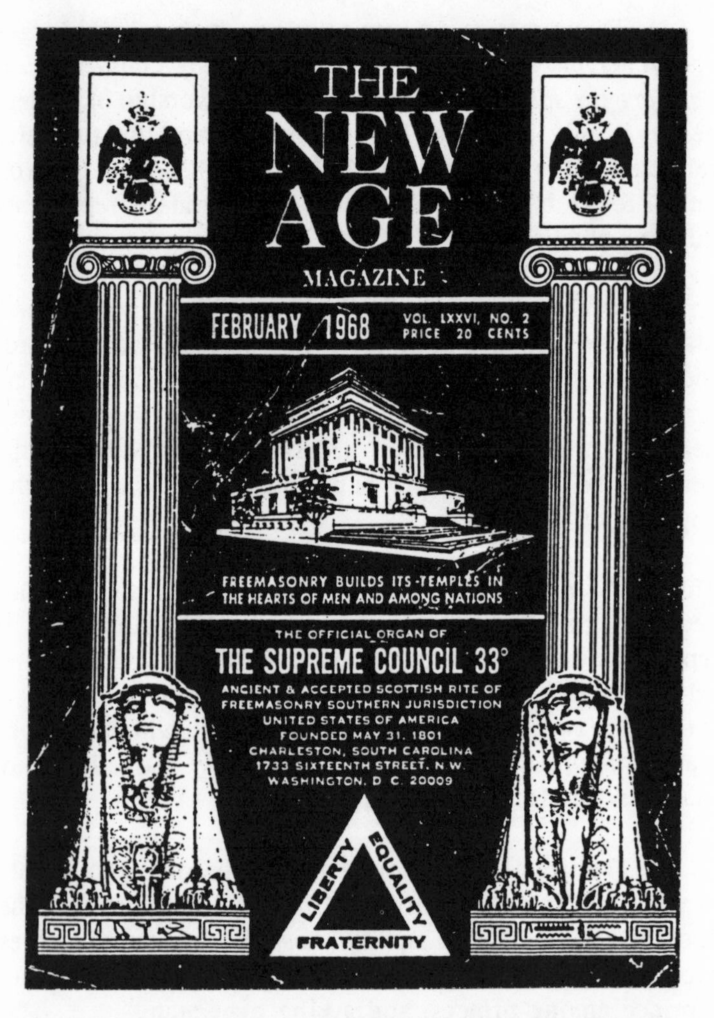

The cover of this 1968 magazine, The New Age, published by the Scottish Rite, the world's largest Freemasonry group, clearly demonstrates its occultic nature. First, note the two double-headed eagles, each crowned. The Egyptian statue at bottom left represents the male principle (Father God "Osiris") and the one at right the feminine principle (Mother Goddess "Isis"). The slogan in the triangle, "Liberty, Equality, Fraternity," was the rallying cry of the Masonic executioners of the French Revolution who sent five million people to the guillotine.

worship of the neutral powers of the universe reposited *within illumined man.*

Service is defined as (a) obedience to one's enlightened Masters; (b) active aid and help to brothers and initiates—fellow illumined ones; and (c) good works and philanthropy to the unenlightened world at large.

5) Since the Illuminati have no special regard for or devotion to any specific deity, it stands to reason that Christianity—or any other organized religion—holds no special merit either. Therefore, the Secret Brotherhood favors no organized religion, but instead recognizes all as coequal. This is why, on the altars of Freemasonry, *either* the Bible of Christianity, the Koran of Islam, or the Bhagavad Gita of the Hindus may be displayed in the place of honor.

This universalist, all-encompassing view of deity means that the initiate of the Secret Brotherhood is welcome to join and participate in any religion he chooses. *But what he cannot do is claim exclusivity or uniqueness for that religion.*

The double-headed eagle of Freemasonry.

That would be the ultimate heresy for tolerant, universalist illumined man.

Thus, a brother of the Order can freely profess Christianity and Christ; he can talk a good game of "Christianity" and show all outward respect and fervent adherence to the God of the Bible. *But in fact, he is not worshipping the same Christ and God as the true Christian, nor does he hold the Bible in the same high, exalted regard.*

Regardless of the outward show of devotion, the Jesus of the illumined is "another Jesus" (see II Corinthians 11:4), and the gospel of the illuminated man is "another gospel." The apostle Paul called it an *"accursed gospel"* (see Galatians 1) and declared that those who believe in it are "bewitched."

A Call to Anarchy

The universalist nature of the Illuminist religion is actually a call to anarchy. Since there are no moral absolutes and no real definition of "spiritual purity," then, in the illuminist view, man is left to his own devices, to do as he wills. Aleister Crowley, the late, infamous British satanist who pridefully called himself "The Beast, 666," stated that the true satanist had only one cardinal commandment which he must obey: "Do as thou wilt shall be the whole of the law!"

Robert Anton Wilson, an authoritative writer of occultism and student of the occult conspiracy, wrote a fascinating novel some years ago called *Masks of the Illuminati*. In that book, Wilson weaved a marvelous tale of the origins, history, and current existence of the conspiratorial elite. Though the book purports to be fiction, there is little doubt that it contains much insight and many hard facts about the Secret Brotherhood.[4]

In one key passage, Wilson suggests that all members of a secret occult society known as the Ordo Templi Orientis—the Order of Oriental Templars—must sign three copies of a very peculiar document. The document is supposedly a concise summary of the group's religious and social creeds. It is handed by a man named "Jones" to "Sir John," the main character in Wilson's *Masks of the Illuminati*, whose mind is sent reeling by what he reads:

> There is no God but Man.
> Man has the right to live by his own law.
> Man has the right to live in the way that he wills to do.
> Man has the right to dress as he wills to do.
> Man has the right to dwell where he wills to dwell.
> Man has the right to move as he will on the face of the earth.
> Man has the right to eat what he will.
> Man has the right to drink what he will.
> Man has the right to think what he will.
> Man has the right to speak as he will.
> Man has the right to write as he will.
> Man has the right to mold as he will.
> Man has the right to carve as he will.
> Man has the right to work as he will.
> Man has the right to rest as he will.
> Man has the right to love as he will, where, when, and whom he will.
> Man has the right to kill those who would thwart these rights.
>
> "But this is anarchy!" Sir John exclaimed.
>
> "Exactly," Jones said. "It is a declaration of war against everything we know as Christian civilization."[5]

The characters portrayed in *Masks of the Illuminati* agreed on the insidious nature of the above declaration. Indeed, this does amount to anarchy, they determined, and it is extremely insidious, although it incorporates a supposed "philosophy of liberty:"

> "Look again at the first line," Jones said. "That is the kernel of the blasphemy: There is no God but man. Do you see how that could lead weak-minded atheists to a kind of humanistic mysticism, and naive mystics to

> atheism, while drawing both into a worldwide plot against both civil government and organized religion? And can you see how this ultra-individualism could even attract some really good minds and noble hearts . . . ?"[6]

Tearing Off the Masks of the Illuminati

Whereas Robert Anton Wilson cloaked the real-life existence of the Illuminati within the context of a novel, which no doubt allowed him a certain maneuverability and greatly-increased literary license, Lady Queensborough (Edith Starr Miller) in 1933 published a book exposing the masks of the Illuminati which was not a novel. Her book, *Occult Theocrasy*, is a literal encyclopedia of Illuminati-related organizations and Masonic groups. Lady Queensborough suggested that her book's value lay in the fact that it unmasks "the means and methods used by a secret world . . . to penetrate, dominate and destroy modern civilization and especially organized religion."[7]

The book is a virtual cornucopia of information about occult secret societies. On pages 510-511 we find some especially interesting material. There reprinted are two letters exchanged between two of the most honored members of English Grand Lodge Freemasonry around the turn of this century, a British subject, William Wynn Westcott and a German, Theodore Reuss.

Apparently, these two esteemed gentlemen were busily laboring at the time to further the Great Work of the Illuminati, which they represented. Their letters contained references to the Illuminati, as well as to Masonry and to the Rosicrucians and "Societas Rosicruciana." One can also observe in their letters references to the "High Council."

As we moved forward into the 20th century we find that there were only a few great men who were able to discern the outlines of the terrible global conspiracy that has confronted honest peoples everywhere for so long. One such man was Sir Winston Churchill. Before Churchill assumed the herculean task of serving as Prime Minister of Great Britain during the dark days of World War II and leading his people on to victory, he wrote, in the February 8, 1920 *London Illustrated Sunday Herald:*

> From the days of Spartacus Weishaupt (code name for Illuminati founder Adam Weishaupt) to those of Karl Marx, to those of Trotsky, Bela Kuhn, Rose Luxembourg, and Emma Goldman, this world-wide conspiracy has been steadily growing. This conspiracy has played a definitely recognizable role in the tragedy of the French Revolution. It has been the mainspring of every subversive movement during the 19th century; and now at last, this band of extraordinary personalities from the underworld of the great cities of Europe and America have gripped the Russian people by the hair of their heads and have become practically undisputed masters of that enormous empire.

The Hidden Hand of the Brotherhood

When Churchill wrote these intriguing words, he was well aware that only three years earlier, the Secret Brotherhood, through its network of Masonic societies, had achieved the unthinkable. They had instigated a bloody revolution in Soviet Russia, taken the Czar and the members of the royal family captive, and grabbed hold of that entire vast empire. The Brotherhood had immediately installed Kerensky as their puppet and set up a provisional "democratic" government.

However, Kerensky was soon ousted by the Bolsheviks (communists) led by Vladimir Lenin, a man who was violently opposed to the leadership of the Secret Brotherhood as it was then constituted. Lenin was in fact sent into Russia from exile by the German general staff, at the urging of secret society factions in Germany. The German secret societies were well aware that they had been upstaged in Russia by a rival Masonic group. Lenin was their revenge, and his plot worked magnificently, Kerensky was overthrown and the communists under Lenin seized power in 1917.

It is a fascinating fact that beginning in the mid-1970's and on into the 1980's and 1990's, Soviet leaders Andropov (now deceased—Gorbachev's mentor and predecessor), Gorbachev, and a small group of conspirators were able to undo everything that Lenin and his bloody successor, Josef Stalin, had done and hand over the rambling Soviet empire to the illuminized leadership of the Secret Brotherhood.

Though the victory of Lenin and his Bolsheviks in Russia caused the Brotherhood to suffer a temporary setback in the 1920's, the Brotherhood sought to mend bridges and regain a stronghold in Russia by financing Soviet industry and construction. Then in 1932-33 a new effort was launched to further the objectives of the world revolution. Franklin Roosevelt, a 33rd degree Mason, had taken office in Washington, D.C. and was joined there by his vice-president, Henry Wallace, also a high-level Mason. These two "blood brothers" were able to do significant damage to the true cause of democracy and Christianity while implementing a number of objectives on behalf of the Brotherhood.

One of the more significant achievements of Roosevelt and Wallace was a revolutionary change in design of the U.S. one-dollar bill. The all-seeing eye of Horus, the great Egyptian sun god, and the unfinished pyramid of the Illuminati were printed for the first time on the dollar bill beginning in 1933. The Latin inscription *Novus Ordo Seclorum*, or *New Secular World Order*, was inscribed on the one dollar currency note directly under the pyramid.[8]

Wallace, a New Age mystic and a follower of Nicholas Roerich, a major occultist of that era, was ecstatic with this because he realized that, now, millions of Americans and indeed, hundreds of millions of people throughout the world were going to be conditioned day-in and day-out by an occultic symbol that, Wallace believed, had powerful magical powers and properties.[9]

The Supermen go Public

Encouraged by successes in the United States and elsewhere in the early 1930's, the Brotherhood for the first time decided to go public in a very limited way. It was determined that the world was ready to be let in on what had up until that time been a very closely guarded secret—that there actually exists a small band of superior, more racially and spiritually developed supermen. It was however, deemed advisable to make the public aware of only the vaguest outlines of the group. The Brotherhood realized that the public was not psychologically prepared and conditioned for the whole sordid truth to come out all at once.

Thus, in 1957, Lucis Trust and World Goodwill founder Alice Bailey published her book *The Externalization of The Hierarchy*, in which she revealed that there exists a secretive group of supermen who are known as the "New Group of World Servers." The year 1934, wrote Bailey, began the monumental task of "the organizing of the men and women" and the "group work of a New Order." In her book, Bailey also used such coded, illuminist terms as "the work of the Brotherhood" and "the Forces of Light." She also used that cryptic phrase which would, in the late 1980's, become a famous cornerstone of President George Bush's supposedly more kind and gentle policies, "Points of Light."[10]

Bailey further revealed that civilization was on the threshold of going through a great period of what she called "spoliation," or ruin and spoil. It is interesting that she would note this because, at that time, Hitler and his Nazi henchmen had not yet kicked-off the first bloody battles of World War II. That was to begin in earnest in 1939 when the Russian storm troopers invaded the territory of Poland. Perhaps Bailey and her brothers in the New Order had some advance information, for she reported that out of "the spoliation of all existing culture and civilization, the New World Order must be built."[11]

The Plan of the Illuminati: An Enduring Dream

To the average Mason, and especially the lower level initiates of the first, second, and third degrees, the evidence that Freemasonry has long been at the forefront in the drive toward world government and that it is ruled by a handful of elitists may be hard to believe. If Masons would, however, read their own literature—most do not—they would be able to discover the amazing plan of the Illuminati right under their noses. This plan, though written in esoteric language, is not extremely well hidden nor is it impossibly disguised. In fact, the design for world revolution has in our lifetime become virtually an "Open Conspiracy."

All that the deceived Masons would have to do, for example, is study the writings of the late Manly P. Hall, a 33rd degree Mason who has been long recognized as one of the greatest philosophers of speculative Masonry of all times. Hall wrote:

> There exists in the world today, and has existed for thousands of years, a body of enlightened humans united in what might be termed, an Order of the Quest. It is composed of those whose intellectual and spiritual perceptions have revealed to them that civilization has a secret Destiny—secret, I say, because this high purpose is not realized by the many; the great masses of people still live along without any knowledge whatsoever that they are part of a Universal Motion.[12]

The quest for a World Order overseen by enlightened god-men is not new, reveals Hall, but has been an enduring dream of the secret societies for centuries. This was touched upon by Hall in his book *The Secret Destiny of America*, in which he discusses the Masonic and Illuminist history of man. This is a history that you will not find described in textbooks, nor is it taught in our public schools and universities. But the men of the secret societies and the Brotherhood are convinced of its authenticity. Hall summarizes this new, mystical history of man when he writes:

> Wise Men, the ancients believe, were a separate race, and to be born into this race it was necessary to develop the mind to a state of enlightened intelligence . . . It is this larger and coming race that will someday inherit the earth . . . the Golden Age will come again.[13]

Manly P. Hall goes on to discuss the evolution of the occult plan. He reveals that the goal is the restoration of a New World to be ruled by men of "enlightened intelligence." He shares with us, for example, concepts of the ideal world-state led by superior men as developed by Englishman Francis Bacon in his novel, *The New Atlantis*, as well as Plato's *Utopia.*

Hall disclosed that the ultimate objective is not only to establish a system in which the illumined rule over a perfect society, the plan also calls for a King (though today we might call him President or Prime Minister of Earth, or perhaps Secretary-General of the United Nations). Here is how Manly P. Hall describes the coming great statesman and leader who is to someday preside over the affairs of all men on earth:

> This king was descended of a divine race; that is, he belonged to the Order of the Illumined; for those who come to a state of wisdom then belong to a family of heroes—perfected human beings.[14]

Whether it's Francis Bacon's *New Atlantis*, Plato's *Utopia*, Marx's communist society with its "new man," or George Bush's New World Order, the threads of the conspiracy remain firm and intact. The world is to edge forward, gradually but surely, toward a Golden Age. When that sun-lit day arrives, the mass of people, dull and unenlightened, will have the satisfaction and benefit of being dictated to and reigned over by an illumined Order of perfected human beings. These are the heroes, the Great Ones, the Illuminati. They are the *Secret Brotherhood.*

The Occult Hierarchy

Foster Bailey, a 33rd degree Mason who authored *The Spirit of Masonry*, which details the New Age occult foundations of Freemasonry, says that behind the flesh and blood, cosmically advanced human beings who have organized themselves as the New Group of World Servers, there exists an even greater group. It is, he says, made up of those who are members of an occult Hierarchy.[15] In a lecture given in London in 1954 entitled *Changing Esoteric Values*, Bailey described the way this occult hierarchy functions. From what he tells us, the occult hierarchy oversees an astute force of international financiers, businessmen and educators who are unparalleled in their organizational and management acumen:

> The occult Hierarchy of the planet functions in a way which is a bit analogous to the way any great international, powerful corporation functions in the world today . . . If an international business concern decides to undertake expansion and investment in a new part of the world, they have to have capital, they have to have the personnel, they have to study the problems involved, they have to lay their plan so that an investment of so many millions will in a certain number of years produce sufficient profits to justify it.
>
> They (the occult Hierarchy) are under the necessity of adjusting their developments to the existing government whatever it may be, good or bad, and that part of the world in which they're proposing to operate. They study the people and the language as well as sources of raw material, availability and quality of labor and transport problems. They send out scouts and they test the reactions to their plans. Finally, when they are ready, they move forward. The Hierarchy functions like that.[16]

Foster Bailey is also a high-ranking official with the Lucis Trust and his publications are published by their press.

One such publication, *Running God's Plan*, gives us an inside look at what will happen to those of us who rebel against the coming New World Order and its society of illumined men in positions of authority. He intimates that those who are unable to accept the inevitable changes occurring in society will become "irreconcilable outcasts."[17] The Aquarian civilization will come into being, and those who are the doubters, skeptics, and resisters will be dealt with.

The Lucis Trust book, *From Bethlehem to Calvary*, also criticizes those who would impede the progress of the New Order. In that book we find that the occult Hierarchy and the Illuminati are divine beings. The illumined one, the book tells us, has experienced "the new birth" and has become "an illumined light bearer and one who can light the way for others." Such a person is said to have experienced the same initiations as did Jesus Christ. He has been symbolically crucified and has become purified in the fires. The person is thus ready to lead the way toward world renewal and restoration. He has become a full member of the Illuminati:

> The Illuminati have ever led the race forward; the knowers, mystics and saints have ever revealed to us the height of racial and individual possibilities.[18]

THIRTEEN

The Science of Mind Control

The story of how an international cartel of super-rich conspirators have been able to induce a form of delusion and hallucination into the minds of men on a mass scale is almost too fantastic to believe. Lt. Col. Archibald E. Roberts, U.S. Army (retired), director of the Committee to Restore the Constitution, is one man who is aware of how the seeds of a new way of thinking have already been implanted secretly into the minds of mass men.

Roberts, whose organization puts out a monthly bulletin exposing the current threat to our freedom posed by the conspiracy, calls the advanced techniques of mind control employed by the Brotherhood, "The Most Secret Science." Testifying before a special joint committee of the Wisconsin State Legislature, Lt. Col. Roberts stated:

> The most secret knowledge, a science which outdates history, is the science of control over people, governments and civilizations. The foundation of this ultimate discipline is the control of wealth.

> Through the control of wealth comes the control of public information and the necessities of life.
>
> Through the control of news media comes fault control.
>
> Through the control of basic necessities comes direct control of people.[1]

"A significant portion of the American public," Roberts notes, "is yet to become aware of the Invisible Government of Monetary Power." Sadly, he observes that, "Americans still believe that they are working toward a better way of life." But, surreptitiously, "social customs and forms of administration in the United States are being carefully and gradually modified. The change from one type of culture to another is thus accomplished without arousing serious public challenge."[2]

Warning that disaster is on the immediate horizon unless more people are made aware of this time bomb in our midst, Roberts told Wisconsin's legislature: "The stark truth is that America is now passing from a constitutional republic into a totalitarian, worldwide government."[3]

Why Do the Masses Not Understand?

If we are descending into a period of darkness in the world in which totalitarian government controlled by the few elite is a reality, as Lt. Col. Archibald Roberts and the Committee to Restore the Constitution suggest, then why is it that the masses do not understand this? The answer is that it is characteristic of a decaying civilization that those most closely associated with it are unconscious of the tragedy that has befallen them.

To the vast majority of Americans and other peoples of the world, the ability to discern good from evil and what is right from what is wrong has been carefully blotted out by the new system of mind control developed by the occult conspirators.

Those at the top of the Secret Brotherhood are not just "on their way" to controlling the masses, *they already possess a firm grip on men's minds*. What William Erwin Thompson, the New Age globalist leader, has called "the planetization of the esoteric" has been going on for some time. The New Culture, which is actually a new spirituality and a new planetary religion, now holds an irresistible fascination for most people. And the mind controllers have been able to accomplish this through a system of illusion, pageantry, and brain shock.

Charles H. Fort once stated that "almost all people are hypnotics." Their beliefs, he said, are induced beliefs. "The proper authority saw to it that the proper belief should be induced, and people believed properly." One of the key beliefs of the Western world today is that acquiring money is the most important thing in a person's life. Given this warped view injected and built into peoples' minds by the image makers, the majority are convinced that those who have a great deal of money are somehow more intellectual, more attractive.

The rich are our idols. Society worships them and adores their eccentricities. As Frenchman Louie Ferdinand Celine once observed, "What does the modern public want? It wants to go down on its knees before money." Today the money men, from Donald Trump and David Rockefeller to H. Ross Perot, are the heroes of society. The masses willingly allow such men to be the puppet masters of their lives.

Greater Gods to Rule Lesser Gods

As it now stands, the Illuminati seek to spread their poisonous doctrines of unity and globalization throughout the body of mankind. Their goal is to develop a *World Mind* or *World Brain*. Their occult, psychological conditioning process, they are convinced, will change all of society and result eventually in a new and universal "cosmic consciousness" which will envelop the globe. Men everywhere, they propagandize, will be transformed into supermen. *Homo sapiens* will become an entirely new species, quite literally a race of divine gods on a divine planet.

Of course if the entire planet and every man and woman on the face of it are their own gods, there must be a small elite of *managerial deities* at the top to coordinate all the god-work that's going on. There must be a way to *manage* the billions of little gods. There must be a hierarchy of gods at the top to make sure that the great kingdom is built properly and operates according to what the "divine reality" should be. The theory put forward by the superior elitists of the Brotherhood is that man can be illuminized and enlightened, but though he may be a deity, the average common man will nevertheless be a *lesser deity*. In the great pantheon of gods and goddesses now being set up by the Secret Brotherhood, there are those who are *greater gods*, whose destiny it is to control, direct, and show the way for the *lesser deities*.

Beware the Inferior Subhuman Species

Therefore, one of the chief ways that the Secret Brotherhood has established a supreme level of control of men's minds is through the employment of *flattery*. It is an axiom that men and women love to be flattered. And to be told that they are a god-like species who are evolving toward divinity is the most dynamic form of flattery. But even though men are flattered today into believing that *they* have control over their own destinies, and that *they* need only do as *they* will, they are also being instructed that not all men and women are divine.

Regrettably, the mind controllers carefully explain, there are some people in this world who are of an inferior species. These *subhumans* are a cancerous stain on humanity. They are the ones responsible for all of the world's ills.

The subhuman species, the claim goes, is polluting our rivers and oceans, and cutting down millennia old forests with reckless abandon. The unfit ones are teaching the children of earth that they must stay bound to the old traditionalist religions such as Biblical Christianity, and even spouting the horrible philosophy that one's own nation should come first. Why, the subhuman, inferior species even believes and teaches that world government is evil!

These subhumans must be stopped, the drumbeaters maintain. They are too competitive, have accumulated negative karma, and are a roadblock to the fulfillment of the dreams of the masses. A system of worldwide control must therefore be established to insure that the inferior species of men does not diminish the Great Work being accomplished by the masses of god-people.

As Brad and Francie Steiger proclaim in their book *The Gods of Aquarius*, "Rigid and foolproof control must be established to eliminate destructive competition." If intelligence is to reign on planet earth, say the Steigers, a system must be devised to eliminate the possibility that those less genetically developed can throw a monkey wrench in the works. The problem, they contend, is to have a system that will transform all of us into "perfect citizens who will behave ideally and love and help everyone else always."

"That is the problem that must be solved. The solutions advanced to date, however, have not solved the problem," complain the Steigers. Therefore, "we must discard them all in search for a new approach."[4]

Their answer to the problems caused by all those "imperfect humans" now alive who are fouling up the system is the *Teilhardian solution*. Pierre Teilhard de Chardin was a Catholic priest in whose writings are found the seeds for the New Age philosophy being promoted by the Secret Brotherhood. That philosophy holds that man is fast evolving toward collective godhood and that the entire planet is gravitating toward what is called the Omega Point. At this stage of human development, de Chardin writes, man and the planet are becoming perfect and god-like. However, the question is what to do with those few rebels, troublemakers, and other inferior beings who are unable to adapt to the "new way of thinking" required to reach this glorious Omega Point.[5]

Toward A World Brain—"Superbrain"

The Steigers believe that man must give up some freedom in exchange for achieving self-divinity. We should listen to what they have to say because my investigation reveals that their solution is exactly what has been promoted for many decades now by the czars of the secret societies: the Secret Brotherhood. First, the Steigers write that, while they "hope for the maximum individual freedom" for mankind, unfortunately, to develop *perfect man* and *perfect world*—individual freedom must be limited. Freedom for humanity must remain "within the constraints of minimum essential inner-individual control."[6]

What does this mean? Well, it means that to overcome the roadblocks to world unity posed by the sub-divine, inferior species who refuse or are unable to go along and adapt, a great levelling must occur. *All men must be linked together into a great World Brain.* Only through a homogenization of men's minds and an interlinking of human potential everywhere can perfection be achieved:

> The only viable solution is to link the brains of all men into one giant superbrain. It is the entire species which has been developing, and it is the entire species which now must be linked into one superbeing.[7]

The linkage of the brains of all men and women into one giant superbrain will be a wonderful event, the Steiger's suggest. It will allow each person to function individually but all are to come "under the control of a single linked-species nervous system." A great by-product of this, they maintain, is that the beings, egos, and personalities of the brains that are integrated will dissolve and merge into one single being, ego and personality. This, they say, will be a great advancement for humanity: "Thus, linkage admirably ends the destructive competition between the formerly separated brains and words like 'we' and 'each other' will no longer exist; there will only be one 'I' in the universe."[8]

It is puzzling to me that such intelligent people as Brad and Francie Steiger cannot see the ominous cloud that hangs over their proposed solution. They are so intent on promoting the globalist unity gospel that they fail to detect the horrors inherent in linking all men's minds into one great superbrain. They have no concept of the repugnance of erasing the consciousness of the individual person by merging his or her individual identity into one great global all-seeing eye. The gospel of globalism has now progressed so far that a tremendous threat to personal freedom and individual liberty and rights has raised its ugly head. That ugly head reveals the traces of the behind-the-scenes work of the Secret Brotherhood.

The men of the Secret Brotherhood understand the reality of global linkage. They know that a World Brain and a unified, planetary way of thinking will allow them to establish the most elaborate and minute form of control over the affairs of men. Finally, the "Great Work" can be achieved: Earth and its peoples will be illuminized and perfected.

Through the science of mind control, the total domination of mankind by a merging of all minds is now made possible. The ability to network and merge people's thoughts, desires, hungers, longings, and even fears is finally being reached. The Omega Point is here, now. That is why a Lucis Trust publication preaches to us that a *synthesis* of human minds is a cardinal requirement for mankind today:

> We need . . . the political synthesis of a World Federation with the . . . World Brain . . . We need also a planetary way of life, a planetary ethics and a planetary way of feeling to supply the powerful drive we shall require for the great tasks that lie ahead of us.[9]

The conspirators are therefore plotting to hypnotize the masses and dissolve all differences so that a unity-conscious World Mind or Global Brain can result. The question is, who will program this World Mind? If the World Mind, made up of billions of human beings as its cells, thinks only one way—the new way—who is it that will determine what is politically correct and spiritually correct? The real crux of the problem is this: *Who* will be at the control center of the Global Brain? Alexander Solzhenitsyn once warned, if the *core* of a tree is rotten the whole tree must be uprooted and destroyed.

Mind as Computer, The Brotherhood as Its Operator

What those who would control men's minds are most desirous of is a type of *computerized universe*. Computer scientist David Foster, an authority on cybernetics, has written about this concept. In his book, *The Intelligent Universe: A Cybernetic Philosophy*, he sets forth a concept that the universe is alive and is intelligent. The universe, Foster writes, is like one, gigantic computer. It is, he adds, a computer that can be controlled by the minds of experts, men of superior minds and intellect.[10] As Foster explains:

> I put forward a new theory of the universe which suggested that the universe was something like a gigantic electric computer and that the energetical and material interactions could be regarded as a sort of cosmic data processing . . . Since man is a part of the intelligent universe then it would be reasonable to suppose that he incorporates cybernetic (computer system) design principles; and indeed, a cursory examination of the structure of the human psyche and body indicate a system basically capable of achieving steersmanship (*cybernetics* comes from the Greek word *kybernetes*, meaning "steersman").[11]

Foster further proposes that the great universal computer can be ruled over by a controller and master. All that is necessary, he contends, is for someone to learn how to "program" the universal computer. Perhaps this idea is why Timothy Leary, LSD drug guru of the 1960's, now has taken on a new project: He has formed a computer software company to promote the powers of the mind. The name for his new company: "Headware."

The God Men Who Program the Universal Computer

In essence, Foster and many new thought, New Age scientists envision the universe as a great computer to be manipulated by the superior wills of fully conscious, New Age exalted men. The Secret Brotherhood is to be the power that tells the universe what to do. These are the men who rule over earth and mankind by knowing the secrets of operating the cosmic computer keyboard.

To those who view the universe as a massive information processing computer and the Secret Brotherhood as the computer's programmer and operator, a computer program (occult mind control) becomes "God's Word." In an obvious distortion and abuse of biblical principles, David Foster states that:

> Some of the dogmas of religion may well be true and especially as to "In the beginning was the *Word*" and "Let there be *Light*." For *light* is the mechanics of information and the *Word* is the utter foundation of computer technology.[12]

Contrary to what Christians know to be true, this distorted theory alleges that superman can take control over both the *Word* and the *Light*. The conspiracy and revolutionary process shall end in "cosmic consciousness," with the expert leadership of the Secret Brotherhood crowned and sitting on the universal throne.

In the language of computers, the Global Brain, composed of the obedient, unified minds of the masses, is to be programmed through occultic magic to comply with the whims and demands of the hidden elite. Malcontents will be seen as similar to a *computer virus*. Programming experts will be called out on a mission to find the computer viruses and destroy them to preserve the global computer program. Only the docile, harmless, cooperative person will be allowed to live and exist in the new Global Community.

The computer model provides sterling advantages to the totalitarian dictatorship that is now shaping up. It puts in the hands of these super-rich megalomaniacs marvelous powers never before available to the Stalins, Pol Pots, Genghis Khans, Neros and Caligulas of history.

After all, if men can, through magic and manipulation of the mind, be seduced into enthusiastically accepting a World Government and international socialism and slavery, the Secret Brotherhood will not be forced into taking the risk of engaging in more bloody and more brutal means of control. As Britain's Jonathan Glover discusses in his thought provoking book, *What Sort of People Should There Be?*, "From the point of view of governments, rule by fear and torture must be a messy affair, generating problems of its own. It would be much simpler if techniques existed to make people *want* to behave in the desired way."[13]

The Manipulation of Human "Meat Machines"

It is apparent that for many years now, the Secret Brotherhood has been operating on the principle that the human body is nothing more than "a meat machine" which readily responds to external forces. The individual human brain, according to this theory, is a machine that can be operated by an outside agency. In other words, to put it bluntly, the Secret Brotherhood believes that it can pull the strings by programming minds and thereby inducing men to effective action in promoting the goals and aims of the Brotherhood.

In a sense this is a form of magic in which the massive organizing power and occultic mind control techniques of the Secret Brotherhood are mobilized in a concentrated assault against individual thought. This is similar to how the medium in a spiritualist seance supposedly mobilizes the energy forces to conjure up an image or apparition which then becomes observable to all those present.

The idea that man is a mere fleshly machine whose mind is highly susceptible to programming and influence by an organized, outside source was once outlined by the famed engineer and inventor, Nikola Tesla. Tesla, a genius who gave mankind the alternating current generating system and therefore brought electric light to the whole world, was a contemporary of Thomas Edison. He was also an occultist and a New Ager of his day who wrote and commented about the human brain and on spiritual matters almost as much as he did on technology. It was Tesla who once wrote:

> We are automata entirely controlled by the forces of the medium, being tossed about like corks on the surface of the water.[14]

Significantly, Tesla maintained that the masses are *blissfully unaware* that impulses from the outside are influencing the way they think and act. Instead, they mistake these impulses for "free will," never suspecting that outside agents prompt their behavior and thought patterns. Tesla used the term "cosmic" to describe these external forces that exist in man's environment. But he emphasized that whereas most men do not even consciously realize they are "meat machines," *some* are much more sensitive machines. These are persons who receive impressions and can understand and interpret these impressions. They possess the ability to discern. Such a man is, in a sense, a "finer automaton" than others, said Tesla.[15]

Tesla also believed that the universe is composed of energy forces, which he called "pranic energy" (*prana* being a Hindu term for God or divine energy). Again we have a reference to the absurd New Age and Masonic theology holding that "God" is simply a force, an inanimate collection of energy vibrations. If mankind is simply part of "God" the energy force, if he, too, is merely a material and spiritual collection of atomic substances, then it stands to reason that an elite group of Wise Men can figure out a way to organize this energy force and direct its work along desired paths.

This has long been the task, then, of the Secret Brotherhood: to devise occult means in which the universal energy force of which mankind is a part can be so directed that men and women labor *willingly* to build the new kingdom. Moreover, it has long been the aim of the Secret Brotherhood to organize this occult energy force in such a way that those who comprise the lower classes will give deference to and put *all authority* in the hands of the few who rule over them.

What's more, if through magical powers and advanced psycho-spiritual techniques of mind control the energy force can be effectively and successfully manipulated so that the masses of people who are its components can be made to believe an *illusion*—that they themselves are in control of their own destiny and that they themselves possess free will—then so much the better.

Thus, a *World Brain* made up of billions of deceived men and women blissfully unaware of its magical manipulation by an outside force (the hidden elite) is exactly what the men of the Secret Brotherhood have in mind.

FOURTEEN

Could This Be Magic?—Alchemy, Illusion, and the Processing of Humanity

The Secret Brotherhood has had centuries to develop its interest in *magic*. Magical knowledge involves the manipulation of "The Force." According to ancient alchemical texts, one who has magical powers is supposedly able to annihilate matter and to reconstruct an entire new structure that is more pleasing. Magic, therefore, is *spiritual alchemy*, an alchemy which takes the baser metals (man) and transmutes, or magically transforms, that baser metal into something greater and of a higher order: pure gold. "Pure gold," in the mysterious and coded, secretive language of magic and alchemy, means that man has achieved a higher state of consciousness, and has realized his divinity.

This is the *Great Work*, the illumination of mankind, the practice of occult transformation practiced by medieval alchemists and sorcerers. Alchemy is also the essence of the *secret doctrines* found in all Renaissance magic textbooks. And alchemy is at the core of the arcane teachings of the secret societies—such as the Rosicrucians, the Skull & Bones, Freemasonry, the Knights of Malta, the Order of the Golden Dawn, and the Knights Templar.

A master magician who knows how to wield the forces of alchemy, the theory goes, understands that the restructuring of reality cannot be brought into being by brute force or by muscle power, or militarism. The true alchemist, notes Peter Partner in his insight-filled book, *The Knights Templar and Their Myth*, is aware that, "the occult world qualities are transmitted by sympathetic contagion, not established by argument."[1]

The art of wizardry calls for the magician to line up materials which he wishes to transmute in such a manner that they will act like contagious bacteria. Each cell must exert an influence on the next so that as a whole (holism) the individual cells will result in a totally new product.

In other words, if magic is to be used to create a *New World Order*, the individual cells—that is, the 6 billion people who make up the planet Earth—must be brought together as one. Though they may be diverse in terms of their cultures, ethnic beliefs, nationalities, religions and languages, their diversity must be harnessed and fitted to become part of the whole.

Unity and Diversity

Thus, the Secret Brotherhood came up with its idea of *Unity and Diversity*, which is sometimes phrased as Unity *in* Diversity. Furthermore, since magic involves willpower, the will to create a new reality, the Secret Brotherhood also came up with a neat ritual formula and expression which has now become universally known. This ritual expression is now in wide use throughout America and in other societies, though only the occultists know its hidden meaning. It goes like this: "*Think Globally, Act Locally.*"

To heighten the development of the World Mind, the magicians of the Secret Brotherhood also came up with an idea to be called *Planetary Meditation*. Planetary Meditation is best achieved by the collective grouping of men's minds through mass gala events and pageantry; for example, *We Are the World; Farm Aid; Live Aid; World Day of Meditation; Harmonic Convergence*; etc. Occult magicians believe that it is through such events that a sustained and concentrated thought-form will grow to eventually envelope the whole planet. All of humanity will then be one giant theatre of deception.

World Goodwill, in its bulletin entitled *A New Vision of Life on Earth*, hints about the magical planetary system that has been developed and now put to use by the Brotherhood. Noting that "the earth is undergoing a profound transformation," the globalist organization touts this as a happy event: "Through this process a thought-form of the oneness of life is being created."[2]

World Goodwill also told its readers that, "At the height of the global meditation a new vision of life on earth is being revealed . . . a soul center of humanity is in the process of being born:"[3]

> When fully developed, this new humanity will be a humanity which celebrates all life in its rituals, its stories, its arts, and its science. It will be a humanity which expresses that unity in its economic, religious and political life.[4]

How will this new vision of life on earth be brought about? World Goodwill says that the environmental movement will go a long way toward creating this new system of collective planetary meditation:

> It involves millions of individuals, and countless local groups of concerned citizens in all parts of the world; it embraces the powerful collective fields of thought formed by such groups as the Worldwide Fund for Nature; Greenpeace; Friends of the Earth. It is fueled by the . . . shifting of political priorities that occur in the

endless round of intergovernmental conferences organized by the United Nations.[5]

The Whole World is a Theater of Illusion

We see then, that the Secret Brotherhood is using various types of powerful magic on a planetary scale. What these men are doing is setting the stage for a great deception. They have organized the whole world into a *theatre of illusion*. The whole world has become *the lie*. In effect, the religion of the Illuminati is *witchcraft*. No wonder Freemasonry often bills itself as "the Craft."

It is not only Freemasonry but *most* secret societies that today are led by men who fervently study magical literature and medieval texts. Freemasons call this branch of work by their leadership "Speculative Masonry," and everyone who becomes a Sovereign Grand Commander of Accepted Scottish Rite Freemasonry (the world's largest Masonic group) will always be a person skilled and trained in Speculative Masonry.

The head of Masonry is, in fact, a *master magician*. Such a person is one who knows how to discern the esoteric and hidden meanings of veiled symbols. He must also understand the latent power of rituals as well as the necessity for the Masonic Order's bloodcurdling oath of secrecy. And he is also required to understand the powerful magic inherent in words and must be able to interpret and create new words of power.

Most of all, the successful leader of the secret society that is controlled by the hierarchy of the Secret Brotherhood must be able to create and enact *pageants*—fantastic and wondrous pageants—which captivate men's minds and motivate men to action. And the most fantastic of all pageants is to create a spectacular celebration of a perpetual nature in which the whole of mankind participates. The most talented of magicians is able to establish the *whole world* as a theatre of action.

The greatest trick, therefore, the most impressive sleight of hand of the magicians and alchemists who are in charge of forming the New World Order, is the supremely deceptive act of creating this massive, global theatre of illuminism. Every technique of magic has been used by the magicians, and they have followed a masterful script and blueprint which has left nothing to chance.

As the result of their handiwork, men's minds have been conditioned to such a drastic degree that, as it now stands, man's free will has practically evaporated. Mass hypnotism has been so successful that men have become like vegetables. Their minds have been robbed of discernment.

The processing of humanity that has occurred from the manipulation of the energy forces by the Brotherhood can best be described as *Planetization.* This is the term used by the globalists, the New Age philosophers, and the masters of the secret societies alike. It is through this process of planetization that the masses have become weak and pliable subjects of a new class of overlords.

Does a New Ruling Class Control the Masses?

William Irwin Thompson, a man widely recognized by fellow New Agers, Sierra Club environmentalists, and Earth religionists as one of their own most distinguished writers and teachers, recently affirmed the existence of a ruling, aristocratic elite. America has led the way and "created a process of planetization of the economy," says Thompson. He also says that this "planetization process" has already resulted in *the takeover of world authority by a new ruling class of the super-rich.*

Interviewed in *Quest* magazine, Thompson, author of such books as *Evil and World Order, Passage About Earth*, and *At the Edge of History*, observed that:

> America has . . . energized and set up our previous enemies, Germany and Japan, and created the system that

> enabled them to very rapidly become wealthy and dynamic.[6]

Thompson, who divides his time between Zurich, Switzerland, and New York, where he is a Lindisfarne associate at the New Age-oriented Cathedral of St. John the Divine, told *Quest* that, "It's sort of a return of the Middle Ages in the sense that nationalism is not as important as it used to be. Money and economic class," said Thompson, "now dictate who reigns over the earth." "Society," he adds, "is beginning to take on very medieval characteristics."

According to Thompson, the caste system of India is almost a role model for what is now transpiring on a global basis. He asserts that:

> There is a ruling class at the time that communicates through oral means, face-to-face . . . and at the bottom there is an underclass. So it's almost like a return of the Vedic (Hindu) caste system.[7]

The "oral" class now in authority, says Thompson, "has the right accent, and has wealth . . . The rich get richer and the poor poorer, and the smaller ruling class just rules the masses through pageantry and illusion."[8]

Pageantry and illusion are the primary ingredients of *magic*. And therefore, it is through magic that the lower classes are being manipulated. In addition to the medieval-style political and economic New World Order that has emerged, Thompson also speaks of a new *planetary religion*. "We have now," he remarks, "a new spirituality, what has been called the New Age Movement."

> The planetization of the esoteric has been going on for some time . . . This is now beginning to influence concepts of politics and community in ecology . . . This is the Gaia (Mother Earth) politique . . . planetary culture.[9]

And just how does this new world religious system, this new "planetary culture" operate? Well, Thompson points out, a prime example is that "Japan got Detroit's automotive industry and the United States got (Buddhist) Zen monasteries in California."

"That's the way cultural exchange always works," explains Thompson, "with Zen coming to America and all the Indian gurus like Yogananda coming to America."[10]

"The esoteric tradition of the New Age has been going on for a long time," Thompson remarked.[11] The emergence of a new ruling class of the elite, combined with the spirituality of the New Age, means that we're in a radical new time. The old world, William Irwin Thompson concludes, is over—"The independent sovereign state, with the sovereign individual in his private property." The Christian fundamentalist days are dead or dying, too, he contends. The planetary culture is here. It's a new day.

Love and Light: Putting On a Happy Face

The Secret Brotherhood is certainly not going to reveal to men that they are being ruled and manipulated through pageantry and illusion. You can count on these diabolical men to put a happy face on what is a very tragic and deadly situation. Accordingly, the Lucis Trust, in announcing a recent World Goodwill symposium, promised that the New Culture brings us love and light through our service to the brotherhood:

> Through this global manifestation of the will-to-serve, a reservoir of spiritual energies has been created which strengthens and vitalizes all that is good in the world. In the language of symbols, humanity's will-to-serve has opened the door to Spiritual Hierarchy, allowing *love and light* from the higher kingdoms on our planet to flow into the consciousness of the human family.[12]

How wonderful all this sounds. Why would we want to fight against "love and light" flowing into the consciousness of the human family? How clever are the magicians. As Lucis Trust goes on to tell us, "Spiritual energies are flowing into the hearts and minds of people throughout the world, awakening the demand for a better way of life for all."[13]

Why, who could possibly be against such an intangible quality as "a better life for all?"

Thus, we are being trained to believe that only an idiot would be against the great possibilities of exalting human potential that are offered by the Secret Brotherhood. After all, if we are to believe the Lucis Trust, a radiant opportunity now presents itself to us:

> We have, now, in this time of great change, a wonderful opportunity to shape the future and harmony with the soul vision of the one world and the one humanity.[14]

But if we are to have harmony and if we are to become *one world* and *one humanity*, we are next told, we will also have to develop a sense of *responsibility*: "We need freedom accompanied by responsibility,"[15] say the masters of the Lucis Trust organization.

In the words of Vaclav Havel, the poet and President of Czechoslovakia—a man who is also a New Age mystic—"Freedom is only one side of the coin, the other side is responsibility."[16] What does "responsibility" mean? Well, explains the Lucis Trust, it means that man has the freedom to act in love but only "for the good of the whole."[17] He must act responsibly by extinguishing any rebellious and separatist personality traits or tendencies he may possess so that his individual will and ego can be merged in with that of the community as a whole.

Thus, Livieu Gota, the Vice Director General of the United Nations, told the members of the Lucis Trust and World Goodwill who were participating in the Arcane School Conference in Geneva, Switzerland in 1990, that man must end his individual will and conform to "common aspirations." According to Gota, a *universal spirituality* must be achieved. Every man must give of himself and serve the global community. Gota also said that the United Nations will play a great part in developing these common aspirations. Spirituality, Gota stresses, is to be the keystone of the work of strengthening the United Nations.[18]

Such groups as the Lucis Trust, World Goodwill, and the United Nations are promoters of good works and service by humanity, but what they are really after is for all of humanity to pledge allegiance to a single set of goals, to comply with the script and blueprint made up in advance by the Brotherhood.

The Role of the Media

How closely are the media following the script written in advance by the Secret Brotherhood? Marlin Maddoux, host of the popular nationally syndicated radio talk show, *Point of View With Marlin Maddoux*, and a man for whom I hold the greatest esteem, has a well-deserved reputation for being one of America's top experts and authorities on the media. In his insight-filled book, *Free Speech or Propaganda?*, he masterfully demonstrates how the media distort the truth. He notes that during the Vietnam War era, the TV networks carried an "unremitting drumbeat of coverage of every riot and rebellion—whether of 20 people or of 20,000."[19]

Marlin states, "Although I watched the evening news for years and years, I never saw the other side presented. The television was dominated by the left. Anyone who dared stand up to the revolutionaries was never given national publicity."[20] He went on to observe that:

> Night after night I had seen the radicals who were calling for the destruction of America being paraded as heroes across my television screen. They were given a national platform from which to spout forth their venom and disdain of our country and its institutions. And all the while they were calling on us, the American people,

> to burn down our society and to build some kind of New Age utopia on its ashes.[21]

Was it just coincidental that the TV networks seemed to have their camera crews on the scene of every riot and commotion, no matter how tiny or inconsequential? Marlin Maddoux reveals that:

> The revolutionaries knew exactly what the networks wanted, and they gave it to them. They let the network assignment editors know where the next riot would be, and they staged it early enough to get pictures on the 6 o'clock news.[22]

The media have been told, obviously, to jump aboard the perpetual campaign to popularize anarchy and revolution and to "illuminate" the masses to further the goals of the Brotherhood. Thus, World Goodwill held a symposium on November 17, 1990 in New York City, with the theme, of "The Psychology of Nations: Revealing the Plan." Interestingly enough, the keynote address, given by Rolland Smith, broadcast journalist and anchor for the Channel 9 news (WWOR-TV and WCBS-TV) in New York City, was "The Role of the Media in Illuminating the Significance of Global Change."

It is fascinating that key people involved in such influential organizations as World Goodwill are now actually coming out of the closet and admitting the role of the media in the illumination of mankind.

Actually, since the era of Abraham Lincoln the American media have been stooges and foils for the conspirators who make up the Secret Brotherhood. Our press is not only biased, it has become expert in *intentionally* manipulating and distorting the truth. The press has become the medium, the occult purveyor in the spiritualistic process of magic being perpetrated on the peoples of the world. It is through the press and the media that the lie is penetrating through to the masses.

Unbelievably, in 1914, John Swinton, editor of the *New York Times*, admitted that the most influential members of the media establishment have been bought up and are now owned body and soul by the secret elite. At a dinner of the American Press Association, Swinton charged:

> There is no such thing as an independent press in America . . . Not a man among you dares to utter his honest opinion . . . You know beforehand that it would never appear in print. It is the duty of New York journalists to lie, to toady at the feet of Mammon (money) and to sell his country and his race for his daily bread (money).
>
> We are the tools and the vassals of the rich behind the scenes. We are marionettes. These men pull the strings and we dance. Our time, our talents, our lives, and our capacities are all the property of these men. We are intellectual prostitutes.[23]

The New Reality Programmed Into Our Brains

With the help of the controlled media, and through their mastery of the arcane knowledge of the occult perennial wisdom and secret doctrine, the Secret Brotherhood has been able to construct the world into what could be called a *new holographic reality*. One can take a laser hologram picture, cut it up into a hundred pieces and amazingly, *each piece will be an exact mirror image of the original.* Likewise, the magicians of the Brotherhood have created a world system in which the residents of planet Earth have lost their God-given individuality. Now they are integral pieces of the hologram, and their thoughts and convictions conform to those of mass man.

Increasingly, it is not considered acceptable for a man to develop and exercise free will or to possess independent knowledge. Instead, he must go along with the crowd and enthusiastically acclaim a universal belief system. A whole culture has collapsed around us. Yet, most men and women are unaware that hidden knowledge and arcane magic have been utilized as weapons to destroy their minds. Our's has become a phantom universe of marvels and wizardry, and illusion and pageantry.

Even a century ago man was fast being propelled by the secret elements toward this miserable condition and state. For example, in his acclaimed *Natural History of Religion*, philosopher David Hume wrote:

> We are placed in this world, as in a great theatre, where the sources and causes of every event are entirely concealed from us; nor have we either sufficient wisdom to foresee, or power to prevent those ills, with which we are continually threatened. We hang in perpetual suspense between life and death, health and sickness, plenty and want; which are distributed among the human species by secret and unknown causes, whose operation is oft unexpected and always unaccountable.
>
> These unknown causes, then, become a constant object of our hopes and fears; and while the passions are kept in perpetual alarm by an anxious expectation of the events, the imagination is equally employed in forming ideas of those powers, on which we have so entire a dependence.[24]

What David Hume revealed is that we have become like a herd of blind mice which are, in unison, rushing over a cliff into a deep and murky sea. The world has become an enchanted place full of magic, and we have become the hapless, hypnotic and mesmerized residents of this world. We are out of touch with the old, more safe reality because a New Reality, one that is not of our own doing, has been substituted for truth.

The Reconstruction of the World

It was the famed composer Mozart who was responsible for a singular work of music that has been acclaimed and praised as "a work of genius" by Freemasonry and the secret societies. I am referring to his Masonic opera, "The Magic Flute," in which Mozart presents to us a vision of the world as a *reconstructed and magical temple*. In his opera, we are presented a temple of reason and nature, which is presided over by a ruler and psychic seer whom Mozart gives the name "Sarasto."

Has our earth today become a great theatre or stage? Are we all becoming programmed, operatic actors and singers whose performance is harmonized and presided over by a ruling elite? Is the goal of this elite to *rebuild the temple*, to make the entire earth into a Freemasonic "temple of reason and nature?" Is a deceived mankind now marching happily forward into the bold new future to the tune of the great musician Pan, the horned god, as he plays marvelous compositions on his Magic Flute?

And more important, consider this: Hitler and his troop of amateur magicians and hypnotists in the 1930's and 1940's were able to *reconstruct* a technologically advanced nation such as Germany into a vast theatre of illusion. They were also able to induce educated and intellectual men into becoming barbarians and oppressors of their fellow men. *What, then, is to become of 1990's men once the Brotherhood is in complete control of our destinies?* What will happen to men in this great operatic production of the Secret Brotherhood when we all reach Act 3, the final, concluding segment of this ages old drama?

A New Barbarism?

Perhaps Irwin Chargaff, a thoughtful man and a Nobel Prize winner who has been called the father of bioengineering, has given us an answer to these questions. Surveying the new world that is galloping toward us with a cloud of fire and dust following in its wake, Chargaff warns:

> I see the beginnings of a new barbarism . . . which tomorrow will be called a "new culture.". . . Nazism was a primitive, brutal, and absurd expression of it. But it was a first draft of a so-called pre-scientific morality that is being prepared for us in the radiant future.[25]

Chargaff's frightening conclusion is that mankind today is teetering on the edge of catastrophe, brought about by determined and calculating men who wish to implant in our minds the seeds of a new reality. These men are builders of the New Culture. But the world they are constructing will push men forward into a dark, black vault of horror.

"Before every catastrophe," Chargaff cautions, "as before an earthquake, there are signs of what is to come."[26]

What is so fantastically preposterous about the illuminized society that now surrounds us is that it comes cloaked with good intentions and altruistic motives. As Chargaff suggests, it comes to us described as a glowing, radiant, and promising new future—and men everywhere are buying into this distorted but seductive picture and image. It is as though mankind has been drugged by powerful hallucinogenic agents, mind control drugs which have induced a severe state of schizophrenia, paranoia, stupor and paralysis. In a manner of speaking, mankind has been given a fatal overdose of mind control drugs and has become the victim of these poisonous "bullets."

Moreover, the victim now needs long-term psychiatric care or confinement in a "government asylum." This asylum is the entire world! And who are the masters, the psychiatrists-magicians who run this supervised and meticulously planned government asylum? Naturally, they are the men of the Secret Brotherhood.

Psychic Chemicals Introduced Into Men's Minds

It is not farfetched to look upon our world and society today as one gigantic, universal nut house. In this global facility for the mentally impaired masses, the hapless and unwitting patients are daily fed dangerous thought-control drugs to alter their memory and heighten their susceptibility. These psychic chemical agents leave them dangerously vulnerable to magical suggestive powers. That would certainly explain why the masses find such horrors as the sadistic torture and fiendishness now routinely depicted in movies, the killing of millions of unborn babies, homosexual acts of perversion, and the creation of World Government not only palatable, but greatly desirable.

We are reminded of a letter smuggled out of one of the Soviet Union's psychiatric hospital prisons by dissident poet V. I. Chernyshov. The communists of the USSR were long engaged in forcing their "malcontents"—those who oppose the monstrous authoritarian system—to be "treated" in crowded psychiatric hospitals. There, confined to a secluded prison ward, they were treated for "mental illness" by being injected with massive doses of mind altering and mind destroying drugs. This, regrettably, was the fate of V. I. Chernyshov.

In his letter smuggled out of his psychiatric hospital prison ward, he unmasked the horrors inflicted on he and his fellow patients. He noted that most of the patients were Christians—honest and good men and women whose only crime was that they had refused to pledge allegiance to the atheistic views of their captors.

Begging Christians around the world to help their brothers in suffering, Chernyshov wrote:

> I'm terribly afraid of torture. But there is a worse torture . . . the introduction of chemicals into my mind . . . I have already been informed of the decision for my treatment. Farewell.[27]

FIFTEEN

The Hidden Persuaders

In every area of our lives, the *invisible powers* are staging furious, pile-driver assaults against us. Their startling goal: To demolish the individual human mind and condition all of humanity to the coming, final takeover of America and the whole earth.

Evidence that our minds and souls are being *processed* and that men have become like sheep led to slaughter can no longer be denied. The hideously frightening truth is that the Secret Brotherhood has been assisted by dark powers in creating a fantastic—yet diabolical—method to mesmerize and control human minds. That method can most accurately be described as the *Processing of Humanity*.

Since the 1950's the business world, through its wizards of public relations and advertising, have worked steadily to discover new ways of bending people's minds. In the corporate world, of course, the motive is to induce the consumer and buyer to purchase one's product. Increasingly, the advertising community has borrowed from the field of psychology and has even employed military psychopathology techniques and methods.

There has come into being a specialized mind control technology which uses techniques of hidden persuasion.

Few of us are aware that such techniques are being utilized against us since we're constantly being led to believe by the hidden persuaders that we are independent, resourceful, intelligent, and fully able to make up our own minds. The fact is, for the vast majority of people, the hidden persuasion of the advertisers *does work*—remarkably so.

Purpose: To Manipulate Our Minds

Hidden persuasion, the ability to influence one's buying habits, has proven so effective a science that in 1956, W. Howard Chase, President of the Public Relations Society of America, warned his colleagues in the advertising community that what they were doing may very well be extremely unethical:

> The very presumptuousness of molding or affecting the human mind through the techniques we use has created a deep sense of uneasiness in our minds.[1]

Vince Packard, whose bestselling book on this topic, *The Hidden Persuaders*, shocked Americans in the 1950's, cautioned that, "Some of these hidden persuaders, in their energetic endeavors to sway our actions—fall into the attitude that man exists to be manipulated."[2]

The incredible propaganda success of Adolf Hitler and his National Socialist Party in Germany, as well as the fascists of Benito Mussolini in Italy, in molding and shaping the thinking of entire populations, greatly influenced psychologists and philosophers after World War II. As a result, many new ways were investigated to determine propaganda and methods that could most effectively be used to promote certain "positive" social goals.

One of the men who gave this subject much thought was Bertrand Russell, a socialist and a member of the Fabian Society of England. Russell pondered the question of how human beings could best be controlled and manipulated for what he considered to be "the good of society." In his 1953 book, *The Impact of Science on Society*, he theorized that an *elite aristocracy* could exercise fantastic power by employing the new advances in mind control:

> It is to be expected that advances in psychology will give governments much more control over individual mentality than they now have . . . Education should aim at destroying free will, so that, after pupils have left school they shall be incapable, throughout the rest of their lives, of thinking or acting otherwise than as their school master would have wished.[3]

Russell, an advocate of a socialist world government and a harsh critic of capitalism, proposed that authorities work on children's minds "from a very early age to produce the sort of character and the sort of beliefs that the authorities consider desirable." If the child is thoroughly indoctrinated, Russell emphasized, any "serious criticism of the powers that be will become psychologically impossible."[4]

But what if, prior to their indoctrination, the masses *did not want to accept the goals of their masters? What then?* Should they be brainwashed to believe? Bertrand Russell's answer reveals the distorted view of the elitists who, in reality, care nothing for human rights:

> Even if all are miserable, all will believe themselves happy, because the government will tell them that they are so.[5]

In shocking passages reminiscent of the Nazi racial experiments, Bertrand Russell also suggested that *genetic selection* would be necessary to develop a more perfect society:

> The System, one may surmise, will be something like this: Except possibly the governing aristocracy, all but 5 percent of males and 30 percent of females will be sterilized . . . As a rule, artificial insemination will be preferred to the natural method. The unsterilized, if they

> desire the pleasures of love, will usually have to seek them with sterilized partners.
>
> Children will be taken from their mothers and reared by professional nurses. To those accustomed to this system, the family as we know it will seem as queer as the totem organization of the Australian Aborigines seems to us. The laboring class will have such long hours of work and so little to eat that their desires will hardly extend beyond sleep and food. The upper-class, being deprived of the softer pleasures, both by the abolition of the family and by the supreme duty of devotion to the state, will acquire the mentality of ascetics: They will care only for power and in the pursuit of it will not shrink from cruelty.[6]

Eventually, Russell explains, the pursuit of power will not require cruelty, for the masses, persuaded to do their "duty"—which means to slavishly serve their upper class rulers—will be so paralyzed in their minds and thoughts that they would not even think of rebelling:

> Gradually, by selective breeding, the congenital differences between the rulers and the ruled will increase until they become almost different species. A revolt of the plebs (lower-classes) would become as unthinkable as an organized insurrection of sheep against the practice of eating mutton.[7]

No Need for Firing Squads in the New World Order

The purpose of mind control is to so condition the minds of the average men and women so that brutality, suppression, and rigid totalitarian powers need never be exercised. The ideal, the Secret Brotherhood realizes, is to have the people willingly and eagerly accepting their fate, convinced that they've got it good, that things are just as they should be, that those who rule over them are chosen to do so by a natural system of selection. The New Culture, said Aldous Huxley, will not need firing squads:

> There is no reason why the new totalitarian state should resemble the old. Government by firing squads . . . is not merely inhuman . . . it is demonstrably inefficient, and in an age of advanced technology, inefficiency is a sin against the Holy Ghost.[8]

According to Huxley, "A really efficient totalitarian state would be one in which the all-powerful executive of political bosses and their army of managers control a population of slaves who do not have to be coerced because they love their servitude."[9]

The Example of the French Revolution

The French Revolution, instigated by the Grand Orient Lodge of Paris, gave the men of the Secret Brotherhood every hope that eventually the entire world could be convinced to willingly become its slaves. The Masonic Order and the conspiratorial Jacobins Society enjoyed tremendous success in convincing the people of France that the monarchs were nothing less than vile insects and enemies of the people. A small group of elitists calling itself "The Committee on Public Safety" was "democratically" formed and began to draw up lists of "Enemies of the People."

At the same time, the Masonic membership of this Committee on Public Safety employed techniques of mass hypnosis, brainwashing, illusion (theater), magic and alchemy to process the common people toward the desired goals.

Ultimately, nearly five million Frenchmen lost their heads in the guillotines as a savage, bloodletting orgy commenced throughout the country. Because of the psychological and spiritual warfare carried out against the people by the Masonic overlords—who convinced the masses that they were democratically chosen and wanted only to bequeath to the people liberty, fraternity, and equality—a mass program of "de-Christianization" was launched. Churches were torched, priests were tortured and sent to the guillotine, and even the average Christians in the pews were tormented by mobs.

These innocent men, women, and children were ridiculed, scoffed and reviled. Anyone who had the audacity to pray to the person of Jesus Christ was branded an "Enemy of the State." Crucifixes were torn off the walls of those churches that weren't torched. Crucifixes were also forcibly removed from the walls of homes, turned upside down on display in the streets, and urinated on by mobs.

A great cloud descended over the nation. If it was not the devil who gripped the minds of the men on the Committee on Public Safety, then who was responsible for these foul things? If it were not the devil, acting through his Masonic agents, whose sophisticated techniques of mind control made these atrocities possible, then how is it possible that they occurred? What type of delusion attacked the minds of millions of common peasants and petty merchants to convince them to participate in such brutal acts of terror against their innocent neighbors?

A Planetary Delusion

From what I have discovered in my studies of the mind control techniques and methods that the Secret Brotherhood is now using against mankind, the mind rape of the people of France over two centuries ago is being repeated today on a global scale. Could it be that somewhere today, in a high-rise office building, a team of "social engineers" hired by the Brotherhood is drawing up lists of people who are to be accused of being "Enemies of the State?"

I am convinced that the techniques of old are now combined with newer psychological advances, the power of words (general semantics), and propaganda. These occult systems are being used to captivate, intoxicate, and totally transform the minds of men.

The Secret Brotherhood now has the capacity to induce a *mass hallucination*, a form of group insanity and planetary delusion, into the minds of the masses. Furthermore, they have also developed certain occultic and magical powers to the maximum and are now able to use the black arts and sorcery to achieve an altered state of consciousness in the minds of entire populations.

A Paradigm Shift: Novus Ordo Seclorum

Effective on a planetary scale, these occult techniques, combined with psychology, mind control, and propaganda, are pushing mankind at a rapid pace down the slippery slope of slavery. What is occurring is a shocking new *paradigm shift*, a change in men's minds. It is through this paradigm shift, our mind controllers believe, that matter can be magically transmuted to spirit. A new consciousness will grab hold of and possess men's minds. The paradigm shift, they believe, signals their supreme success in the alchemical processing of humanity.

The Great Work, the illumination of all mankind, is finally on the threshold of completion. The New Order of the Ages (*Novus Ordo Seclorum*) is on the immediate horizon.

The men who intend to rule over us have no desire to smash us into submission. Rather, they are confident and are looking forward to our rapturous embracing of the solutions that they offer us to resolve the chaotic problems and crises now besetting our planet. They arrogantly believe that mankind will, in desperation, turn to them for salvation.

The hidden persuaders are not interested in becoming Hitlers and Mussolinis. Their way is not that of China's Mao, Russia's Stalin, or Cambodia's murderous Pol Pot. They use the velvet-gloved fist, the satin-smooth turn of words, and the magical frame of thinking to gain their objectives. Theirs is the route of hidden persuasion to change and alter men's minds.

As Vicomte Leon de Poncins writes in *The Secret Powers Behind Revolution*, "The role of Freemasonry is to create the *revolutionary state of mind* rather than to act directly."

We may well recall the dilemma of Winston, the heroic character from George Orwell's book *1984*. When it was found out that he was a rebel, an insurrectionist who was able to discern the lies of Big Brother and who sought to combat the oppressive forces of the elitists, Winston was arrested. Thrown into a prison cell, he was tortured unmercifully. His captors could have ended it all by simply dispatching Winston with a bullet to the back of the head. But they chose not to do so.[10]

Instead, they began to work on his mind and to remold his thoughts. Winston, Big Brother's police state ruled, was guilty of "thought-crime." His thoughts had to be made "pure" so that once again, he would love Big Brother and also love and respect the system that Big Brother had created for the good of society. It was only when Winston was able to totally and unconditionally accept these principles— in other words, only when his mind was thoroughly cleansed, purged, and changed, that Big Brother could be appeased.

In the world of *1984's* Big Brother, the Party, comprised of the elitists, felt it necessary to create a Ministry of Truth. The bureaucrats of this ministry were housed in an enormous pyramid-shaped building of glittering white concrete, which soared up, terrace after terrace, 300 meters into the air. On the white face of this pyramidal structure, in elegant lettering, were the three slogans of the Party:

War is peace

Freedom is slavery

Ignorance is strength

Mandatory: A "New Way of Thinking"

What the Secret Brotherhood is insisting is that Americans and the peoples of the earth adopt a "new way of thinking." Even some ostensibly Christian groups are falling for this ploy. For example, in the *Plain Truth* magazine published by the Worldwide Church of God, a religious cult founded by the late Herbert W. Armstrong, was a special section, entitled, "Needed for the '90's . . . A New Way of Thinking!"[11] In this special section, a number of authorities were quoted as recommending that a "new way of thinking," a "new ecological and cultural ethos," and a "new kind of mind," be adopted by the peoples of the world. According to the *Plain Truth*, "We need this new mind because the old mind is proving incapable of handling the world we've made for ourselves."[12]

Everywhere we turn it seems that authorities are encouraging us to develop this "new way of thinking." Robert Ornstein and Paul Ehrlich, in their book, *New World, New Mind*, claim that the human mind is now "mismatched for the world it has created." They say that the population explosion and the environmental crisis cannot be solved unless the human mind is changed and upgraded. In the *UNESCO Charter*, we also find an appeal that men change their minds: "Since wars begin in the minds of men, it is in the minds of men that we have to erect the ramparts of peace."

Gorbachev Promotes a "New Way of Thinking"

Mikhail Gorbachev, the former Soviet President who is now head of a think tank organization with centers in both Moscow and the United States, obviously has been told by his mentors in the New World Order to hammer out a similar refrain. Gorbachev has become a superhero to New Agers around the world who love to hear him preach on his favorite theme: that the world desperately needs a "higher consciousness."[13]

Gorbachev also continues to stress the topic of world unity, to trumpet and proclaim that "we are all one." As he puts it: "We are all passengers aboard one ship the Earth, and we must not allow it to be wrecked. There will be no second Noah's Ark."[14] Strange words indeed for a man who says that he is an atheist and a dedicated communist.

To promote these ideas, Mikhail Gorbachev wrote his book, *Perestroika: New Thinking For Our Country and the World,* which promptly became a smash hit on the *New York Times* bestseller list in 1987 and 1988. In his book, Gorbachev explained that *Perestroika* meant that the world must be *reconstructed,* and that mankind must rally behind the formation of a "global consciousness." The former bully of the Kremlin also called for "a worldwide revolution" so that mankind would have a "new way of thinking."[15] This revolution, he added, must "begin in the mind." Gorbachev's claim is that such a revolution will insure peace and harmony for all the peoples of the world because, along with this "new way of thinking" will come "*universal values* to take advantage of man's spiritual capital."[16]

Gorbachev has proven to be one of the greatest parrots and evangelists imaginable for the New Age masters of the Secret Brotherhood. The good comrade from Moscow no doubt recognizes that the term "global consciousness" simply means that the entire world is to be propagandized into believing in the necessity of the "worldwide revolution" that he and fellow conspirators so stridently propose. That revolution, he tells us, "must begin in the mind."[17]

This is exactly what Vicomte Leon de Poncins revealed as the true goal of Freemasonry: the creation of the *revolutionary state of mind.* It is interesting also that Gorbachev talks about "spiritual capital" for, as de Poncins notes, "The inner nature of the struggle is spiritual." It is a conflict between the Christian idea—between God—and the men who would exalt themselves to godhood.

German Banker Calls for a "New Way of Thinking"

Another prominent figure in the New World Order, the fabulously powerful German banker F. Wilhelm Christians, has also joined the rising crescendo of voices urging this "new way of thinking." Christians just happens to be the chairman of the supervisory board of Deutsche Bank. As such he is virtually the equal of Great Britain's wealthy Lord Rothschild and America's banking and corporate magnate David Rockefeller in the international banking sweepstakes.[18]

It was Christians who broke down the walls of communism by having his bank and other banking syndicates which he controls lend billions of German marks to the Soviets to help them build the Siberian Pipeline and the Yamal Pipeline, among other projects. Over the years, Christians has traveled back and forth to the Soviet Union, both before the fall of communism and since. He has held secret and open meetings with Soviet leaders like Brezhnev, Andropov, and Gorbachev, as well as American Presidents Carter, Reagan, and Bush.

Truly a financial insider, Christians authored a penetrating book, *Paths to Russia: From War to Peace*, which has a foreword by Helmut Schmidt, the former Chancellor of West Germany. In it, Christians heaps praise on Gorbachev's doctrine of *Perestroika* (reconstruction) and on his "new way of thinking." Christians writes that he is in full agreement with these goals, which, he notes, also include such elements as "a new morality and a new psychology."[19]

Thus, we have it from one of the hidden persuader's own top spokesmen: The "new way of thinking" is the wave of the future—the path not only to conquest over the hardline communists of Russia, but over the peoples and nations of the whole world.

The Secret Brotherhood is convinced that its hidden blueprint for world domination will be achieved by the year 2000, as mankind enters the "New Millennium." So appropriately, F. Wilhelm Christians says that it is significant that we are about to enter the third millennium, "a new millennium," he says, that "exerts a powerful suggestive effect on people."[20] Christians is positive that this new era, the New Millennium, has great possibilities. He happily notes that, "There are signs of changes in world events, signs that were inconceivable until very recently." These changes, Christians' adds, mean that "Long familiar absolutes and fixed positions are shifting, becoming relative; they are no longer suitable."[21]

F. Wilhelm Christians stresses his belief that Gorbachev's *Perestroika* and "new way of thinking" must be adopted by Europe, America and the whole world and not just in Russia alone. He says that he is so glad that Gorbachev (a coworker with him in the Secret Brotherhood), understands the "vibrations" which are causing the world to change so dramatically:

> Unlike millions of indolent (Communist) Party members, Gorbachev feels the vibrations that are announcing the new international system of the coming millennium.[22]

World Government is Needed

If we are "to attain an irreversible peace on this planet," Christians writes, "all human beings will cooperate in implementing the new geopolitical vision now offered to us."[23] And what is meant by this new "vision?"

> More than anything else, we have to cast off the traditional national structures. The European Economic Community is set on this course, which will eventually effect the other European countries. The Eastern European countries, having long been deprived of self-determination, are urgently intent on emphasizing their inviolable borders. But ultimately they will have to yield, slowly but inevitably, to the global lifting of such demarcations.[24]

What Christians is proposing is what every other member of the Secret Brotherhood is hungering for, from Mikhail Gorbachev and George Bush to David Rockefeller, Henry Kissinger, Helmut Kohl, James Baker, and Lord Rothschild: "*World Government.*" Their consistent theme is that national sovereignties must be torn down.

How to Deal With Fundamentalists

World Government is not the only goal of the Brotherhood. They also want to put an end to Western forms of spirituality. The religions of the East must take prominence in the spirituality of man. As Christians suggests, "In the course of mutual give and take, the West will remember the spiritual and cultural values of the East."[25]

Like other members of the invisible college who prides themselves on being labeled the "Wise Men," Christians warns that there are certain elements that will have to be suppressed and eliminated if the world is to see its way clear to global harmony and the preferred "new way of thinking." He lists such problems as "religious fanaticism" (fundamentalist Christianity, fundamentalist Islam, and fundamentalist Judaism are always the three baddies mentioned by the Brotherhood) as well as worldwide ecological problems. Last but not least, he lists epidemics such as AIDS and the escalating global catastrophe of drug addiction.[26]

Christians also states that, "we must help the plight of the poor in the Third World, especially black Africa and Latin America." No longer is it acceptable for a nation to close off its economy to others. The needs of both "economy and ecology," he insists, "require vast cooperation that transcends national borders."[27]

What we have then is a formula for the "new way of thinking" and a severe criticism of the "old way of thinking." The new way includes World Government, a new Global Economic Order, the unity of the religions of the mystical East and apostate versions of the Christian West, and the rise of a new "global consciousness." The old way of thinking, which includes patriotism, pride in one's race and country, and belief in a living, personal God are all to be tossed into the wind.

Farewell to the Old Way of Thinking

The Lucis Trust, one of the subsidiary organizations of the Secret Brotherhood, has a special code-phrase to describe the unacceptable "old way of thinking." It calls the outmoded ways, "world glamour." In her book, *The Reappearance of the Christ*, Lucis Trust founder Alice Bailey states that world glamour (the old way of thinking), "will be dissipated and world illusion dispelled."[28] She suggests that such concepts as love for one's country, the traditional family, and pride in one's race are old-fashioned and even dangerous. They are all part of what the Hindus call *maya*, or illusion, the negative world on the mental plain.

In the place of world glamour and world illusion must come a new way of thinking, so that, "The present world order can be so modified and changed that a *New World Order* and a *new race of men* can gradually come into being."[29]

What is necessary, Bailey explains, is that man accept "a point of light, a new illumination." She adds that with the world changes now occurring, this illumination is fast being achieved: "Men are being rapidly disillusioned and will consequently see more clearly. World glamour is being steadily removed from the ways of men."[30]

Keep in mind that the alchemists of the occult world and the higher-level initiates of the Secret Brotherhood operate from a totally opposite frame of thinking than normal people. Therefore, when Bailey says that, "Men are being rapidly disillusioned and will consequently see more clearly," what she is *really* telling us is that men are going to be required to change and adopt the "new way of thinking." The old way (world glamour) "is being steadily removed from the ways of men."

Like her Russian counterpart Gorbachev, Bailey says that man must have instilled in his mind a *new global consciousness:*

> When the consciousness which is (the collective New Age) Christ has been awakened in all men, then we shall have peace on earth and goodwill among men . . . The expression of our divinity will bring to an end the hatred rampant upon earth and break down all the separating walls which divide man from man, group from group, nation from nation, religion from religion.[31]

Identifying the Insane, Inferior Species

The advocates of the "new way of thinking" believe that men who cannot change are unfit for survival. They are, in fact, *insane* and are members of an inferior species as far removed from human beings as the ant is from a bear. We of the old way of thinking are also dangerous and must be harshly dealt with if we cannot change or if we stubbornly refuse to do so. We must be separated and purged because, it is claimed, we are infecting the rising generation with our old-fashioned morality and our negative, evil thoughts. As Professor Chester Pierce of Harvard University's Department of Educational Psychiatry suggested to a national teacher's convention:

> Every child of America entering school at the age of five is mentally ill, because he comes to school with certain allegiances toward his founding fathers, towards his elected officials, towards his parents, toward a belief in a supernatural being, towards the sovereignty of this nation as a separate entity. It's up to you teachers to make all these children well, by creating international children of the future."[32]

It is we, who believe strongly in nation and patriotism, who are convinced that there are moral absolutes of right and wrong, and who profess belief in a true God, that are to be branded as hopelessly insane and mean-spirited. The masses are being taught to detest and revile us. Meanwhile, propagandized by the Secret Brotherhood's campaign of mass hypnosis and hallucination, the masses now picture themselves as virtuous, modern, and progressive lovers of the Earth.

Benjamin Creme, head of two New Age, socialist groups, the Tara Center and International Sharing, has been touring the United States for some years now promoting these themes. In a newsletter published by the Tara Center, Creme boasted that, "A new spirit is awakening in humanity. Growing throughout the world is a new sense of interdependence, a desire for *saner* modes of living and a commitment to the well-being of the planet."[33]

The Tara Center moans about all of the crises and problems that have befallen mankind—ranging from AIDS, political and business corruption, and alienation, to drugs, crimes, and natural disasters. But, the editor of the Tara Center newsletter assures its readers, "The problems of mankind are real, but solvable."[34]

And how may they be solved? The solution, we are told, is to "demonstrate that humanity is one." Then, we must take the "first step toward lasting peace . . . by sharing the world's resources among all peoples."[35]

Here we see yet another delusion sponsored by the mind controllers of the Brotherhood: that if we simply *take from* the people of America and the other developed countries and *give to* the Third World nations, an age of peace will be achieved. But, the mind controllers warn, if we struggle against this needed world revolutionary movement and the ongoing march of socialism, we old-timers are in for a bit of trouble. The Tara Center makes it clear that the forces of a "new way of thinking" are ready "to do battle with ignorance and fear, division and want." What's more, in a superb example of Brotherhood double-think, we are told by the same group that those weapons are merely "spiritual understanding, knowledge, and love."[36]

Destruction Just Ahead?

But do the propagandists of the Secret Brotherhood really intend to solve the world's problems with "spiritual understanding, knowledge and love," or is there a more chilling solution on the drawing boards? We find the answer in the amazingly frank book, *The Armageddon Script*, by Peter Lemesurier, who writes that the new vision must be pursued amidst a time of turmoil such as the world has never seen. Because of the resistance of those (we who resist the "New Way of Thinking") who do not want to enter the New Age of prosperity and world harmony and therefore do not adjust their minds accordingly, a calamity of monstrous proportions will occur:

> The massed forces of the Old Age, however, will be unable to check their (the New Age forces) headlong onrush. In large measure they will go on to destroy each other in a massive, mutual venting of long pent-up aggression . . . they will succumb, while the vision and its bearers survive.[37]

Evidently, what the Secret Brotherhood has on the docket is to drive a wedge between and instigate a series of bloody conflicts on a global scale between the various groups that now oppose the New World Order. We're already beginning to see the ominous, early warning signs of the clashes that are to come. The Secret Brotherhood will continue to use the media and all of the weapons in its vast, propagandistic armory to inflame passions and thereby encourage Afro-Americans and white Americans to fight pitch battles in the streets of our major cities. They are now arming both the Arab Moslems and the Jews in anticipation of total warfare in the Middle East that will wipe out any remaining opposition to the New World Order.

They are also pitting Christian fundamentalists against the fundamentalists of Islam and Judaism, and they are arranging society so that the gays, radical feminists, abortionists, and other socially-deviant groups will gang up on and aggressively war against fundamentalist (Biblical) Christianity.

Just as significant, they are stirring up public sentiment against those who still insist that their country is best. Patriotism has to go, the Secret Brotherhood has ruled. So increasingly, nationalistic feeling will be stifled and suppressed. Ethnic groups everywhere, including the peoples of the new, fledgling nations of Eastern Europe and those who have freed themselves from the communist oppression of the old Soviet Union, must be taught a lesson. They must be forced to understand that nationalism *cannot* be tolerated in the New World Order.

To insure that this understanding is achieved, we can expect the Brotherhood to encourage and even provoke border clashes and disputes among many smaller nations in Europe and the old Soviet empire. Nuclear weapons will be covertly sold to Iran, Iraq, Syria, and other Islamic nations by the former Soviet republics and may actually be unleashed.

Horrid acts of terrorism and bloody violence will fill our TV screens and our newspapers. Then and only then, the Brotherhood reasons, will man, in his misery, cry out for World Government and an end to "poisonous" national sovereignty and independence, and the bloody ethnic and religious strife.

The Secret Brotherhood uses propaganda-laden terms to describe these crises and volatile clashes. Their agents speak of "a great cleansing" to take place as the earth catapults into the New Age, that glorious era which President Reagan once described as "the new sunlit day." According to the Secret Brotherhood, this great cleansing will occur as a result of intense conflict between the "sons of light" and the "sons of darkness:"

> And it will occur after the wars between the Sons of Light versus the Sons of Darkness that a "New Age" will occur for all mankind surviving the great, great changes . . . of this planet.[38]

The Coming Planetary Cleansing Operation

Those who cannot adjust to the "new way of thinking," who refuse to become partakers of the planetary hallucination induced by the mind-rapers of the Secret Brotherhood, are deemed insane, defective, and even dangerous to the world system. They are chaff, virtually human waste. They *must be eradicated* if the world is to go forward and fulfill the enduring dream of the secret societies:

> The fetus of the New Humanity is already stirring in the Womb of Time and like the human mother, humanity must learn to eliminate its waste materials and poisons and give the fetus proper nourishment or the life of both the child and the mother will be in danger . . . This is the work of the present transitory conditions.[39]

Those of us unfit for the New Age kingdom because we're unable to "think correct" are such a dangerous and unhealthy blot on humanity that we are viewed as something akin to cancer cells. The new man, properly educated, says Alice Bailey in *Education in the New Age*, will practice "global citizenship" and promote the harmony of all religions as one. "If not," she writes, "then they will have to go, for they have become impediments to world peace and threats to a proper human society:"[40]

> A violent streptococcic germ and infection . . . makes its presence felt in infected areas in the body of humanity.

> Another surgical operation may be necessary . . . to dissipate the infection and get rid of the fever . . .
>
> Let us never forget . . . that when a life-form proves inadequate, or too diseased, or too crippled . . . it is—from the point of view of the Hierarchy—no disaster when that form has to go.[41]

Isn't it interesting that Bailey makes the revealing statement, "*Another* surgical operation may be necessary." Is she referring to the holocaust of World War II, when Jews and many Christians and other persons adjudged to be unsuitable for Hitler's "new way of thinking" were destroyed in the concentration camps? I believe that is exactly the case.

In the past, extreme measures were taken to rid the earth of those deemed to be undesirable for assimilation into the New Order. These grotesque methods of eliminating the unfit will no doubt be employed once again. Peter Lemesurier writes in *The Armageddon Script*:

> Those human beings who refuse to accept the new archetype will, naturally enough, not partake of it. Only those who accept it will make up the New Man, the Second Adam, or Ultimate Messiah; the rest, inevitably, will therefore not enter the promised kingdom.[42]

Who will enter the new kingdom now being prepared so assiduously by the super rich elite who intend to be our absolute masters? Well, says Lemesurier, "All those who enter the New Kingdom will, by definition, be co-rulers . . . the collective Christ," which he describes as "that supreme entity."[43]

FOOTNOTES AND REFERENCES

Preface

1. Alexander Solzhenitsyn's Nobel Prize speech, as quoted in *MRA For a Change*, March 6, 1992.

Chapter 1: The Illuminati—Secret Brotherhood of Destiny

1. In addition to my own original research, among the sources used to document and prove the history, purpose, organization, rituals, leadership, membership, and other facts revealed in *Dark Majesty* regarding the *Skull & Bones Society* were the following:

Steven M. L. Aronson, "George Bush's Biggest Secret," *Fame* magazine, August, 1989, pp. 82-89.

The Catholic Intelligencer newsletter, June/July, 1991, p. 9.

"Skull and Spare Ribs," *The Economist* magazine, November 2, 1991.

"God, Men, and Bonding at Yale," *Newsweek* magazine, April 29, 1991, p. 66.

"Yale Women Barred From Secret Society," *Los Angeles Times* newspaper, September 6, 1991, p. A28.

Roger Javens, *Skull and Bones and the Secret Society System at Yale* (unpublished paper).

"So George, What About Those Swastikas?," from the *Winnipeg Free Press* newspaper, reprinted in *Sun*, October 17, 1989.

Antony C. Sutton, *America's Secret Establishment: An Introduction to the Order of Skull & Bones* (Published by Liberty House Press, 2027 Iris, Billings, Montant, 59102,1986).

Antony C. Sutton, *Two Faces of George Bush* (Published by Wiswell Ruffin House, Inc., P.O. Box 236, Dresden, New York, 14441).

James J. Drummey, *The Establishment's Man* (Appleton, Wisconsin: Western Islands, 1991).

Webster G. Tarpley and Anton Chaitkin, *George Bush: The Unauthorized Biography*, published by Executive Intelligence

Review, 1992; and see excerpts of this book in *The New Federalist*, December 16, 1991.

Curtis Lang, "Bad Company: How Speculators, Spooks, and Con Men Helped Build the Bush Dynasty," *Village Voice* newspaper.

Ron Rosenbaum, "The Last Secrets of the Skull & Bones," *Esquire* magazine, September, 1977.

Walter Isaacson and Evan Thomas, *The Wise Men* (New York: Touchstone Books edition, 1986).

Christopher Hutchens, "Old New World Order?," *The European* newspaper, June 14-16, 1991), p. 10.

2. Roger Javens, *Ibid.*
3. *Ibid.*
4. *Ibid.*
5. *Ibid.*
6. See article by Dennis L. Cuddy, "New World Order," *Wisconsin Report* newspaper, December 27, 1990. Malachi Martin's comments about George Bush being one of the "Wise Men" were made in a September 1, 1990 interview.
7. "Time is Running Out for Bush, Too," *Guardian Weekly* (insert of *Washington Post* newspaper, January 6, 1991), p. 14.
8. Harmon Taylor, "Freemasonry at the Bush Inauguration," HRT Ministries Newsletter, January-March, 1989. Also see Allan Boudreau, "Why the St. John's Lodge Bible?," *The Royal Arch Mason* magazine, Spring, 1991, p. 15.
9. A. Ralph Epperson, *The New World Order* (Published in 1990 by Publius Press, Suite B, 3100 South Philamena Place, Tucson, Arizona, 85730), p. 289.
10. Kenneth T. Walsh, "Bush's Man With the Hawk's Eye View," *U.S. News & World Report*, October 7, 1991, pp. 28-29.
11. Guy Molyneau, quoted by Harold Meyerson, "The Peripheral President: Bush at Midterm," *LA Weekly*, January 4-10, 1991, p. 13.

Chapter 2: **World Conspiracy: A "Novel Idea"**

1. My sources for facts presented in this chapter regarding Maurice Strong include the following:

Roy Livesey, "The Baca Grande in Colorado," *New Age Bulletin* newsletter (published in Great Britain), June, 1988.

Miro Cernetig, "Baca Troubled: Water Wars Disrupt New Age Valley," *The Globe and Mail* newspaper (Canada), July 9, 1990, p. A-1.

Gregg Easterbrook, "Why Rio Will Make History," *Newsweek* magazine, June 15, 1992, pp. 29-35.

Jayne Schindler, "So Much for Saving Mother Earth," *The Eagle Forum* newspaper, Denver, Colorado, Fall, 1991, p. 1.

Samantha Smith, article in *The Eagle Forum*, Denver,Colorado, April-June, 1991.

2. Daniel Wood, *West* magazine (Canada), May, 1990; reprinted by Roy Livesey in *New Age Bulletin* (Great Britain), July, 1990.
3. *Ibid.*
4. See Chapter 5 of *Dark Majesty.*
5. Gaetan Delaforge, *The Templar Tradition in the Age of Aquarius* (Putney, Vermont: Threshold Books, 1987), p. 136.
6. *Ibid.*, p. 56. Also see John J. Robinson, *Born in Blood: The Lost Secrets of Masonry* (New York: M. Evans and Company, 1989); and Michael Baigent and Richard Leigh, *The Temple and the Lodge* (New York: Arcade Publishing/Little, Brown and Co., 1989), pp. 266-267.
7. Gaetan Delaforge, *op. cit.*, pp. 136-138.
8. See footnote 1 above.
9. See Texe Marrs, *New Age Cults and Religions* (Austin, Texas: Living Truth Publishers, 1990), p. 190. Also see David Ellis, "Gorby, the New Age Guru?," *Time* magazine, June 18, 1990.
10. Gaetan Delaforge, *The Templar Tradition in the Age of Aquarius, op. cit.*, pp. 136-138.
11. Thomas Ehrenzeller, *Solar Man* (Winona, Minnesota: Apollo Books, 1985).
12. *Ibid.*
13. Robin Waterfield, "Julius Evola: An Interpreter of the Grail," in the book, *Household of the Grail*, edited by John Matthews (England: The Aquarian Press/Thorsen's Publishing Group, 1990), p. 163.
14. Maurice Strong, remarks at Cathedral of St. John the Divine (Episcopal) Church, New York City, "Theology of the Earth" sermon series. (See *The New Federalist* magazine, "Changing Christians Into Pagans," 1990, p. 32).
15. See Texe Marrs, "Investigating 'The Octopus' Can Be Deadly!," *Flashpoint* newsletter, November/December, 1991.
16. A. K. Chesterton, *The New Unhappy Lords*, 3rd American Edition, January, 1970 (reprinted 1979).
17. *Ibid.*
18. *Ibid.*
19. *Ibid.*
20. *Ibid.*
21. *Ibid.*

Chapter 3: **What International Evil Lurks in Vaults of Banks?**

1. Steve Daley, "What International Evil Lurks in Vaults of Banks?," *News Journal*, Mansfield, Ohio (*Chicago Tribune News Service*), August 7, 1991, p. 7-A.
2. Meg Greenfield, "Time For The Grand Finale," *Newsweek* magazine, August 19, 1991, p. 64.
3. *Ibid.*
4. *Ibid.*

5. *Ibid.*
6. *Ibid.*
7. *Ibid.*
8. *Ibid.*
9. *Ibid.*
10. *Ibid.*
11. *Ibid.*
12. Quoted by Don Oldenburg, "International Plot or Happenstance?," *American Statesman* newspaper, Austin, Texas (*Washington Post News Service*), February 16, 1992, pp. 6-14.
13. *Ibid.*
14. *Ibid.*
15. *Ibid.*
16. Lady Queensborough (Edith Starr Miller), *Occult Theocrasy.*
17. See the account by Mark Lane, *Plausible Denial: Was the CIA Involved in the Assassination of JFK?* (New York: Thunder's Mouth Press, 1991), pp. 324-334, 371-374. Also see Joseph McBride, "The Man Who Wasn't There: George Bush, CIA Operative," in *Nation* magazine, July 16/23, 1988; and August 13/20, 1988.
18. Quoted in the *McAlvany Intelligence Advisor* newsletter, February, 1991.
19. *Ibid.*
20. Jacques Attali, *Sigmund Warberg: A Man of Influence* (France: Fayard, 1985). Also see article by Lewis Pauwels, *Figaro* magazine, January 13, 1990.
21. Jacques Attali, *Ibid.*, pp. 14, 86.
22. *Ibid.*, p. 15.
23. *Ibid.*, p. 3.
24. *Ibid.*
25. Emanuel M. Josephson, *The Federal Reserve Conspiracy and the Rockefellers* (New York: Chedney Press, 1968), p. 1.
26. *Ibid.*
27. *Ibid.*
28. "Banking Man at the Top," *Time* magazine, September 7, 1962.
29. *Ibid.*
30. E. J. Kahn, "Profiles, Resources, and Responsibilities," *New Yorker* magazine, January 9, 1965.

Chapter 4: **The Great Work: The Magic of A Thousand Points of Light**

1. Robert Anton Wilson, "Cosmic Trigger II," *Magical Blend* magazine, July, 1991, pp. 25-30.

2. Quoted in Sir John Sinclair, *The Alice Bailey Inheritance* (Wellingborough, Northamptonshire, England: Turnstone Press Ltd., 1984), p. 174.
3. *Ibid.*, p. 145.
4. Gaetan Delaforge, *The Templar Tradition in the Age of Aquarius*, p. 140.
5. Malachi Martin, *Keys of This Blood* (New York: Simon & Schuster, 1990), p. 364.
6. The entire text of George Bush's speech accepting the Republican Party's nomination as President of the United States was published in the *New York Times*, August 19, 1988.
7. Alice Bailey, *Esoteric Psychology* II (New York: Lucis Publishing, 1970), p. 396.
8. "Becoming Sun-like," *The Beacon*, Vol. LI, #10, July/August, 1986, p. 289.
9. Corinne Heline, *Mysteries of the Grail* (Santa Monica, California: New Age Bible and Philosophy Center), p. 114.
10. Alexander Hislop, *The Two Babylons* (reprinted, New York: Loizeaux Brothers, 1959; original edition published 1916 in England), p. 194.
11. *Ibid.*, pp. 162-163.
12. John Randolph Price, *The Planetary Commission* (Austin, Texas: Quartus Books, 1984, p. 68).
13. John Randolph Price, *Practical Spirituality* (Austin, Texas: Quartus Books), p. 33.
14. Alice Bailey, *Discipleship in A New Age*, quoted by Sir John Sinclair, in *The Alice Bailey Inheritance*, *op. cit.*, p. 127.
15. Alice Bailey, *The Externalization of the Hierarchy* (New York: Lucis Publishing Company, 1957).
16. Thomas Ehrenzeller, *Solar Man*.
17. See *Beacon*, July/August, 1986, p. 289.
18. *Ibid.*, p. 293
19. *Ibid.*
20. Joshua Halpern, *Children of the Dawn: Visions of the New Family* (Bodega, California: Only With Love Publications, 1986).
21. John G. Bennett, quoted by Barry McWaters, *Conscious Evolution* (San Francisco: Evolutionary Press, 1982), pp. 84-85.
22. LaVedi Lafferty and Bud Hollowell, *The Eternal Dance* (St. Paul, Minnesota: Llewellyn Press, 1983).
23. Francis Huxley, *The Way of the Sacred* (London: Bloomsbury Books, 1989), pp. 188-190).
24. *World Monitor* magazine, February, 1992.
25. See Isadore Kozminsky, *Numbers: Their Meaning and Magic*.
26. Alexander Hislop, *The Two Babylons*, p. 115.
27. Barbara Walker, Jr., *The Women's Encyclopedia of Myths and Secrets* (San Francisco: Harper & Row, 1983), p. 550.
28. D. C. Yermak, *The Axis of Death* (published in Greece, 1985), p. 207.

29. Joseph Campbell (with Bill Moyers), *The Power of Myth* (New York: Doubleday, 1988), pp. 7, 24-30, 162-163, 202-204, 213, 223.
30. *Ibid.*
31. *Ibid.*
32. Quoted by M. H. Reynolds, *Foundation* magazine, November/December, 1986. Also see Anuradha Vittachi, *Earth Conference: Sharing A Vision For Our Planet* (Boston: Shambhala Press, 1989); Charles W. Sutherland, *Disciples of Destruction* (Buffalo, New York: 1987); Abbe Daniel LeRoux, *Pope John Paul II: Pope of Tradition or Pope of Revolution?*; Malachi Martin, *Keys of This Blood* (New York: Simon & Schuster, 1990); Gerald and Patricia Mische, *Toward a Human World Order* (New York: Paulist Press, 1977), pp. 274-306; *Sangre de Christo Newsnotes*, published by Father Daniel E. Jones, No. 65, July 1990; and the newspaper column by Mikhail Gorbachev, "Pope Had a Key Role in Freeing Eastern Europe," *St. Petersburg Times*, March 9, 1992.
33. R. S. Sagar, "Let Your Light Shine Forth," *The Royal Arch Mason* magazine, Fall, 1990, pp. 341-344.
34. Rex Hutchens, *A Bridge to Light* (Washington, D.C.: Supreme Council, 33rd Degree of the Ancient and Accepted Scottish Rite of Freemasonry).
35. *Ibid.*
36. *Ibid.*, p. 253. Also see Albert Pike, *Morals and Dogma* (Washington, D.C.: Supreme Council, 33rd Degree of the Ancient and Accepted Scottish Rite of Freemasonry), p. 734.
37. Rex Hutchens, *Ibid.*, p. 252.
38. *Ibid.*, p. 254.
39. Joseph Campbell, *The Power of Myth.*
40. Malachi Martin, *Keys of This Blood*, p. 364.
41. *Ibid.*
42. H. G. Wells, *Experiment in Autobiography* (1934). Also see H. G. Wells' *The Open Conspiracy: Blueprints For A World Revolution* (1928).
43. George Bush, speech reprinted in *New York Times*, August 19, 1988.
44. Alice Bailey, *A Treatise on the Seven Rays* (New York: Lucis Publishing Company), p. 294.
45. Ronald Reagan, speech reprinted in *New York Times*, August 16, 1988, p. 12.
46. Shirley Marlow, "Bush Has a Date With a Pyramid," *Los Angeles Times*, January 3, 1989, p. 10. Also see "Millennium Group Expects Bush at '99 Egypt Bash," *The Arizona Daily Star*, Tuscon, Arizona, January 3, 1989, Section A, p. 5.
47. Ronald Reagan, *op. cit.*.

Chapter 5: **The Bilderbergers and Other Conspirators**

1. Accounts were published in several French newspapers and publications, but except for an edition of the newsletter published by the Committee to Restore the Constitution (December, 1991), and

several issues of the *Spotlight*, there was almost a blackout of coverage of this event and other Bilderberger meetings by the news media throughout the United States. See especially Michael C. Piper, "Quayle Gets Nod From Post," *The Spotlight*, January 27, 1992; James P. Tucker, "Bilderbergers Meet in Secret," *The Spotlight*, June 1, 1992. Also see *Washington Post*, issue of January 12, 1992.

2. *Ibid.*
3. *Ibid.*
4. *Ibid.*
5. Michael Howard, *Secret Societies: Their Influence and Power in World History* (Rochester, Vermont: Destiny Books, 1989), p. 169.
6. *Ibid.*
7. Nicolo Nicolov, *The World Conspiracy: What the Historians Don't Tell You* (Published by Nicolo Nicolov, Box 784, Portland, Oregon, 97207), pp. 220-225.
8. *Ibid.*
9. *Ibid.*
10. William Sutton, *The Illuminati 666* (The Institute of Religious Knowledge: 1983), pp. 243-244.
11. Series published by *Washington Post*, 1991.
12. "Hate Laws Target Gospel," *The Chrisitian World Report*," July, 1990, p. 1. Also see "Forum--President Bush, the Great Pretender," *The Christian News*, January 27, 1992, p. 17.
13. *Ibid.*
14. Jose Arguelles, interviewed by John-Alexis Viereck, "Earth Speaks: The Great Return," *Meditation* magazine, Summer, 1987, pp. 7-15.
15. Morton Kaplan, "Steps Toward A Democratic World Order," *The World and I* journal, January, 1990.
16. *Ibid.*
17. *Ibid.*
18. *Ibid.*
19. *Ibid.*

Chapter 6: International Network of Light

1. David Allen Lewis, *Dark Angels of Light* (available from David Allen Lewis Ministries, 304 E. Manchester, Springfield, Missouri, 65807).
2. *Ibid.*
3. Emile G. DeGivry, *Picture Museum of Sorcery, Magic, and Alchemy* (New Hyde, New York: University Books, 1963), p. 347.
4. *Ibid.*, pp. 347, 367.
5. Albert Pike, *Morals and Dogma.*
6. *Ibid.*, p. 819.
7. Manly P. Hall, *Lectures on Ancient Philosophy*, p. 433.

Chapter 7: **The Supermen of the Imperial Brain Trust**

1. Alice Bailey, *From Bethelem to Calvary* (New York: Lucis Publishing Company), p. 40.
2. *Christian World Report* newspaper, "A Council of Wise Persons May be in the Making," April, 1991, p. 19.
3. *Ibid.*
4. *Initiator* newsletter, published by The Planetary Initiative for the World We Choose, Volume 1, No. 1, 1982.
5. Quoted by Peggy S. Cuddy, "Transformation Toward New Age Synthesis," *Distant Drums*, March, 1986, p. 8.
6. *Ibid.*

Chapter 8: **Strange Glory: What are They Hiding Inside That Tomb?**

1. See footnote 1, Chapter One, of *Dark Majesty.*
2. For an excellent account of Adolf Hitler and the Nazis and their occultic and satanic reign, see Joseph Carr, *The Twisted Cross* (Huntington House Publishers).
3. Christopher Hitchens, "Old New World Order," *The European* newspaper, June 14-16, 1991, p. 10.
4. *The Iconoclast*, Vol. 1, No. 1, New Haven, Connecticut, October 13, 1873.
5. See footnote 1, Chapter One, of *Dark Majesty*; and see Mark Lane, *Plausible Denial: Was the CIA Involved in the Assassination of JFK?.*
6. Alexander Hislop, *The Two Babylons.*
7. Steven M. L. Aronson, "George Bush's Biggest Secret," *Fame* magazine, August, 1989.
8. See Joseph Carr, *The Twisted Cross*, and Fred Gettings, *Secret Symbolism in Occult Art* (New York: Harmony Books, 1987), p. 11. Also see Texe Marrs, *Mystery Mark of the New Age* (Crossway Publishers, 1988).
9. See John J. Robinson, *Born in Blood: The Lost Secrets of Freemasonry*; and Gaetan Delaforge, *The Knights Templar in the Age of Aquarius.*
10. Shirley Marlow, "Bush Has a Date With a Pyramid," *Los Angeles Times*, January 3, 1989, p. 10. Also see "Millennium Group Expects Bush at '99 Egypt Bash," *The Arizona Daily Star*, Tuscon, Arizona, January 3, 1989, Section A, p. 5.
11. Roger Javens, *Skull & Bones and The Secret Society System at Yale University.*
12. Antony C. Sutton, *America's Secret Establishment: An Introduction to The Order of Skull & Bones* (Published in 1986 by Liberty House Press, 2027 Iris, Billings, Montana, 59102). Also see Steven M. L. Aronson, "George Bush's Biggest Secret," *Fame* magazine, August, 1989.

13. Ron Rosenbaum, "The Lost Secrets of the Skull & Bones, *Esquire* magazine, September, 1977.
14. *The Iconoclast, op. cit.*.

Chapter 9: The Pleasant Adventures of a Bonesman...Or How George Bush Made it all the Way to the White House With Just a Little Help From His Friends

1. For a list of sources and documentation to support the information found in this Chapter, see footnote 1, Chapter 1, *Dark Majesty*.
2. *Ibid.* Especially, see Antony C. Sutton, pp. 8-17; Curtis Lang, *Bad Company*: "How Speculators, Spooks, and Con Men Helped Build the Bush Dynasty," *Village Voice* newspaper; and Webster G. Tarpley and Anton Chaitkin, *George Bush: The Unauthorized Biography*, 1992.
3. Antony C. Sutton, *The Two Faces of George Bush*, pp. 8-17.
4. *Ibid.* Especially see Antony C. Sutton, *The Secret Establishment: An Introduction to the Order of Skull & Bones.*
5. Steven M. L. Aronson, "George Bush's Biggest Secrets," *Fame* magazine, August, 1989.
6. For documentation that George Bush was deeply involved in both the "October Surprise" scandal and the Iran Contra affair, see "One Man, Many Tales," *Newsweek*, November 4, 1991, pp. 36-38; *Jewish World*, Broward, Florida, October 11, 1991; and *Spotlight* newspaper (issues of May 13, May 20, June 3, and June 17, 1991). Also see the book *October Surprise*, by Barbara Honneger, the book; *My Turn to Speak*, by Abol Hassan Bani-Sadr, who was the president of Iran during the U.S. hostage crisis (New York: Brassey's, 1991); and see the *American Freedom Movement* newsletter (P.O. Box 309, Irwin, Pennsylvania, 15642), July, 1991 edition.
7. *Ibid.*
8. For example, see Webster G. Tarpley and Anton Chaitkin, *George Bush: The Unauthorized Biography.*
9. *Ibid.*

Chapter 10: The Skull & Bones Lineup: A Rogues' Gallery of Questionable Characters

1. For a list of the sources used in compiling data and facts on this chapter, see footnote 1, Chapter One, *Dark Majesty*. For additional information about Senator John Kerry, see "The Senator Who Knew Too Much," *Newsweek*, August 12, 1991, p. 21.
2. *Ibid.*
3. *Ibid.*
4. *Ibid.* Also see *World Federalist* newsletter, Spring, 1989, p. 2.
5. *Ibid.*

6. Reference is to the *Masonry Altar Bible* which sits on the altar of worship in all Masonic lodges in the U.S.A. (published by A. J. Holman Company, Philadelphia, Pennsylvania). See page 5 of this Bible.
7. Roger Javens, *Skull & Bones and the Secret Society System at Yale University* (unpublished paper).

Chapter 11: **The Skull & Bones "Good Old Boys" Club— Not Just A Fraternity**

1. James J. Drummey, "The Internationalist," *The New American* magazine, March 12, 1991; and see the book by James J. Drummey, *The Establishment's Man.*
2. For insight into the business, government, and diplomatic career of Averall Harriman, see the book by Evan Thomas and Walter Isaacson, *The Wise Men*, 1986.
3. See William McIlhany, "The WCC: A Haven for Marxists?," *Family Protection Scorecard* (P.O. Box 10459, Costa Mesa, California, 92627), p. 21. Also see the pamphlet, "The World Council of Churches: An Ecumenical Tower of Babel," by M. H. Reynolds (Fundamental Evangelistic Association, P.O. Box 6278, Los Osos, California, 93402).
4. Fritz Springmeier, *Be Wise As Serpents* (Published by Fritz Springmeier, 5316 Southeast Lincoln, Portland, Oregon, 97215.)

Chapter 12: **They Worship a God Whose Name They Conceal**

1. See Nesta Webster, *Secret Societies and Subversive Movements* (Christian Club of American, 1923).
2. *Ibid.*, pp. 215-216.
3. *Liberty* (New York: Madison Square Press, 1986), pp. 1-7.
4. Robert Anton Wilson, *Masks of the Illuminati* (New York: Pocketbooks, 1981), p. 174.
5. *Ibid.*, p. 174
6. *Ibid.*.
7. Lady Queensborough (Edith Starr Miller), *Occult Theocrasy.*
8. For a fascinating account of this little known but important episode in American history, see the book, *The Coming of the New Deal*, published in 1958 (pp. 31-33), by noted Harvard University historian Arthur Schlesinger, Jr.. Schlesinger was a key advisor and insider in the administration of President John F. Kennedy.
9. *Ibid.*
10. Alice A. Bailey, *The Externalization of the Hierarchy* (New York: Lucis Trust Publishing).
11. *Ibid.*
12. Manly P. Hall, *The Secret Destiny of America* (Los Angeles: Philosophical Research Library, 1972), pp. 23-24.

13. *Ibid.*, p. 45.
14. *Ibid.*, p. 59
15. Foster Bailey, *The Spirit of Masonry* (New York: Lucis Publishing Company, 1957).
16. Foster Bailey, lecture entitled "Changing Esoteric Values," London, England, 1954.
17. Foster Bailey, *Running God's Plan* (New York: Lucis Trust Publishing Company).
18. Alice A. Bailey, *From Bethlehem to Calvary: The Initiations of Jesus* (New York: Lucis Trust Publishing Company, 1965; first printed 1937).

Chapter 13: **The Science of Mind Control**

1. Archibald E. Roberts, Bulletin of the Committee to Restore the Constitution, No. 347, January, 1991, p. 1.
2. *Ibid.*
3. *Ibid.*
4. Brad and Francie Steiger, *Gods of Aquarius* (New York: Berkeley Books, 1981), p. 260.
5. See Claude Cuenat, *Pierre Teilhard de Chardin, A Biographical Study* (Baltimore: Helican Press, 1965).
6. Brad and Francie Steiger, *Gods of Aquarius*.
7. *Ibid.*
8. *Ibid.*
9. Alice Bailey, *Education in the New Age* (New York: Lucis Trust Publishing Company, 1954), pp. vi-vii.
10. David Foster, *The Intelligent Universe: A Cybernetic Philosophy* (New York: G. P. Putnam, 1975), pp. 16-17.
11. *Ibid.*
12. *Ibid.*
13. Jonathan Glover, *What Sort of People Should There Be?* (New York: Penguin Books, 1984).
14. Quoted by John J. O'Neill, *Prodigal Genius: The Life of Nikola Tesla* (Hollywood, California: Angriff Press), pp. 259-261.
15. *Ibid.*

Chapter 14: **Could This be Magic?—Alchemy, Illusion, and the Processing of Humanity**

1. Peter Partner, *The Knights Templar and Their Myth* (Rochester, Vermont: Destiny Books, 1990), pp. 92-94.
2. *World Goodwill* newsletter No. 4, "A New Vision of Life on Earth," 1990.
3. *Ibid.*
4. *Ibid.*
5. *Ibid.*

6. William Irwin Thompson, interviewed in *Quest* magazine, Spring, 1991.
7. *Ibid.*
8. *Ibid.*
9. *Ibid.*
10. *Ibid.*
11. *Ibid.*
12. Letter and flyer from Lucis Trust to its membership, September, 1990, announcing a World Goodwill symposium, "The Psychology of Nations: Revealing the Plan."
13. *Ibid.*
14. *Ibid.*
15. *Ibid.*
16. Vaclav Havel, quoted in Lucis Trust letter, *Ibid.*
17. *Ibid.*
18. Livieu Gota, quoted in Lucis Trust letter, *Ibid.*
19. Marlin Maddoux, *Free Speech or Propaganda?* (Nashville, Tennessee: Thomas Nelson Publishers, 1990), pp. 10-11.
20. *Ibid.*
21. *Ibid.*
22. *Ibid.*
23. John Swinton, quoted in the *McAlvany Intelligence Advisor* newsletter, "Encouragement for the Remnant," December, 1991, p. 2.
24. David Hume, *Natural History of Religion.*
25. Irwin Chargaff, quoted by Michael Saloman, *Future Life* (New York: MacMillian, 1983).
26. *Ibid.*
27. V. I. Chernyshov, quoted by John Barron, *The KGB Today: The Hidden Hand* (Pleasantville, New York: Reader's Digest Press).

Chapter 15: **The Hidden Persuaders**

1. W. Howard Chase, quoted by Vance Packard, *The Hidden Persuaders* (New York: Pocket Books, 1957, p. 219).
2. Vance Packard, *The Hidden Persuaders*, p. 219.
3. Bertrand Russell, *The Impact of Science on Society*, 1953.
4. *Ibid.*
5. *Ibid.*
6. *Ibid.*
7. *Ibid.*
8. Aldous Huxley, *Brave New World* (New York: Bantam Books, 1968 edition; first published in 1939), p. xii.
9. *Ibid.*
10. George Orwell, *1984* (New York: New American Library edition).
11. "Needed for the '90's . . . A New Way of Thinking," *Plain Truth* magazine, January, 1990.

12. *Ibid.*, p. 10.
13. Mikhail Gorbachev, *Perestroika: New Thinking For Our Country and the World* (New York: Harper & Row Publishers, 1987).
14. *Ibid.*
15. *Ibid.*
16. *Ibid.*
17. *Ibid.*
18. F. Wilhelm Christians, *Paths to Russia: From Wart to Peace* (New York: MacMillan Publishing Company, 1991).
19. *Ibid.*
20. *Ibid.*
21. *Ibid.*, p. 214.
22. *Ibid.*, p. 221.
23. *Ibid.*
24. *Ibid.*
25. *Ibid.*
26. *Ibid.*, pp. 218-219.
27. *Ibid.*
28. Alice A. Bailey, *The Reappearance of the Christ* (New York: Lucis Trust Publishing, 1948), p. 132.
29. *Ibid.*
30. *Ibid.*, pp. 129-133.
31. *Ibid.*
32. Chester Pierce, quoted in *Christian Awareness Newsletter*, Summer/Fall, 1991, p. 10.
33. *Network News*, published by the Tara Center, Hollywood, California, November/December, 1988, p. 3.
34. *Ibid.*
35. *Ibid.*
36. *Ibid.*
37. Peter Lemesurier, *The Armageddon Script*.
38. See J. J. Hurtag, *The Keys of Enoch*, (Los Gatos, California: The Academy for Future Science, 1977; revised 1982), pp. 173, 332.
39. F. Homer Curtiss and Harriette Curtiss, *Coming World Changes* (Albuquerque, New Mexico: Sun Publishing Company, 1981), p. xii.
40. Alice Bailey, *Education in the New Age* (New York: Lucis Publishing Company, 1954), pp. 111-112.
41. *Ibid.*
42. Peter Lemesurier, *The Armageddon Script*, p. 251.
43. *Ibid.*

For Our Newsletter

Texe Marrs offers a *free* newsletter about Bible prophecy and world events, secret societies, the New Age Movement, cults, and the occult challenge to Christianity. If you would like to receive this newsletter, please write to:

Living Truth Ministries
8104-D Caisson Circle
Austin, Texas 78745

About the Author

Well-known author of the #1 national bestseller, *Dark Secrets of The New Age*, **Texe Marrs** has also written 30 other books for such major publishers as Simon & Schuster, John Wiley, Prentice Hall/Arco, Stein & Day, and Dow Jones-Irwin. His books have sold over a million copies.

Texe Marrs was assistant professor of aerospace studies, teaching American defense policy, strategic weapons systems, and related subjects at the University of Texas at Austin for five years. He has also taught international affairs, political science, and psychology for two other universities. A graduate *summa cum laude* from Park College, Kansas City, Missouri, he earned his Master's degree at North Carolina State University.

As a career USAF officer (now retired), he commanded communications-electronics and engineering units. He holds a number of military decorations including the Vietnam Service Medal, and served in Germany, Italy, and throughout Asia.

President of Living Truth Publishers in Austin, Texas, Texe Marrs is a frequent guest on radio and TV talk shows throughout the U.S.A. and Canada. His monthly newsletter, *Flashpoint*, is distributed around the world.